A Collection of Sufi Rules of Conduct

Other Translations of Sufi titles by the Islamic Texts Society

The Key to Salvation

The Secret of Secrets

The Speech of the Birds

The Way of Abū Madyan

A Collection of Sufi Rules of Conduct

Jawāmiʿ Ādāb al-Ṣūfiyya

Translated by Elena Biagi

THE ISLAMIC TEXTS SOCIETY

This edition first published 2010 by
The Islamic Texts Society
Miller's House
Kings Mill Lane
Great Shelford
Cambridge CB22 5EN, U.K.

Reprint 2013

British Library Cataloguing-in-Publication Data.
A catalogue record for this book is
available from the British Library.

ISBN 978 1903682 56 2 cloth
ISBN 978 1903682 57 9 paper

Miniature on cover : V& A Images/Victorya and Albert Museum,
London (2006AM2573, IM. 7-1920, INDIAN PAINTING C. 1700)

DEDICATION

To my parents, who gave me passion for life, and to Hisham and Nabila who are a constant inspiration to me

CONTENTS

Transliteration Keys

Arabic letter	Eng.	Arabic letter	Eng.
ء	ʾ	ط	ṭ
ا	ā	ظ	ẓ
ب	b	ع	ʿ
ت	t	غ	gh
ث	th	ف	f
ج	j	ق	q
ح	ḥ	ك	k
خ	kh	ل	l
د	d	م	m
ذ	dh	ن	n
ر	r	و	w
ز	z	ه	-a
س	s	ي	y
ش	sh		
ص	ṣ		
ض	ḍ		

	Arabic letter	English equivalent
Long vowels	ا or ى	ā
	و	ū
	ي	ī
Doubled	يّ	iyy final form ī
	وّ	uww final form ū
Dipthongs	وَ	aw
	يَ	ay
Short vowels	َ	a
	ِ	i
	ُ	u

Abbreviations:

EI: *The Encyclopaedia of Islam*, new edition, ed. by H. A. R. Gibb et al., Leiden: E. J. Brill, 1960–.

GAL: C. Brockelmann, *Geschichte der Arabischen Litteratur*, Weimar: Verlag Von Emil Felber, 1898.

GAS: F. Sezgin, *Geschichte des Arabischen Schrifttums*, Leiden: E. J. Brill, 1967.

PREFACE

The growing interest of the Western world in classical Sufism has been linked to a greater awareness of the significant role played by Abū ʿAbd al-Raḥmān al-Sulamī (d. 412/1021) in the development of Arabic Sufi literature. During the second half of the twentieth century, many of Sulamī's writings were edited and studied by Western scholars, who sought in this way to shed more light on the personality and work of this Sufi author. Yet, until now, a thorough appreciation of Sulamī's literary achievement has only been possible for a restricted public of Arabic readers, as only few of Sulamī's works have hitherto been translated into English or into other European languages. Therefore, I thought of focusing my research on the translation of a text, the *Jawāmiʿ ādāb al-ṣūfiyya*, which had never been translated, and whose peculiar nature, I believe, makes it one of the most attractive of Sulamī's works. The aim of my research, however, was not merely the translation of a work of literature; rather, through the translation I have tried to interpret the text and understand its purpose within both the traditions of Arabic literature and of Islamic mysticism.

In the introduction to his work, Sulamī says that he wrote the *Jawāmiʿ* with the clear intention to provide the reader with an accurate formulation of Sufi attitudes and beliefs so that 'those who criticise them [i.e., the Sufis] without really knowing the truth can learn about them, their way of life and their customs' and thus 'think about them as they deserve.'[1] I believe that the

[1] Kohlberg, Etan, *Jawāmiʿ Ādāb al-Ṣūfiyya and ʿUyūb al-Nafs wa-Mudāwātuhā by Abū ʿAbd al-Raḥmān al-Sulamī*, The Max Schloessinger Memorial Series, Texts 1, Jerusalem: Jerusalem Academic Press, 1976, section 2, p. 1 (Arabic).

need for a sincere understanding of Sufism is as urgent today as it was in Sulamī's time: in fact, it is frequent nowadays (and, paradoxically, especially in Muslim countries) to hear people pass judgements on Sufism which do not really reflect the truth of it. Such judgements often show a substantial ignorance of the original and authentic expressions of this complex phenomenon called Sufism, which indeed represents one of the most diverse and attractive manifestations of Islamic belief. The more extremist trends of Sufism, which emerged since the very beginnings of the movement, contributed to the development of the idea that Sufism is opposed to Islamic orthodoxy. Furthermore, over many centuries the gradual combination of its original spiritual elitism with social populism brought about a certain vulgarisation, and seldom did the popularised and institutional Sufism reflect the genuine spirit of the early mystics of Islam. This can explain why criticism of the unorthodoxy of Sufism—which spurred Sulamī to the composition of this book—is still present today. For these reasons, I believe this particular text is of great relevance: not only does it provide contemporary readers with a clear explanation of what Sufism is, but it also gives them a picture of Islamic mysticism as it originally developed from within Sunni orthodoxy. Finally, both its contents and its language are free from the technicality typical of many Sufi treatises, which makes the *Jawāmiʿ* a book that can be easily understood and enjoyed both by those acquainted with its subject and by the general public.

Sulamī was a prolific author: according to his biographers, he wrote more than a hundred different books and treatises over a period of some fifty years from around 360/970 onwards. The text taken into consideration in my research represents a significant attempt to harmonise Sufism with Islamic orthodoxy by describing Sufi attitudes and manners (*ādāb*) and demonstrating their compatibility with the Qur'ān and the Sunna. Indeed, the nature of this and of most works by Sulamī may be best understood by considering their context in the history of Sufism and the particular circumstances under which they were written.

Throughout its history, Sufism has manifested itself as a complex phenomenon. It began as a form of practical piety, which lacked any interest in speculative thought and which developed as a response of the religiously minded to what they saw as the corruption of a society where, after the succession of the first Umayyad caliph Muᶜāwiya (d. 60/680), worldly considerations had come to replace the original aspirations as the basis of government and social life. Calling for a return to the austerity of the first years of Islam, these pious men, among whom stands the theologian and spiritual master al-Ḥasan al-Baṣrī (d. 110/728), devoted themselves to ascetic practices and lived a life of self-denial and total renunciation (*zuhd*). However, during the eighth century a gradual transition began to affect the character of Sufism and disregard of the world was transfigured into complete absorption by fear, then service and finally absolute loving devotion to God. The language of love and the idea of extinction in God (*fanā'*), which found beautiful expression in the works of many 'sober' mystics, such as Junayd (d. 298/910), also led other Sufis to disclose the secret of their mystical experience in their attempt to convey in human language their total and inexpressible encounter with God. Among these daring mystics were the Persian Abū Yazīd al-Bisṭāmī (d. 261/874) who, transported with the rapture of mystical ardour, found God within himself and *in persona Dei* uttered theopathic locutions (*shaṭḥiyyāt*)[2], and the famous Ḥusayn ibn Manṣūr al-Ḥallāj (d. 309/922). The latter, in particular, became the supreme example of the 'intoxicated' mystic: accused of having betrayed the 'discipline of the Arcanum', he was condemned to death for heresy. At the same time Sufism was gradually developing into a vast movement where man's striving toward spiritual realisation was variously expressed and codified. The tenth century witnessed the most successful attempts to 'systematise' mystical thought, which

[2] On Bistami and his 'locutions divines', cfr. Massignon, Louis, *Essai sur les origines du lexique technique de la mystique musulmane*, Paris: Les Editions du Cerf, 1999, pp. 273–286.

indicates that the mystical movement was now established well enough to allow description and discussion. Moreover, Sufism was now torn by a struggle between its extremist and its more orthodox manifestations and, after the scandal which ended in the execution of Ḥallāj, many mystics felt the need to rehabilitate the movement by setting down some of the main lines of moderate Sufism. These same motives seem to have prompted Sulamī throughout: at a time when Sunni doctrine was being defined and defended, he endeavoured to establish the bases of the orthodox foundations of Sufism by showing how Sufi beliefs were based directly on the Qur'ān and on the Prophet's behaviour. Thus he became one of the most outstanding personalities of Sufism as accepted by Sunni tradition, followed approximately half a century later by the great Abū Ḥāmid al-Ghazālī (d. 505/1111), the renowned theologian and Sufi who finally succeeded in ensuring the mystical perspective a place within formal Islam. For all these reasons, in his works Sulamī intended to reach a number of different audiences, from the Sufi élite to the general public, and this accounts for the wide range and varied nature of his literary production.

The dominant trend in Sulamī's works is represented by his treatises on Sufi customs and practices. In his many books dealing with practical aspects of Sufism, the author aimed to define the foundations of Muslim morality by describing particular Sufi attitudes and manners. Usually free of any esoteric terminology, these works contain numerous maxims, poems and Sufi sayings to which citations from the Qur'ān and the Sunna were added in support of the claimed orthodoxy of Sufi behaviour. The material gathered by Sulamī was tremendously varied: from books of poetry and collections of Hadith, to the many treatises dealing with manners and behaviour which appeared in the ninth and tenth centuries. Although addressed principally to a Sufi audience, these miscellanies of Muslim ethics had an evident popular appeal and formed an interesting link between the Sufi literature and the Arabic literary tradition of *adab*. The text taken into consideration here well represents this trend in Sulamī's writings. Nonetheless, it is of interest too as it differs from all of Sulamī's other works and from the works of Sufi classical authors in general.

Having noted the affinities between the *Jawāmiʿ ādāb al-ṣūfiyya* and *adab* literature, I thought it proper to precede my translation with a brief analysis of Sulamī's work within the *adab* literary tradition in Arabic. The term '*adab*' has been used by historians of Arabic literature to describe a body of medieval works, which is considered to constitute a specific literary genre. Yet, this term is also applied to writings of very different nature and form: monographs and wide-ranging miscellanies; essays on disparate literary, philosophical and social issues; and edifying works abundant with aphorisms and anecdotes. In my analysis I have referred primarily to the literary production connected with the earlier use of the term *adab* for training and for the social and ethical virtues. In this sense, I have considered Nallino's interpretation of *adab* as 'rules of conduct'[3] pertaining to a particular social group or to be observed while engaged in some social activities. At the same time, works of an edifying nature were composed by ascetics and Sufis where sayings of kings, sages and Sufi masters were collected along with Hadiths and Qur'ānic passages to illustrate rules of moral behaviour and practical ethics. Therefore, the intention, through this brief survey of *adab* literature, has been that of defining more clearly the place of Sulamī's work within Arabic literary tradition and trying to understand the heterogeneity of the source material from which the author probably drew his inspiration.

Although the *Jawāmiʿ* is a work of an edifying nature, in which Sufi topics function mainly as a means of moral education, it is also a Sufi treatise, intended to illustrate the ideal conduct of a Sufi society. Besides the content, the element that is indicative of the Sufi nature of this work is its language. Therefore, a general glossary of Sufi technical terms has been provided for those readers who are unfamiliar with the Sufi idiom, and who need

[3] See my discussion on *adab* in the chapter 'The *Adab* Literary Tradition'.

a quick reference to facilitate their understanding of the text. For each term I have explained first its meaning in general Sufi terminology, by referring to some of the classical Sufi works in Arabic, in particular the *Kitāb al-lumaᶜ fi'l-taṣawwuf* by Sulamī's contemporary Abū Naṣr al-Sarrāj (d. 377/988), along with the *Kashf al-maḥjūb* and *al-Risāla al-Qushayriyya*, written half a century after Sulamī by the two great theorists of Sufism, Hujwīrī (d. 463/1071) and Qushayrī (d. 466/1074) respectively. After that, I have included the specific meaning and connotation the term acquires in the *Jawāmiᶜ*.

Finally, the bibliography lists the various books which I have used as source material for my research: these include reference works, primary sources and secondary source studies on Sufism. The bibliography comprises those works which I have actually cited in this book as well as sources consulted during my research.

INTRODUCTION

The Life and Works of Sulamī

Sulamī's full name was Abū ʿAbd al-Raḥmān Muḥammad b. al-Ḥusayn b. Muḥammad b. Mūsa b. Khālid b. Sālim b. Zāwiyya b. Saʿīd b. Qabīṣa b. Sarrāq al-Azdī al-Sulamī al-Naysābūrī. He was born in 325/937 or 330/942 at Nishapur (i.e., Arabic: Naysābūr, Persian: Nīshāpūr) and died in the same city in 412/1021. He was one of the most prominent personalities of Sufism in the tenth century. The information we have on the life of Sulamī is very scanty.[1] We know that he belonged to the tribe of the Azd on his father's side and to that of the Sulaym on his mother's side. In his early youth he was instructed by his father, al-Ḥusayn b. Muḥammad b. Mūsā al-Azdī; afterwards, when his father settled at Mecca, Sulamī continued his education under his maternal grandfather, Abū ʿAmr Ismāʿīl b. Nujayd b. Aḥmad b. Yūsuf b. Khālid al-Sulamī al-Naysābūrī (d. 366/976–7). The latter, a prominent figure among Sufis, had become a renowned scholar of Hadith and one of the leaders of the *Malāmatiyya* movement.[2] It was probably the influence of his grandfather which first drew Sulamī towards the ascetic doctrine.

Sulamī was formally initiated into Sufism by the Ḥanafī judge Abū Sahl Muḥammad b. Sulaymān al-Ṣuʿlūkī (d. 369/980), from whom he received a certificate of competence (*ijāza*) authorising him to instruct novices (*murīdūn*). He continued his education as a Sufi with Abū'l-Qāsim Ibrāhīm b. Muḥammad b. Maḥmawayh al-Naṣrābādhī (d. 367/977–8), a Shāfiʿī scholar of Hadith who had become a Sufi at the hands of Abū Bakr al-Shiblī (d. 334/946) at Baghdad.[3] Sulamī also received the Sufi frock of investiture (*khirqa*) from him, some time after 340/951.

Sulamī was also thoroughly trained in the study of Hadith. Always in search of traditions, he travelled widely throughout Khurasan and Iraq, where he visited Baghdad for long periods of time, and as far as the Hijaz, and soon he became a specialist in the field. His extensive travels, which confronted him with the ideas and thoughts of many different Sufi schools, proved an important factor in forming Sulamī's education. Sulamī's expertise in the field of traditions is evident in his works.[4] Some Hanbalī scholars, such as Ibn al-Jawzī (d. 596/1200) and Ibn Taymiyya (d. 728/1328), levelled against Sulamī the accusation of forging traditions;[5] such allegations, however, have been proved to be without foundation.[6]

Sulamī's education was also supported by a thorough training in religious law and theology, Ashᶜarī *kalām* in particular, which he learned from the *qāḍī* Abū Bakr al-Bāqillānī (d. 403/1013). In *fiqh*, Sulamī followed the Shāfiᶜī school, which during that period was in many ways connected with Sufi circles at Nishapur.[7]

Sulamī went to Mecca, where he performed the pilgrimage in 366/976 with Abū'l-Qāsim al-Naṣrābādhī. He returned to Nishapur in about 368/977–8 where he established a small Sufi convent (*duwayra*), which had its centre in the library left to him by Ismāᶜīl ibn Nujayd after his death.[8] Sulamī spent the remaining forty years of his life in Nishapur, and became renowned and highly regarded as a Shāfiᶜī scholar and a collector of traditions.

Sulami's popularity among his contemporaries is evident from the large number of his disciples, among whom were well-known figures such as Abū'l-Qāsim al-Qushayrī (d. 465/1073), who quotes him frequently in his famous *al-Risala al-Qushayriyya*.[9] However, the significance of the role played by Sulamī in the development of Sufi tradition is best demonstrated by his many works and how they influenced the succeeding generations.

The literary production of Sulamī is vast: he composed all his works—amounting to more than a hundred—over a period of some fifty years from 360/970 onwards.[10] However, only about thirty of his works are known to be extant;[11] some of them have appeared in print.[12] Sulamī's writings may be divided into three main categories: Sufi biographies, commentaries on the Qur'ān, and treatises on Sufi customs and practices. Each category seems to be represented by a major work.[13]

In his *Ta'rīkh al-ṣūfiyya* the author registered the biographies of a thousand Sufis; however, this work is lost and known only through quotations and extracts of it in other sources. A shorter version of it is the *Ṭabaqāt al-ṣūfiyya*, a collection of hagiographies of some one hundred Sufis, including selections of their sayings. It was edited and analysed by Johannes Pedersen in 1960 with an extensive introduction to Sulamī's life and work.[14] Sulamī's *Ṭabaqāt* represents without doubt a significant contribution in the history of Sufi hagiographical literature. Although works of this kind had already been compiled before our author's time,[15] Sulamī was the first compiler to use systematically the method of *isnād*, i.e., the detailed chain of authorities on which a reported saying is based.[16] In his preface, Sulamī affirms that for each of the Sufis mentioned he will report of his sayings, his traits of character, and his biography all that can cast a light on his method (*ṭarīqa*), his mystical state (*ḥāl*) and his knowledge; however, as Pedersen observes, 'le texte est constitué, en très grande majorité, par les adages du ṣūfī, la narration se limitant à des indications données, sous forme d'une introduction, sur son nom, en général aussi sur son lieu d'origine et la date de sa mort, son intérêt particulier, et un jugement, qui se réduit le plus souvent à des louanges assez stéréotypées.'[17] Throughout the *Ṭabaqāt*, some of the central themes of Sufi *adab* literature are also dealt with, such as *taṣawwuf*, or the mystic's method of achieving spiritual realisation; gnosis (*maʿrifa*); the ideal of *futuwwa*, man's relationship with people and his dealing with them; and love (*maḥabba*).

Sulamī's principal commentary on the Qur'ān, entitled *Ḥaqā'iq al-tafsīr*, is an extensive work of Sufi Qur'ānic exegesis, which has not been published yet, although extracts from it have appeared in works by Louis Massignon and Paul Nwyia.[18] An interesting analysis of this work has been done by Gerhard Böwering in his article 'The Qur'ān Commentary of al-Sulamī'.[19] According to Nwyia, the *Ḥaqā'iq* was most probably one of the first works compiled by the author, as its esoteric nature does not conform to that tendency of harmonisation with the orthodox points of view which characterises Sulamī's later works.[20] The peculiar feature of the *Ḥaqā'iq* lies in its structure, as well as in the fact that it substantially embodies the development of centuries of mystic exegesis on the Qur'ān.[21] In this work Sulamī selects some three thousand Qur'ānic verses, recording after each a rich sequence of interpretative glosses quoted from authors who were esteemed by Sufis at that time. The glosses incorporated in the commentary are basically of two types: *āyāt*, or illustrative comments on Qur'ānic passages, and *aqwāl*, or Sufi sayings, quoted when the issues discussed more strictly relate to mysticism. In collecting the glosses, Sulamī avoided including those items of interpretation connected with the exoteric sciences (*al-ʿulūm al-ẓāhira*),[22] and concentrated only on those explanations which to him best mirrored the genuine mystic understanding of the Holy Book. This method of exegesis, to which Sulamī gave ample space in his commentary, represented the literary genre of Sufi allusive Qur'ānic interpretation. Those privileged people, who had been accorded the blessing of understanding the spiritual realities (*ḥaqā'iq*) hidden in the Sacred Text, would afterwards reveal such realities by way of allusions (*ishārāt*):[23] such allusions were then condensed in brief explanations, which would strike the Sufi's mind when reading them and listening to the Qur'ānic text. Moreover, in compiling the vast material for his commentary, the author included almost exclusively the interpretive metaphorical comments, thus referring to only one level of Qur'ānic meaning, i.e., the inward one, or *al-bāṭin*.[24] It was this kind of esoteric exegesis that provoked the reaction of the orthodox Sunni scholars, some of whom critically judged Sulamī's work and tried to discredit him altogether.[25] Yet, as Böwering observes, the significance and value of the *Ḥaqā'iq* as a whole is undeniable. In fact, as a Sufi source, it is of primary importance in giving us information about

Sufi thought and its development up to Sulamī's time; second, as a commentary, the work established a specific literary genre, that of Sufi exegesis, distinguished from the traditional method of Qur'ānic interpretation. Finally, being a systematic collection of Sufi Qur'ānic items of interpretation, the *Ḥaqā'iq* is an important reference in the history of exegesis and an extensive basis for Sufi Qur'ānic interpretation.

Some time after the completion of the *Ḥaqā'iq*, probably some years after 370/980, Sulamī wrote a separate Qur'ān commentary entitled *Ziyādāt ḥaqā'iq al-tafsīr*, 'The Additions to the Realities of Qur'ānic Interpretation'. This minor commentary is extant in a unique manuscript, which was edited with an introduction by Gerhard Böwering in 1995.[26] As Sulamī himself explains in the *incipit* of his work, the *Ziyādāt* was conceived as an appendix to the *Ḥaqā'iq*, where he added those items of interpretation (*ḥurūf*) which were lacking in the first commentary.[27] Therefore, the *Ziyādāt* is similar in both content and style to the *Ḥaqā'iq al-tafsīr*. In fact, like the *Ḥaqā'iq*, the *Ziyādāt* contains a selection of Qur'ānic passages, reported mostly in the actual order of the *sūras* and verses: the phrases selected for comment are about six hundred and, after each, is recorded a sequence of interpretive glosses, along with Sufi sayings.

The third category of Sulamī's works is represented by a variety of treatises and writings on Sufi customs and practices, some of which have appeared in print.[28]

The *Kitāb ādāb al-ṣuḥba wa-ḥusn al-ʿishra*, 'The Book on the Rules of Companionship and Good Social Intercourse', was edited with an introduction by M. J. Kister in 1954.[29] As the title says, the book discusses the rules of behaviour (*ādāb*) which a man must follow in his dealings with people in order to be a good companion and brother to those around him. The book begins with a short introduction, where Sulamī stresses the goodness of the Prophet's moral character and behaviour, which he sees as conforming at the highest degree with the ethics laid down in the Qur'ān.[30] Hence, the author invites his readers to imitate the Prophet's behaviour and follow his Sunna. For this reason, from here on, the book becomes mostly a collection of Hadiths on the Prophet's morals and his dealing with people, which Sulamī quotes to legitimate each rule of behaviour. Almost all passages of the *Kitāb* begin with the formula *wa-min ādābihā* ('one of the rules of companionship is ...'), which opens a short heading, where the rule is set out.[31] The opening sentence is then followed by one or more Hadiths, as well as verses from the Qur'ān, and Sufi sayings, through which the initial statement is supported and illustrated. Verses of poetry are also quoted frequently. The *Kitāb ādāb al-ṣuḥba* contains some eighty Hadiths, some hundred sayings of well-known and esteemed Sufis or other personalities, and about forty poetic quotations.[32] The principles of social behaviour (*ṣuḥba wa-ʿishra*) and brotherliness (*ukhuwwa*) outlined in the *Kitāb ādāb al-ṣuḥba* mostly resemble those delineated in the *Jawāmiʿ*, which will be the object of my analysis further on. In brief, according to the *Kitāb*, the good companion should respect those who are above him and revere his spiritual master (29, 75, 76),[33] speak well of his brethren (49–50) and forgive them their mistakes (28–9, 38, 49), shun the company of those who are attached to this world and associate instead with those who live for the Hereafter (30); he should be generous (44), god-fearing (33), humble (44), and calm (49) and should always keep a cheerful face; he should be ready to give and accept advice (33, 46), keep his friends' secrets (45) and avoid disputing with them, especially on worldly matters (47–8). The book ends with two long passages. The first explains the different kinds of companionship with the various types of persons one befriends, and the *ādāb* to be followed accordingly. Thus, for instance, the *ṣuḥba* with God consists essentially in following His commands and prohibitions, remembering His name always, studying His book, and guarding His secrets (80); the *ṣuḥba* with the friends of God (*al-awliyā'*) consists in revering them and that with the ruler in obeying him (81); also, are described the kinds of *ṣuḥba* to be kept with one's children, with one's servants, and so on. In the second passage (85–6), the author explains that every single part of one's body must follow distinct rules of behaviour, the eye, as well as the ear, the tongue, the hands and feet. Sulamī concludes his *Kitāb* with an observation (86–7) which he will fully develop in the *Jawāmiʿ*, i.e., that in a sincere companion, as well as in a sincere mystic, the external rules of discipline relating to one's outward behaviour (*ādāb al-ẓāhir*) must be in total harmony with the rules pertaining to one's innermost attitudes and beliefs (*ādāb al-bāṭin*).

The *Kitāb al-futuwwa*, or 'The Book of (Sufi) Chivalry' was edited by F. Taeschner in 1953, and by S. Ateş in 1977;[34] it has also been translated into English, French and Italian.[35] In this treatise Sulamī describes the virtues of spiritual chivalry (*al-futuwwa*)[36] and the rules of conduct (*ādāb*) to be followed by the *fatā*.[37] The structure of the book follows that of the *Kitāb ādāb al-ṣuḥba*, and of many other of Sulamī's works on *ādāb*: each passage opens with a heading, which begins with the same formula and where the main rule of behaviour is outlined; then follows a series of sayings, whose aim is to elucidate the rule. Yet, unlike the *Kitāb ādāb al-ṣuḥba*, the *Kitāb al-futuwwa* is characterised by the preponderance of sayings of Sufis, or other leading personalities, over the Prophet's Hadiths. The figure of the *fatā*, as delineated in this book, is essentially that of someone who strives to destroy the idols of his own individuality (*nafs*), who fights his passions and acts solely for God. The path of *futuwwa* is similar to the path of Sufism: as we shall see, many of the *ādāb* described in the *Kitāb al-futuwwa*, in fact, closely resemble those described in the *Jawāmiʿ*. Like the Sufi, the *fatā* must be wholly concentrated on God and trust Him unreservedly (*K. al-Futuwwa*, II, 31; III, 6);[38] strive to attain total harmony between his exterior and his interior conduct (IV, 28); have a good opinion of people and a bad opinion of his own self (IV, 14); honour those senior to him, and show mercy to those junior to him. One of the basic qualities of the *fatā* is described as placing others above oneself, *īthār ʿalā nafsihi*, also known as preference, i.e., 'preferring others to oneself' (III, 12). This virtue, which holds a special place in Sufi *ādāb* literature, finds expressions in other complementary qualities forming a genuine chivalrous man, such as liberality, superiority to disappointment, indulgence to the faults of brethren, self-denial and altruism.

A work by Sulamī which has been the object of special interest is the *Risālat al-malāmatiyya*, or 'The Epistle of the People of Blame'. The work has been edited and published more than once,[39] and it has also been translated into both French and Italian.[40] The treatise opens with a long introduction, where the author explains the attitude and mode of behaviour of the *Malāmatī*,[41] i.e., the one who draws blame (*malāma*) upon himself. In Sufi tradition, the attitude of the *Ahl al-malāma* consisted in dissimulating one's spiritual states (*talbīs al-ḥāl*) by assuming an outward behaviour that would be as similar as possible to that of the common people (*al-ʿāmma*). Indeed, the higher the spiritual station of the mystic, the more ordinary would be his exterior condition and conduct in his dealings with people. The *Malāmatī*s would shun fame and renown and eschew the opinion and approval of people, which in their view were based only on appearances and can easily lead the mystic to self-conceit. Yet, such an attitude was taken to the extreme by some ascetics, who aimed at drawing the contempt of the world upon themselves by showing an immoral conduct and by committing unseemly, even unlawful actions. This indulging in blameworthy habits only for the sake of attracting the attention of people and their reproval was condemned by some mystics, who denounced the subtle hypocrisy of the *Malāmatiyya*'s behaviour.[42] Such an extreme connotation, however, is not present in Sulamī's *Risāla*. In fact, in the second part of his work, Sulamī outlines the basic principles (*uṣūl*) of conduct to be followed by the 'People of Blame': there, the *malāmatī* mystic is described mainly as the one who conforms to people's behaviour in his outward conduct but preserves absolute sincerity (*ikhlāṣ*) in his inward heart and loves God without thought for other.[43] In this sense, Sulamī seems to suggest the *malāmatī* attitude as an effective method against the evils of self-satisfaction and the subtle traps of vanity (*ʿujb*). According to Sulamī, the *malāmatī* is the mystic who has reached the stage of proximity (*qurb*) to God: he is free from spiritual pretensions (*daʿāwā*) and, by disguising his inward state, he guards the secret (*sirr*) between him and the divinity. The *malāmatī* is distinguished from the *ṣūfī*, who is on a lower degree of proximity to God because he makes manifest in his outward conduct the light of his intimate state, and from the *ʿālim*, the expert in the exoteric sciences of religion, who is on the lowest rung of spiritual realisation.[44]

Sulamī also composed a treatise with the title *ʿUyūb al-nafs wa-mudāwātuhā*, or 'The Defects of the Soul and their Remedy', which has been edited by Etan Kohlberg in 1976 along with the *Jawāmiʿ Ādāb al-Ṣūfiyya*.[45] In this work the author describes many human sins and base qualities and suggests a cure for them. The author begins with a discussion of the Qur'ānic notion of the three parts of the soul (*nafs*):[46] the 'soul which orders evil-doing' (*al-nafs al-ammāra bi'l-sū'*), the 'self-accusing soul' (*al-nafs al-lawwāma*), which blames itself for every action, and the 'soul at peace' (*al-nafs al-muṭma'inna*), which has found tranquillity and peace in belief. Sufi *adab* literature on *nafs* usually focused on the meaning of the word as the lower soul, the 'ego-self', which is the locus of man's appetites and base inclinations. Throughout the treatise, Sulamī uses and interprets the term mostly in this Sufi sense; frequently he refers to it also as man's personality as a whole, although a negative connotation seems to be constantly present. After the brief introduction, the author describes the diseases (*ʿuyūb*) of the soul, which arise usually from the absence of a sincere faith in God, and the remedies (*mudāwāt*) through which salvation can be achieved. The structure of the work is similar to that of other treatises: in each section the defect is introduced with the formula *wa-min ʿuyūbihā*, followed by *wa-mudāwātuhā*, after which the cure is described. Moreover, verses from the Qur'ān, Hadiths and Sufi maxims are quoted to illustrate each passage. Unlike in the *Jawāmiʿ*, quotations from the Qur'ān (41 times) and from Hadiths (48 times) are preponderant over Sufi sayings (39 times).[47] According to the *ʿUyūb*, some individual defects originate from the absence of a sincere trust in God and in His providential arrangements (6,

33),[48] which leads to indifference (*ghafla*, 61) or lack of inward conviction when performing religious obligations (16, 42, 48). The temptations of this world (*al-dunyā*) are also described as causing disease, in that they easily lead to desires (40), anger (50), deceit, envy (56), ambition (27), greed (55, 59) and avarice (52). However, most defects result from self-satisfaction (*riḍā ʿan al-nafs*), which brings with itself conceit and vaunting, and leads man to abandon any attempts at self-improvement (45). Freedom from the diseases of the soul can be achieved through a constant struggle against hypocrisy (*riyāʾ*) and pride (*ʿujb*): such struggle must be accompanied by a total sincerity in one's inward heart (*ikhlāṣ*) and sustained by a firm belief in God. Finally, a prerequisite to that is adherence to *ādāb*, the body of rules of conduct, which combine rigorous physical and psychological discipline: only by complying with these rules can the Sufi attain a thorough spiritual realisation. For this reason, many of the passages of the *ʿUyūb* dealing with the remedies for the disease of the soul closely resemble sections of the *Jawāmiʿ ādāb al-ṣūfiyya*.

The *Adab* Literary Tradition

Having discussed the similarities between Sulamī's *Jawāmiʿ* and the works of *adab* literature, I will precede my translation of the text with a survey of the *adab* literary tradition in Arabic. The aim of this brief historical survey has been first to define the meaning and use of the term *adab*; while doing that, I have also looked at the development of *adab* literature until Sulamī's time and I have tried to outline its main features by mentioning some major works that belong to this genre. This survey, I believe, will allow us to understand more clearly the place of Sulamī's work within the *adab* tradition as well as the diversity of his sources.

The dictionaries register many different meanings for the Arabic word *adab*, and its plural *ādāb*, such as 'culture', 'good breeding', 'good manners', 'courtesy', as well as 'humaneness' and 'the humanities' or 'belles-lettres'. In fact, the term *adab* has been often used by scholars to designate a body of Arabic medieval works, which have been considered as constituting a specific literary category. As well, we encounter this term in a variety of applications denoting writings of very different nature and form: monographs and wide-ranging miscellanies, essays on disparate literary, philosophical and social issues, and edifying works abundant with aphorisms and anecdotes. It was probably the medieval usage of the term *adab* as literary scholarship and philology which finally led nineteenth-century scholars to choose the term *adab*, especially in the plural *ādāb*, to designate literature or belles-lettres. Yet, in my review, I have referred primarily to the earlier use of the term for moral training and the social and ethical virtues, following Sulamī's *Jawāmiʿ*. Hence, I have considered the literary production connected with this application of the term and I have focused on the writings with a clear didactic connotation intended to define rules of conduct.

In my attempt to trace the medieval history of the word *adab* I have referred particularly to Nallino's discussion of the term in the introduction to his work *La letteratura araba: dagli inizi all'epoca della dinastia Umayyade*.[49] An interesting analysis of this issue, also including many references to Nallino's work, is found in Bonebakker's '*Adab* and the concept of *Belles-lettres*' in the *Cambridge History of Arabic Literature*.[50] Nallino suggests that *adab* originally meant 'ancestral custom' and, in this sense, it was used as a near-synonym of *sunna*, or 'customary procedure or practice'. Therefore, during pre-Islamic times and in the seventh century, the term *adab* was used as meaning 'the body of the ancient habits, which, in the opinion of the Arabs of the *jāhiliyya*, was incumbent upon everyone to follow.'[51] At the same time, *adab* acquired the meaning of 'knowing something', and the verbal noun *ta'dīb* that of 'informing someone of something, instructing and educating someone in something'; similarly, the word *adīb* meant 'someone who is informed of, educated in something.' Such application of *adab* both as 'custom' and 'the knowledge and teaching of custom' finds evidence in early poetry as well as in the Hadiths, where the association of *adab* with education is often explicit. This is, for example, the case of a famous Hadith, which has gained wide popularity in Sufi circles, '*Inna 'Llāha addabanī fa-aḥsana adabī* (*or ta'dībī*)' ('God educated me and perfected my education'), where the verb *addaba* is used in the sense of 'to educate', 'to bring up', 'to discipline' especially in the moral sense.[52] Other examples from seventh century literary production reveal a use of *adab* for 'diplomacy, courtesy' as social virtues, and 'refinement, grace' in the ethical sphere.

The association of *adab* with social and ethical virtues becomes more evident in the eighth and ninth centuries and is supported by two works. The first is a small treatise by ʿAbd Allāh ibn al-Muqaffaʿ (d. c. 140/757), called *Kitāb al-adab al-ṣaghīr*. The book contains teachings and suggestions on practical morals and the terms *adab* and *ādāb* mean 'way of behaving', especially if laudable, 'inward grace', 'beauty of character' which one acquires through education, as well as 'learning', 'education' in the passive sense.[53] This same interpretation of *adab* is evident also in the third chapter of the *Ḥamāsa*, an anthology of Bedouin poetry compiled by the ʿAbbasid poet Abū Tammām (d. c. 231/845). As Nallino observes, this chapter, called '*Adab*', contains verses dealing with moral precepts and good qualities of the soul (fear of incurring blame, abhorrence of immoral actions, courtesy, indulgence towards friends, etc.), i.e., all that guides people in their conduct.[54] Therefore, once again *adab* is used as a synonym for good character and wisdom and the related qualities. The application of *adab* as nobility of character and good conduct finds evidence also in other works. Thus, for example, Abū ʿAbd Allāh al-Bukhārī (d. 256/870), in his *al-Jāmiʿ al-ṣaḥīḥ*, dedicates the *Kitāb al-adab* to 'practical morals and to the social rules' (duties towards one's parents; taking care of widows, orphans and the poor; duties towards one's neighbours; hospitality, etc.).[55] In a similar way, moral precepts are the subject of the *Kitāb al-adab* by the poet Ibn al-Muʿtazz (d. 296/908).

During the eighth century, and the beginning of the ninth, new meanings came to be applied to the term *adab*. For the first time, *adab* appears in relation to literature, as referring either to literary talent, or literary scholarship, i.e., knowledge of literature as a sign of good education, or, more particularly, literary production, mainly poetry.[56] This association of *adab* with learning continues until the tenth century, especially in relation to knowledge of classical literature, as well as philology, grammar and lexicography. However, the new concepts of creative talent and literary erudition were never separated from the original ones of taste and beauty of character. This is evident in the usage of the term *adab* by the beginning of the ninth century, when it came to indicate certain social graces which implied the ability to entertain people with witticism, anecdotes, proverbs, aphorisms, elegant verse and stories, and to use quotations and digressions to make one's conversation attractive and pleasant. Hence, the *adīb* became 'he who takes the best of everything and puts it together,'[57] i.e., he who possesses a general erudition in all matters.[58] The social connotations of the literary erudition of the *adīb* appear clearly in the *Kitāb al-muwashshā* by Abū'l-Ṭayyib Muḥammad b. Isḥāq b. Yaḥyā al-Aʿrābī, known as al-Washshā' (d. 325/937).[59] In it the term *adab* somehow loses its original moral connotation and rather designates all that must be known and observed by those who want to be in the company of the people of elegance and distinction. Therefore, *adab* acquired the meaning of grace in one's outward behaviour, affability, elegance in the way of dressing, eating and drinking, eloquence, and ability to embellish one's talk through literary quotations. This is also the use of *adab* in the *Kitāb al-ʿiqd al-farīd* by Aḥmad ibn ʿAbd Rabbihi al-Andalusī (d. 328/940), especially in the chapter dealing with the *ādāb* of the erudite men.

To satisfy the need for *adab* in this sense, many books were written, which contained collections of passages of poetry, anecdotes and bizarre stories intended to entertain the reader as well as to provide the apprentice 'man of *adab*' with material for his training. Among them were the many works of Abū ʿUthmān ʿAmr b. Baḥr al-Jāḥiẓ (d. 255/869), and the above-mentioned *al-ʿIqd al-farīd* by Ibn ʿAbd Rabbihi. However, this usage of the term often included the application of *adab* as meaning 'all literary composition of style and distinction, and not simply elegant extracts.' In this sense, one could explain how *adab* progressively came to acquire the active sense of literary skills (eloquence being deemed the Arab characteristic *par excellence*) as well as the passive sense of literary scholarship and the classical literary heritage that was the object of such scholarship.[60]

A further stage in the development of the term *adab* is its application in the sense of what a certain class of people must know and the rules of conduct pertaining to a particular social group. This usage of the term, which can be dated as early as the ninth century, is of special interest to us, as it is somehow closer to Sulamī's use of *adab* (and *ādāb*) in the *Jawāmiᶜ ādāb al-ṣūfiyya*. As examples for this particular usage, Nallino quotes Ibn Qutayba al-Dīnawarī's (d. 276/889)[61] *Adab al-kātib* or *Adab al-kuttāb*, a book collecting the kind of knowledge, and especially linguistic notions, required for secretaries, and Kushājim's (d. c. 350/961) *Adab al-nadīm*, a treatise on rules of conduct for boon-companions. Other works were composed as well, with such titles as *Adab al-wuzarā'* ('Rules of Behaviour for the Vizier'), or *Adab al-qāḍī* ('What the Judge Should Know and Do'). By the end of the ninth century, many other instances can be quoted, which confirm the application of *adab* in the sense of the way of conducting oneself while engaged in some specific art, science, or other activity.[62] Such are, for example, the chapters on *ādāb al-ḥukamā' wa'l-ᶜulamā'* ('The Conduct of Sages and Men of Learning'), on *al-adab fī'l-ḥadīth wa'l-istimāᶜ* ('How to Converse and How to Listen'), and on *al-adab fī'l-mujālasa* ('The Rules of Social Intercourse'), in Ibn ᶜAbd Rabbihi's *al-ᶜIqd al-farīd*. However specialised the contexts in which this usage of *adab* appears to have been applied in these works, *adab* was mostly intended in a more general sense and it was used as well to refer to 'some general concept of human activity, either as an object of observation or as a model for behaviour.'[63]

A remark needs to be made here for the sake of clarity. As we have seen, by the ninth century the term *adab* had acquired a variety of meanings and applications in which the socio-ethical and the literary concepts progressively tended to merge. In the light of this, it is natural to question whether the terms '*adab* literature' and '*adab* works' can be properly used—as western scholars have usually done—to define a literary category and a specific genre of Arabic literature. Although the definitions of this genre are disparate and various, 'it is generally felt', as Bonebakker puts it, 'that *adab* works are usually miscellanies of one sort or another and are encyclopedic and didactic in their aims, though non-technical in their approach;'[64] in this sense, the works of Jāḥiẓ are seen as representative of *adab* literature. However, we find the word *adab* applied to writings of quite different nature and structure, from those having a merely entertaining character to those requiring expertise from their audience, from works dealing with practical morals to works narrower in scope. Thus, for instance, although the *Kitāb al-maḥāsin wa'l-masāwi'* ('The Book on Good and Bad Qualities') by Ibrāhīm b. Aḥmad al-Bayhaqī (d. 320/932), includes discussions on literary topics, it generally deals with good and evil, and has mainly an edifying purpose. On the other hand, Abū Isḥāq b. Ibrāhīm al-Ḥuṣrī's (d. 413/1022) *Zahr al-ādāb*, which is also considered an *adab* work, is a selection of pieces of eloquence from poems, stories and prose extracts, and has therefore a marked literary connotation. Other so-called *adab* works are too technical in content and restricted in scope to justify such designation: this is the case, for example, of the mystic Abū Ḥayyān al-Tawḥīdī's (d. 414/1023) *al-Ishārāt al-ilāhiyya*, which has a marked Sufi character. For this reason, throughout my work I have referred to the category '*adab* literature', while I am fully aware of the heterogeneity of this kind of literature and of the difficulties raised by the use of the term *adab* as applied to a specific genre.

The development in the applications of the term *adab*, which we have observed in this brief review, highlights a certain polarity between secular and religious learning. Nallino points out that the type of *adab* as applied to literary scholarship usually comprised 'all existing types of knowledge, exclusive of matters pertaining to religion.'[65] Moreover, as we have seen, the first usage of the term as 'customary practice' originally referred to the customs of the pre-Islamic period. Yet, if in the sense of literary skills the religious connotation was actually kept out from the usage of *adab*, in the other sense of 'custom' and 'education based on such custom' the absorption of *adab* into the Islamic context was immediate and spontaneous. Thus, those virtues which were typical of ancient Arab society and constituted the traditional practice (*adab*) were progressively assimilated into the religious sphere, in so far as they were in harmony with Islamic tenets and morals. Therefore, religious ethical attitudes were gradually absorbed into the literary framework of *adab* and an originally popular philosophy of morality came to acquire an evident religious connotation. Thus, for instance, Washshā', in giving an exposition of the sentiments and manners of the ideal man of culture (*ẓarīf*) in his *Kitāb al-muwashshā,* already quotes the Qur'ān and the Hadith; ethical treatises, such as the *Adab al-dunyā wa'l-dīn* by the famous constitutional theorist of Baghdad, Mawardī (d. 450/1058), were abundant with wise sayings of the Prophet and the Companions.[66] Later on, the use of the term *ādāb* began to appear in relation with specifically Islamic notions of morality and in the course of time this connection became more and more systematic. Thus, works of an edifying nature were composed by ascetics and Sufis where sayings of kings, sages and Sufi masters were collected along with Hadiths and Qur'ānic passages to illustrate rules of moral behaviour and practical ethics. Some western scholars have designated this kind of early edifying Islamic literature by the term *zuhd*[67] and have accordingly classified these works as *zuhd* works. Such are, for instance, the books of Ibn Abī'l-Dunyā (d. 281/894), in which popular material is used to impart moral guidance. The boundary between this kind of literature and *adab* literature is not easily definable: indeed, many *zuhd* works could as effectively be classified as *adab* works or also *zuhd-ṣūfī* works. All these categories include those kinds of works dealing with practical morals and providing guidance and advice for the pious believer. As Kinberg explains, 'some works of this kind focus on distinguished figures of *zuhd* and early Sufism, and as such share certain features with biographical dictionaries. Others follow thematic lines and concentrate on duties to be performed and virtues to be preserved. Yet others combine both methods and present the pious Muslims of the first centuries of Islam as models of conduct, whose way of life should be cherished and followed.'[68] The works which are of interest to us in this survey are those belonging to what I may finally call the '*zuhd-ṣūfī*' literature, i.e., the literature dealing more strictly with religious Islamic morals. For example: *al-Zuhd wa'l-raqā'iq* by ᶜAbd Allāh b. al-Mubārak (d. 181/797), *Kitāb al-zuhd* by Wakīᶜ b. al-Jarrāḥ (d. 197/812), *al-Zuhd* by Aḥmad b. Ḥanbal (d.241/855), *Kitāb al-zuhd* by Hannād b. al-Sarī (d. 243/857), some works of the aforementioned Ibn Abī'l-Dunyā, *Kitāb al-miḥan* by Abū'l-ᶜArab al-Tamīmī (d. 333/944), *Kitāb al-zuhd* by Ibn al-Aᶜrābī (d. 340/951), and *al-Fawā'id wa'l-zuhd* by Khuldī (d. 348/959). The authors of early *zuhd-ṣūfī* works figure as the literary ancestors of Sulamī and some interesting similarities could be drawn between these works and the *Jawāmiᶜ ādāb al-ṣūfiyya*.

As an example of that, I have considered the *Kitāb al-manām* by Ibn Abī'l-Dunyā and I have tried to show some analogies between this work and Sulamī's *Jawāmiᶜ*. Ibn Abī'l-Dunyā's *Kitāb al-manām*[69] is 'a unique collection of edifying anecdotes recorded as dreams that present Islamic piety.'[70] There, the author uses the descriptions delivered by dreams as a literary means for supplying moral counsel, and, by focusing on specific values, he aims to provide the pious believer with a moral code to be followed. The set of virtues and duties of the *Kitāb al-manām* closely resembles that of the *Jawāmiᶜ*: we find amongst them, for instance, the love for God and the desire to draw near Him; confidence in providence (*ḥusn al-ẓann bi'Llāh*); contentment (*riḍā*); total trust in God (*tawakkul*) and remembrance of Him (*dhikr*); gratitude (*shukr*); scrupulousness (*waraᶜ*); patience (*ṣabr*); and awareness of imminent death (*qiṣar al-amal*).[71] The nature of Sulamī's *Jawāmiᶜ* is obviously different from that of the *Kitāb al-manām*, as the former is a collection of Sufi rules of behaviour and is intended mostly for a Sufi audience, while the latter deals more specifically with eschatological[72] material and has been conceived as general guidance for the pious Muslim. Therefore, if in the *Jawāmiʿ* the above mentioned virtues and duties are dealt with at length and are described in detail, in Ibn Abī'l-Dunyā's *Kitāb* they are just mentioned within the description of the dream as a means for directing the individual towards a way of conduct that will grant him a reward after death and will lead him eventually to a pleasant life in the Hereafter. Yet, the structure and main contents of the books are quite similar. Both are collections of existing material: they include quotations from Qur'ānic verses (or allusions to Qur'ānic phrases) and quotations from Hadiths, as well as sayings of pious people and spiritual masters, to which a careful *isnād* is always attached. The material is organised in an unsystematic way and very often sayings from the same transmitter and sections dealing with the same subject are reported separately.[73] Moreover, both works contain material dealing with the human–divine relationship as well as with interpersonal relationships. Finally, although concerned primarily with *zuhd* topics, they both take a popular form and concentrate on the descriptive aspect rather than on the theological one.[74]

Finally, we find works on specific Sufi *ādāb* which were written by Sufis long before Sulamī's time. Unlike the other *adab* works, these works dealt particularly with Sufi customs, attitudes and rules of conduct (*ādāb*) and were intended mostly for a restricted audience, being usually addressed to the novice at the beginning of the Sufi path.[75] Among those which are extant in manuscript are the *Adab al-muftaqir ilā Allāh* ('The *adab* of those who need God') by Junayd (d. 298/910),[76] the *Kitāb adab al-nafs* ('The book on the *adab* of the *nafs*') by al-Ḥakīm al-Tirmidhī (d. after 318/930),[77] and the *Adab al-faqīr* ('The *adab* of the poor' or 'The *adab* of the mystic') by Abū ʿAbd Allāh al-Rūdhbārī (d. 369/979).[78] We also find writings dealing with more specific Sufi issues. Thus some authors dealt with the subject of *nafs*, first in the form of aphorisms and then with real treatises: one can mention, for instance, the *Dawā' dā' al-qulūb wa-maʿrifat himam al-nafs wa-ādābihā* ('The remedy for the disease of the heart and the knowledge of the intentions of the *nafs* and the *ādāb* of it') by Abū ʿAbd Allāh al-Anṭākī (d. 220/835)[79] and the *Ādāb al-nufūs* ('The *ādāb* of the *nafs*') by al-Ḥārith al-Muḥāsibī (d. 243/857).[80] These works, along with the heterogeneous *adab* production of which a brief outline has been given above, represent the literary tradition preceding Sulamī and constitute the vast source material from which the author probably drew his inspiration.

SULAMĪ'S *JAWĀMIʿ ĀDĀB AL-ṢŪFIYYA*

As we have seen above, treatises on Sufi manners and customs were written long before Sulamī's time. Sulamī himself composed many works of this kind, such as the aforementioned *Ādāb al-ṣuḥba wa-ḥusn al-ʿishra* and the *Ādāb al-faqr wa-sharā'iṭuhu.*[81] Yet, the best known work of Sulamī which deals extensively with Sufi conduct and practice, the *Sunan al-ṣūfiyya*, is lost today.[82] Extracts of the *Sunan*'s contents are found in the *al-Sunan al-kubrā*, the *Kitāb al-zuhd al-kabīr*, and the *Shuʿab al-īmān* of Abū Bakr Aḥmad b. al-Ḥusayn b. ʿAlī al-Bayhaqī (d. 458/1066). The *Kitāb al-zuhd al-kabīr* includes about 150 passages on Sulamī's authority out of a total of about 990 passages, whereas the much more extensive *Shuʿab al-īmān* contains more than 500 such passages. The material on Sulamī's authority integrated in the *al-Sunan al-kubrā* is as considerable as that in Bayhaqī's other two works.[83] As Böwering observes, judging by these excerpts, 'Sulamī's *Sunan* appears to have been similar to a variety of minor treatises on Sufi practice, some of which have been edited.'[84] Of these minor treatises the *Jawāmiʿ ādāb al-ṣūfiyya* is probably the one which is closer in content and structure to the lost *Sunan*.

The *Jawāmiʿ ādāb al-ṣūfiyya*[85] is 'a collection of Sufi rules of conduct', intended to provide the reader with an accurate formulation of Sufi attitudes and beliefs[86] so that 'those who criticize them [i.e., criticise the Sufis] without really knowing the truth can learn about them, their way of life and their customs' and thus 'think about them as they deserve' (2).[87] As we see, the composition of this treatise seems to have been prompted by the author's awareness of the need for a clear and systematic formulation of the Sufi discipline at a time when Sufism was being attacked and its orthodoxy was being questioned by many.[88] Therefore, in the introductory sections of the *Jawāmiᶜ* (1–7), Sulamī emphasises a basic concept which also underlies many of his other works, i.e., that Sufi *ādāb* not only are in keeping with the orthodox position, but are based directly on the Qur'ān and on the character and behaviour of the Prophet himself. In fact, as Sulamī explains by quoting some significant Qur'ānic passages, *adab* was given by God to mankind when He commanded 'the doing of good, and liberality to kith and kin' and when He forbade them 'all shameful deeds, and injustice and rebellion' (4). The highest degree of conformity to the morals as laid down in the Qur'ān was achieved by the Prophet Muhammad, whose character (*khuluq*) is, in Sulamī's words, 'the most splendid ornament in the *adab*' (4). The Prophet's behaviour, as well as that of his Companions, has then become the model to be followed by the Sufis, and the Muslims in general, through a faithful adherence to the traditional practices and norms of the Sunna (110). Moreover, in section 7 Sulamī shows the importance of *adab* to the mystics by quoting maxims and sayings of some early Sufi masters. There, it is said that 'the faith of the godservant does not prove true except through *adab*' and 'through *adab* man reaches the most sublime states and the highest ranks in this world and the next'; therefore, the acquisition of discipline must be regarded as more excellent and laudable to the Sufi 'than keeping oneself thirsty for a long time in the midday heat or staying awake always at night.'

The structure of the *Jawāmiᶜ* is similar to that of other works by Sulamī.[89] The introduction is followed by 163 sections: each one has a heading that begins with the formula *wa-min ādābihim* and sets out a specific rule of conduct. The section proper is intended to sanction and illustrate this rule by quoting Qur'ānic verses, Hadiths, sayings of early Sufi masters and poems: the *Jawāmiʿ* contains 26 quotations from the Qur'ān, 19 Hadiths, some 250 Sufi sayings, and four passages of poetry. The sections are arranged arbitrarily, except in a few cases,[90] and they differ greatly in length.

The topics dealt with in the *Jawāmiʿ* are various and cover the wide range of themes which were discussed among Sufis in the tenth and eleventh centuries, such as the relationship between master and novice and between fellow Sufis, the Sufi's struggle against the baser appetites and his rejection of worldly pursuits. The various topics develop a theme which is common to many mystic traditions and which represents the leitmotif of the book, namely the necessity of proper behaviour (*adab*) to help achieve a thorough spiritual realisation. Sulamī's concept of *adab* can be well summarised in the saying of Muḥammad b. ʿAlī al-Tirmidhī (26): '*Adab* is to be careful how you act so that your masters may not reprove you, to take nothing from this world that the ascetics would blame you for, never prefer this world to the Hereafter, lest the men of wisdom condemn you, and to behave with your Lord during your retreat in such a way that the Recording Angels need not reproach you. The basis of *adab* and its perfection consist in contemplating in your secret-heart nothing but your Lord and seeking nothing either in this world or in the Hereafter but His satisfaction.'

In order to keep proper behaviour the Sufi must follow specific rules of conduct (*ādāb*). Indeed, the *ādāb* dealt with in the *Jawāmiʿ* are so numerous and diversified that it would be difficult to summarise them all here. Some of them are strictly related to Sufi practices, such as those concerning the invocation of God (*dhikr*, 84, 160) and the mystical audition (*samāʿ*, 125); others deal with topics having a universal validity, as they belong to the principles of common ethics and moral practice and could be as well applied to everyone.

Two key terms in Sulamī's collection are *adab al-ẓāhir* and *adab al-bāṭin*: the first designates the discipline of one's external behaviour and the second the discipline of one's interior. On these two terms is developed the basic idea of the book, i.e., that the mystic, and man in general, should be constantly striving toward attaining total harmony between his exterior conduct and his intimate attitude to God (30, 57, 153). The *adab* with God (119) consists basically in 'being perseverant in his dealing (with God)', i.e., performing acts of devotion without negligence, and 'rectifying his dealing (with Him) through the contemplation of Him', i.e., always directing one's inward thoughts to the thought of Him (149). The *adab* with the godservants is dealt with at great length in the *Jawāmiʿ* and entails the using of kindness (18, 22–3) and generosity (15, 20), being good company (*ḥusn al-ṣuḥba*, 17), having a good opinion of people (122, 141–2) and forgiving them their faults, and always preferring others to oneself (*īthār*, 31, 103).

On his way to God, the Sufi must constantly fight against the inclinations of the ego-self (*nafs*) and always be aware of its faults and defects (10, 16, 88); he must rely on God and in His providential arrangements unreservedly (*tawakkul*), and therefore he should abandon self-direction (*tark al-tadbīr*) and avoid planning independently for his life (36, 74, 86). Being aware of the prospect of death (*taqṣīr al-amal*, 9, 78, 91), he should live for the present moment (*waqt*) and always occupy it in fulfilling his duties toward the Lord (25, 40, 78, 91, 139, 159, 162). The mystic's way of eating and speaking is also regulated (27, 100, 102, 104, 108, 126), and rules are set as well for his travelling (17, 28, 50, 58, 97).

Although the *Jawāmiʿ* contains many exhortations to detach one's self from this world and live a life of isolation (*tajrīd*) for the purpose of contemplation (39, 118), work is not rejected altogether: rather, the Sufi is advised not to renounce gaining his living except after he has perfected his trust in God (47). Therefore, both the attitudes of the *mutasabbib* (i.e., he who gains his living) and the *mutajarrid* (i.e., he who isolates himself) are regarded as commendable, as long as the former gets 'as much sustenance as suffices him, without indulging pleasure and desire' (45), and the latter does not resort to begging (*su'āl*, *kudya*) as a profession

(51, 53, 144, 154). In any case, poverty (*faqr*) must be practised constantly. Many are the rules set out in the book which relate to the Sufi's duty of poverty and regulate its *ādāb*, both when practising it (15, 68) and when staying with those who practise it (20, 13, 39). As said by Abū ʿAbd Allāh b. Khafīf, 'the *adab* of poverty is to be happy in it, conceal one's neediness, and be content with every circumstance that comes to one because of it, knowing as a certainty that poverty is a favour bestowed by God upon those of His servants whom He loves most' (148).

The Sufi must 'travel' (*salaka*) along the spiritual Path with a sound attitude and an authentic desire for the truth, abstaining from false claims and deceitful expectations. In many passages of the *Jawāmiʿ*, Sulamī exhorts the Sufi to 'rectify his mystical states' (*taṣḥīḥ al-aḥwāl*), that is to say, to maintain an attitude of integrity and purity of heart, while experiencing the spiritual path. Therefore, the sincere Sufi should strive for absolute honesty towards himself and towards his fellows, abstaining from false claims and spiritual pretensions (*tark al-daʿāwā*). Thus, for instance, he should not claim to have experienced mystical illumination if he has not (117) or to have reached a state of ecstasy during a *samāʿ* session (125), and he should avoid talking about states which he has not experienced.

It is interesting to note that the attitude of *tark al-daʿāwā* is described in Sulamī's *Risālat al-malāmatiyya* as a distinctive feature of the *malāmatī* mystics, whereas the Sufis are alleged to disclose their spiritual experiences.[91] As Kohlberg observes,[92] this can be explained by the fact that Sulamī uses the word '*ṣūfī*' in two different senses in the two books. In the *Jawāmiʿ*, a '*ṣūfī*' is anyone who has gone through the first stage of novitiate (*irāda*) and who abides by the Sufi rules of conduct. In the *Risālat al-malāmatiyya*, the term '*ṣūfī*' refers instead to a person 'who stands one rung below the top of the spiritual ladder', which is occupied by the *Malāmatī*.[93] Hence, the term '*ṣūfī*' in the *Jawāmiʿ* is synonymous with the term *malāmatī* in the *Risālat al-malāmatiyya*, and, as concludes Kohlberg, 'it is hardly surprising, then, to find that many of the *ādāb* described in the *Jawāmiʿ* as incumbent on ṣūfīs closely resemble the *uṣūl* of the *Malāmatīs*.'[94] The same can be said if we consider Sulamī's discussion of the mystical rule concerning the concealment of one's inward states. In the *Risāla* the attitude of hiding one's spiritual condition is said to be the distinctive mark of the *Malāmatī*, whereas the Sufi is described as the one who manifests outwardly the light of his interior state. In the *Jawāmiʿ*, by contrast, it is said that it is the duty of every sincere Sufi to guard his secret heart (*ḥifẓ al-sirr*, 30) and be constantly vigilant and attentive in keeping it hidden (10, 25, 53, 113, 150). This attitude, which helps the mystic escape the traps of self-complacency and preserve the secret of his condition, is seen as one of the fundamentals of Sufi behaviour and is mentioned frequently among the rules to be followed by anyone who aims at attaining spiritual realisation.

The *Jawāmiʿ* forms somehow a link between those works by Sulamī having an evident popular appeal, such as the *Ādāb al-ṣuḥba*, and the works having an explicit esoteric nature and intended exclusively for the Sufi élite, such as the *Ḥaqā'iq al-tafsīr*. In the *Jawāmiʿ*, these two attitudes are well combined together, which contributed to make this work of interest both for the Sufi élite and the general public.

The originality of the *Jawāmiʿ* lies in the basic subject matter of the book as well as in the author's approach, which is rather different from that of most Sufi writers. As regards the content, the *Jawāmiʿ ādāb al-ṣūfiyya* is seemingly 'the first single work ever entirely devoted to describing many disparate *ādāb*.'[95] In fact, Sufi treatises generally dealt with *adab* as one of the many stations in the Sufi path: indeed, they usually used the word *adab* to mean 'good conduct' or 'decorum', and therefore they dedicated to it only a separate section within a wider discussion on Sufi conduct and virtues.[96] The *Jawāmiʿ* instead was conceived as a work on *adab* specifically and therefore it was wholly devoted to illustrating the many rules concerning Sufi life and behaviour. Moreover, unlike other works by Sulamī, where the author discusses the *ādāb* pertaining only to one virtue or one set of virtues,[97] the *Jawāmiʿ* is intended to cover all the *ādāb* concerning both the Sufi's inward conduct and his outward behaviour with people, as well as his intimate relationship with God.

As for the author's approach to the subject, I have already mentioned the particular 'in-between' nature of the *Jawāmiʿ*, which can be read both as a popular edifying work and as a Sufi book. On the one hand, the *Jawāmiʿ ādāb al-ṣūfiyya* forms a link between the *adab* and Sufi literature and it belongs to the kind of the edifying Sufi works in which the Sufi esoteric themes were not much emphasised. Therefore, although intended for the novice, the book does not have the exclusive character typical of many Sufi manuals for the *murīd*. The vocabulary used is in general free of esoteric connotations and on the whole the construction and the style resemble those of *adab* works. On the other hand, it is a Sufi book, intended first and foremost for the *murīd*, and conceived basically for a high moral Sufi society whose norms of behaviour it aims to outline. The *ādāb* described in Sulamī's collection concern both the Sufi's relationship with himself and with his fellows; the outer world is mentioned only sporadically. This feature, which Kohlberg calls the 'inward-looking aspect of the *Jawāmiʿ*',[98] represents a very peculiar trait of the book in evident contrast to other works of this kind, usually concerned with setting out 'outward' rules of social behaviour regulating man's conduct in his dealings with other people.[99] Therefore, as Kohlberg observes,[100] the author's special interest in discussing the Sufi's attitudes to himself and to his fellow mystics rather than to the outside world as well as the preponderance of Sufi sayings over Hadiths[101] mark the book as essentially a Sufi work. Finally, besides the content, the element that is truly indicative of the Sufi nature of the book is its language. The vocabulary used by the author, although free of the esoteric technicality typical of many Sufi works, is often charged with meanings and connotations, which can be best understood by those acquainted with the Arabic language and with Sufi idiom in particular.

In dealing with the subjects, Sulamī adhered to the role of a compiler: in fact, the *Jawāmiʿ ādāb al-ṣūfiyya* is mainly a collection of Sufi sayings representing the views of more than five generations of thinkers and accompanied by Qurʾānic verses and Hadiths, which are quoted with an illustrative intent. The author culled the sayings and maxims constituting the *Jawāmiʿ* from a vast material heard by him from his masters and colleagues in the course of many years of thorough study and activity in the field of Hadith and in that of Sufism. Therefore, the main contribution of the author—as it can be judged by his *Jawāmiʿ*—lies not in the presentation of new material, but rather in the compilation of early material, and in the selection and arrangement of it. Indeed, the *Jawāmiʿ* appears as a faithful mirror of a whole tradition of Sufi thought and that accounts for the importance attached to this work within the history of Arabic Sufi literature.

Unlike other known treatises on Sufi practices and virtues, the *Jawāmiʿ* is a relatively short work, and the topics are not treated extensively, which probably accounts for it usually being classified among Sulamī's 'minor' works. While the *Sunan al-ṣūfiyya* must have played a significant role in the transmission of Sufi material,[102] the *Jawāmiʿ* seems not to have been taken into much consideration by Sulamī's successors.[103] However, because the *Sunan* is lost, that surely makes the short *Jawāmiʿ* more important today than it was before. Finally, I believe a work of this kind is of great significance to Arabic Sufi literature. Its contribution lies in its embodying a whole tradition of Sufi thinking, as well as in the author's distinctive treatment of this subject, and above all in his emphasis that the essence of Sufism is close adherence to God's *adab* as known through the Qurʾān and Sunna. At a time when an increasing number of people are interested in Sufism, and may be confused by its many varieties, this book remains a useful guide to the principles of Islamic mysticism, as originally developed within Sunni orthodoxy.

Notes to Introduction

[1] For Sulamī's biography see: Pedersen, Johannes, *Kitāb Ṭabaqāt al-Ṣūfiyya: Texte arabe avec une introduction et un index,* Leiden: E. J. Brill, 1960, pp. 19–23; Böwering, Gerhard, 'Al-Sulamī' in *EI* (*The Encyclopaedia of Islam*), new edition, ed. by H. A. R. Gibb et al., Leiden: E. J. Brill, 1998, v. IX, pp. 811–12; *id.*, 'The Qur'ān Commentary of Al-Sulamī', in W. B. Hallaq and D. P. Little (eds.), *Islamic Studies Presented to Charles J. Adams*, Leiden 1991, pp. 41–56; Kohlberg, Etan, *Jawāmiᶜ Ādāb al-Ṣūfiyya and ᶜUyūb al-Nafs wa-Mudāwātuhā by Abū ᶜAbd al-Raḥmān al-Sulamī*, edited with an introduction, The Max Schloessinger Memorial Series, Texts 1, Jerusalem: Jerusalem Academic Press, 1976, pp. 7–8; Kister, M. J., *Kitab Ādāb aṣ-Ṣuḥba by Abū ᶜAbd ar-Raḥmān as-Sulamī*, Jerusalem: The Israel Oriental Society, 1954, pp. 1–2 (English) and pp. 3–4 (Arabic).

[2] On *Malāmatiyya*, see in this chapter my discussion of Sulamī's *Risālat al-malāmatiyya*.

[3] See Sezgin, Fuat, GAS, Leiden: E. J. Brill, 1967, I, p. 663, n. 35.

[4] See, in particular, his collection of Hadiths known as *Ḥadīth* (or *Juz'*) *al-Sulamī*, GAS I, p. 674, n. 24; the *Kitāb Ādāb aṣ-Ṣuḥba*, Kister, M. J., *op. cit*; *Kitāb al-arbaᶜīn fī'l-taṣawwuf*, Ḥaydarābād 1369/1950.

[5] On the accusations against Sulamī, see Pedersen, J., *op. cit.*, pp. 61–62; Böwering, G., 'The Qur'ān Commentary of al-Sulamī', pp. 51–52.

[6] See Kister M. J., *op. cit*; pp. 6–9 (Arabic) and 3–5 (English). According to Kister, in fact, most of these accusations were levelled by the opponents of the Sufi movement, who did not approve of Sulamī's interpretation of the Qur'ān in his work *Ḥaqā'iq al-tafsīr* and of his use of the method of *ta'wīl* (allegoric interpretation), and therefore opposed him by alleging that he forged traditions. As Kister states, 'there is hardly any ḥadīth cited by him, which did not appear prior to as-Sulamī's time in one of the collections of Ḥadīth, the Adab literature or the Sufi writings.' 'Of course,' Kister continues, 'there are in his works many ḥadīths transmitted by men unreliable according to Islamic tradition, but it is certain that as-Sulamī did not do more than innocently repeat the ḥadīths' [Kister, *op. cit.*, p. 4 (English)].

[7] See Meier, Fritz, 'Ein wichtiger Handschriftenfund zur sufi: Abū ᶜAbdarraḥmān Muḥammad b. al-Ḥusayn as-Sulamī (gest. 412/1021)', in *Oriens* 20 (1967), p. 106.

[8] Cf. Pedersen, J., *op. cit.*, p. 32.

[9] For the quotations from Sulamī in Qushayrī's *Risāla*, see Pedersen, J., *op. cit.*, pp. 53–54. The fact that a later famous Sufi, Abū Saᶜīd b. Abī'l-Khayr

(d. 440/1049), was sent by his teacher to Sulamī, in order to be invested by him with the *khirqa*, tells us clearly of the high respect and esteem our author enjoyed among his contemporaries [see, Nicholson, R. A., *Studies in Islamic Mysticism*, Cambridge: Cambridge University Press, 1921, p. 14].

[10] The long list of his works has been left by Sulamī himself, in the hand of his scribe Abū Saʿīd Muḥammad b. ʿAlī al-Khashshāb (d. 456/1064) [see Böwering, 'The Qur'ān Commentary of Al-Sulamī', p. 45].

[11] For a list of Sulamī's works in manuscript, see Brockelmann, Carl, GAL (*Geschichte der Arabischen Litteratur*), vol. 1, Weimar: Verlag Von Emil Felber, 1898, p. 200–201, and *Supplement Bände*, vol. 1, Leiden: E. J. Brill, 1937, p. 361–362 and p. 955; Sezgin, Fuat, GAS, 1, pp. 671–674. To these we should add Sulamī's *Nasīm al-arwāḥ* and *Risāla fī kalām ash-Shāfiʿī fī'l-taṣawwuf,* described by F. Meier, *op. cit.*, pp. 91–106. Two other works are also mentioned by Kister as ascribed to Sulamī, although they seem not to have survived: *al-Miḥan aṣ-ṣūfiyya* and *al-Maknūn fī manāqib dhī 'n-Nūn* [Kister, *op. cit.*, p. 2].

[12] See the list of Sulamī's edited works in Böwering, G., 'Al-Sulamī', in *EI*, p. 812.

[13] See Böwering, 'The Qur'ān Commentary of Al-Sulamī', p. 45; *ibid.*, p. 50, for the chronological sequence of Sulamī's writings.

[14] *Kitāb Ṭabaqāt al-Ṣūfiyya: Texte arabe avec une introduction et un index* by Johannes Pedersen, Leiden: E. J. Brill, 1960. In 1969, in Cairo, the *Ṭabaqāt* was also edited by Nūr al-Dīn Sharība with an introduction to the author, his life and his work [See Böwering, 'The Qur'ān Commentary of Al-Sulamī,' p. 45, n. 11]. In his preface to the *Ṭabaqāt*, Sulamī mentions another work of the same kind, the *Kitāb al-zuhd*, where he says he dealt with the generations of the ascetics of Islam from the Prophet's time through the following centuries till the period of full development of Sufism. Although this work is not extant in manuscript, it is known through the quotations of it made by other authors [see Pedersen, J., *op. cit.*, p. 50].

[15] See, for instance, the *Ta'rīkh al-mashā'ikh* or *Ṭabaqāt al-ṣūfiyya* by Tirmidhī (285/898), the *Ḥikāyāt al-mashā'ikh* by Jaʿfar al-Khuldī (d. 348/959), the *Ṭabaqāt al-nussāk* by Abū Saʿīd b. al-Aʿrābī (d. 341/952), and the *Ta'rīkh* by Muḥammad b. ʿAbd Allāh Abū Bakr al-Rāzī (376/986). This last one is often quoted by Sulamī in his *Ṭabaqāt* [see Pedersen, J., *op. cit.*, pp. 24–25].

[16] Cf. Pedersen: 'La haute valeur de son ouvrage tient à ce qu'il est le plus ancien du genre qui nous soit conservé et qu'il donne les références des sentences qu'il cite, at aussi à ce qu'il est tout proche de la période créatrice.' [Pedersen, J., *op. cit.*, p. 25]

[17] Pedersen, J., *op. cit.*, p. 39.

[18] Massignon, L., *Essai sur les origines du lexique technique de la mystique musulmane*, Paris: J. Vrin, 1954; Nwyia, P., 'Le Tafsīr mystique attribué à Jaʿfar

al-Ṣādiq' in *Mèlanges de l'Université Saint-Joseph*, XLIII (1968), pp. 181–230. For the other works containing quotations from Sulamī's *Ḥaqā'iq*, see Böwering, *EI*, *op. cit.*, p. 812.

[19] Böwering, Gerhard., 'The Qur'ān Commentary of Al-Sulamī', in W. B. Hallaq and D. P. Little (eds.), *Islamic Studies Presented to Charles J. Adams*, Leiden: E. J. Brill, 1991, pp. 41–56.

[20] *Ibid.*, p. 49.

[21] The literature of Sufi *Tafsīr*, or Qur'ānic exegesis, is voluminous. In the eighth century, fragments of Qur'ānic commentary were attributed to authors, who were the forebears of Sufi exegetes, such as Ḥasan al-Baṣrī (d. 110/728) and Ja'far al-Ṣādiq (d. 148/765). During the ninth and early tenth centuries prototypes of Sufi Qur'ān commentary were written by famous mystics, such as Dhū 'l-Nūn al-Miṣrī (d. 246/861), Abū Saʿīd al-Kharrāz (d. 286/899), Junayd (d. 298/910), Shiblī (d. 334/946), and most of all, Sahl al-Tustarī (d. 283/896), Ibn ʿAṭā' (d. 311/923), and Abū Bakr al-Wāsiṭī (d. 320/932). For a brief historical survey of Sufi exegesis of the Qur'ān and an analysis of the principal sources of Sulamī's *Ḥaqā'iq*, see Böwering, G., 'The Qur'ān Commentary of Al-Sulamī', pp. 41–43 and pp. 52–55.

[22] That is to say, the traditional (legal and philological) forms of Qur'ānic exegesis.

[23] Böwering, 'The Qur'ān Commentary of Al-Sulamī', pp. 50–51.

[24] Although in his attempt to justify the Sufi method of interpretation, Sulamī himself refers in his work to four levels of meanings: the literal (*ẓāhir*), the metaphorical (*bāṭin*), the moral (*ḥadd*), and the anagogical or mystical (*muṭṭalaʿ*) [cf. Böwering, *id.*, p. 52].

[25] On criticism against Sulamī, see above, notes 5 and 6.

[26] Böwering, G., *The Minor Qur'ān Commentary of Abū ʿAbd ar-Raḥmān Muḥammad b. al-Ḥusayn as-Sulamī (d. 412/1021)*, Recherches (Collection publiée sous la direction de la Faculté des Lettres et des Sciences Humaines de l'Université Saint-Joseph, Beyrouth), Vol. XVII-Nouvelle Série: Language Arabe et Pensée Islamique, Beyrouth: Dar el-Machreq Éd., 1995.

[27] *Ibid.*, p. 19.

[28] For a list of Sulamī's writings on Sufi manners, see Böwering, G., *EI*, p. 812; *id.*, 'The Qur'an Commentary of al-Sulamī', p. 45, n. 12.

[29] Kister, M. J., *Kitab Ādāb aṣ-Ṣuḥba by Abū ʿAbd ar-Raḥmān as-Sulamī*, Jerusalem: The Israel Oriental Society, 1954.

[30] *Ibid.*, pp. 22–23 (Arabic).

[31] For instance: *Wa-min ādābihā al-ṣafḥu ʿan ʿatharāti 'l-ikhwān*: 'One instance of good manners is to forgive brethren their faults', [Kister, *op. cit.*, p. 29 (Arabic)].

[32] Kister, *op. cit.*, p. 6 (English).

[33] I have indicated within brackets the page numbers (in Kister's edition of the Arabic text), where the mentioned rule appears.

[34] *Kitāb al-futuwwa*, ed. by F. Taeschner in *Studia Orientalia J. Pedersen septagenario* (Copenhagen, 1953), pp. 340–351; ed. by S. Ateş, Ankara 1397/1977.

[35] Bayrak, Tosun, *Kitāb al-Futuwwa: The Way of Sufi Chivalry*, New York, 1983; Faouzi, Skali, *Futuwah: Traité de chevalerie soufie*, Paris: Albin Michel, 1989; Sassi, Giuditta, *La Cavalleria spirituale: Kitāb-ul-Futuwwa*, Milan: Luni Editrice, 1998.

[36] On *futuwwa* and its connection with Sufism, see Glossary. Cf. also Taeschner's article in *First Encyclopaedia of Islam 1913–1936*, Leiden: E. J. Brill, 1987, vol. III, pp. 123–124, and G. Sassi's preface to her translation of *K. al-Futuwwa*, *op. cit.*, pp. 7–13.

[37] On *fatā*, see Glossary (*futuwwa*).

[38] I have referred here to Sassi's translation: I have indicated within brackets the number of the chapter (in Roman numerals) and the number of the section in which the mentioned rule appears.

[39] The first edition of the *Risāla* is that by Abū'l-ʿAlā' al-ʿAfīfī (*al-Malāmatiyya wa-'l-ṣūfiyya wa-ahl al-futuwwa*, Cairo: Dār Iḥyā' al-Kutub al-ʿArabiyya, 1364/1945); later, it has been edited, along with other works by Sulamī, by Süleyman Ateş in *Tisʿat kutub li-Abī ʿAbd al-Raḥmān Muḥammad b. al-Ḥusayn b. Mūsā al-Sulamī* (Ankara, 1401/1981), pp. 1–212; more recent is the edition by ʿAbd al-Fattāḥ Aḥmad al-Fāwī in his book *al-Taṣawwuf: al-wajh wa'l-wajh al-ākhar, maʿahu taḥqīq Kitāb uṣūl al-malāmatiyya wa-ghalaṭāt al-ṣūfiyya, li'l-imām Abī ʿAbd al-Raḥmān al-Sulamī (412 H)*, Cairo: Maktabat al-Zahrā', 1995.

[40] See the French translation of the *Risāla* by Roger Deladriere, *La lucidité implacable* (Paris, 1991) and the Italian translation by Giuditta Sassi, *I custodi del segreto: Risālat-ul-Malāmatiyya, ovvero, Epistola della Gente della riprovazione*, Milan: Luni Editrice, 1997. See also Honerkamp's translation of Sulamī's *Darajāt al-ṣādiqīn* ('Stations of the righteous') and *Zalal al-fuqarā'* ('The stumblings of those aspiring') in Honerkamp, K. L., Heer, N., *The Early Sufi Texts*, Louisville: Fons Vitae, 2003, pp. 83–172.

[41] On the *Malāmatiyya* and the meaning of the word, see: Molé, Marijan, *I Mistici Musulmani*, Milan: Adelphi, 1992, pp. 85–93 (the book also contains some quotations from Sulamī's *Risāla*); Sassi's preface to her translation of the *Risāla*, *op. cit.*, pp. 7–15; Schimmel, Annemarie, *Mystical Dimensions of Islam*, Chapel Hill: The University of North Carolina Press, 1975, pp. 86–87.

[42] Among them Ḥujwīrī, who stated: 'The ostentatious man purposely acts in such a way as to win popularity, while the *Malāmatī* purposely acts in such a way that the people reject him. Both have their thoughts fixed on mankind and do not pass beyond that sphere'. [al-Hujwīrī, ʿAlī ibn ʿUthmān al-Jullābī, *The*

Kashf al-maḥjúb, the oldest Persian treatise on Sufiism, translated by R. A. Nicholson, E. J. W. Gibb Memorial Series vol. XVII, London: Luzac, 1967, p. 67].

43 G. Sassi, *I custodi del segreto*, p. 38.

44 *Ibid.*, pp. 19–23.

45 The two texts are contained in the same volume: Kohlberg, Etan, *Jawāmiᶜ Ādāb al-ṣūfiyya and ᶜUyūb al-Nafs wa-Mudāwātuhā by Abū ᶜAbd al-Raḥmān al-Sulamī*, edited with an introduction, The Max Schloessinger Memorial Series, Texts I, Jerusalem: Jerusalem Academic Press, 1976. See pp. 14–18 for the editor's introduction to the *ᶜUyūb al-Nafs wa-Mudāwātuhā*.

46 On *nafs* and its meanings, cf. E. E. Calverley's article, 'Nafs', in *EI*, new edition, ed. C. E. Bosworth et al., Leiden: E. J. Brill, 1993, vol. VII, pp. 880–883.

47 See Kohlberg, *op. cit.*, p. 17.

48 Numerals within brackets refer to the appropriate sections in the text edited by Kohlberg.

49 Nallino, Carlo Alfonso, *La letteratura araba: dagli inizi all'epoca della dinastia Umayyade. Lezioni tenute in arabo all'Università del Cairo*. Traduzione italiana di Maria Nallino (Estratto da C. A. Nallino, *Raccolta di scritti editi ed inediti*, vol. VI), Rome, 1948, 'Introduzione', pp. 1–17.

50 Bonebakker, S. A., '*Adab* and the concept of *Belles-lettres*' in the *Cambridge History of Arabic Literature: ᶜAbbasid belles-lettres*, ed. by Julia Ashtiany et al., Cambridge: Cambridge University Press, 1990; Chapter 1, pp. 16–30. A discussion of the term *adab* and its application, especially in Washshā''s *Kitāb al-muwashshā*, is found also in Vadet, Jean-Claude, *L'Esprit courtois en Orient dans les cinq premiers siècles de L'Hégire*, Paris: Ed. Maisonneuve & Larose, 1968, Livre II, ch. V, pp. 327–339.

51 Nallino, *op. cit.*, p. 4. For the sake of clarity, the quotations from Nallino's *La letteratura araba* have been translated into English.

52 Examples from pre-Islamic times and from the first century of Islam, confirming the association of *adab* with education and training are quoted both in Nallino's work (pp. 4–5) and in the *Cambridge History of Arabic Literature* (pp. 17–19).

53 See Nallino, *op. cit.*, pp. 6–7.

54 *Ibid.*, p. 7.

55 *Ibid.*, p. 7.

56 Examples of this new application of *adab* are quoted by Bonebakker, *op. cit.*, pp. 20–21.

57 Quotation from Yāqūt al-Ḥamawī's *Kitāb irshād al-arīb* in Nallino, *op. cit.*, p. 11.

58 Except those matters related to religion, which were considered as falling within the competence of the *ᶜālim*.

[59] On Washshā' and his *Kitāb al-muwashshā* see, Vadet, *op. cit.*, Livre II, ch. IV, pp. 317–326.

[60] Bonebakker, *op. cit.*, p. 23.

[61] Ibn Qutayba is also known as the author of another famous *adab* work, the *ʿUyūn al-akhbār*, an anthology, aiming at providing the reader with a broad general education on a wide range of topics.

[62] Nallino, *op. cit.*, p. 9.

[63] Bonebakker, *op. cit.*, p. 27.

[64] *Idem.*

[65] Nallino, *op. cit.*, p. 9.

[66] Cf. Hitti, Philip K., *History of the Arabs: from the earliest times to the present*, New York: Macmillan St Martin's Press, 1970, p. 401.

[67] In this sense, the word *zuhd*, which in Sufi terminology properly designates 'ascesis' or 'renunciation of worldly things' (see Glossary), has been interpreted as meaning 'practical ethics'. On this application of *zuhd*, see Kinberg, Leah, 'What is Meant by *Zuhd*', in *Studia Islamica* 61 (1985), pp. 27–44.

[68] Kinberg, Leah, *Ibn Abī al-Dunyā: Morality in the guise of dreams: A critical edition of Kitāb al-Manām*, Leiden: E. J. Brill, 1994, p. 41.

[69] An accurate edition of Ibn Abī'l-Dunyā's *Kitāb al-manām* has been done by Leah Kinberg (see above, *op. cit.*). Kinberg's edition is preceded by an extensive introduction (pp. 11–58), where the editor scrupulously examines the characteristics and structure of the *Kitāb al-manām* and its contribution to Arabic literature.

[70] Kinberg, *op. cit.*, p. 9.

[71] The cross-references to the *Kitāb al-manām*, which I have reported in footnote to my translation of the *Jawāmiʿ*, are intended to highlight this similarity between the two works.

[72] As Kinberg does in her introduction to the *Kitāb al-manām,* I have used here the term 'eschatological' to mean '*popular* descriptions of Death, the Day of Judgement, Paradise and Hell, rather than *theological* examination of the same topics' (Kinberg, L., *op. cit.*, p. 12, n. 1).

[73] Cf. below, 'Sulamī's *Jawāmiʿ ādāb al-ṣūfiyya*'.

[74] For a description of the *Kitāb al-manām*'s contents and style, see Kinberg, L., *op. cit.*, pp. 11–28.

[75] Although every pious individual could also find in them a precious guide for his life.

[76] Sezgin, Fuat, GAS, Leiden: E. J. Brill, 1967, I, p. 649, n. 13.

[77] *Ibid.*, I, p. 656, n. 21. This work has been edited by Arberry and ʿAbd al-Qādir (Cairo, 1947). On it, see also, *The Concept of Sainthood in Early Islamic Mysticism: Two works by al-Ḥakīm al-Tirmidhī (Bad' and Sīrat al-awliyā')*. An

annotated translation with introduction by Bernd Radtke and John O' Kane, Richmond: Curzon Press, 1996, p. 4, n. 10.

[78] GAS, I, p. 663, n. 2. For other Sufi works on *adab*, see, *ibid.*, I, p. 656.

[79] GAS, I, p. 638. However, according to Prof. van Ess (*Die Gedankenwelt des Ḥārith al-Muḥāsibī*, Bonn 1961, pp. 16–18), the work was written by Muḥāsibī, and Anṭākī only transmitted it (cf. Kohlberg, Etan, p. 26).

[80] See GAS, I, p. 641, n. 5, and Kohlberg, *op. cit.*, pp. 10, 14.

[81] GAS, I, p. 673, n. 9. In his introduction Kohlberg (*Jawāmiʿ Ādāb al-Ṣūfiyya and ʿUyūb al-Nafs wa-Mudāwātuhā*, *op. cit.*, p. 10) mentions another treatise by Sulamī with the title *Ādāb al-taʿāzī*, which he believes is probably lost.

[82] As Böwering observes in *The Minor Qur'ān Commentary of Abū ʿAbd ar-Raḥmān Muḥammad b. al-Ḥusayn as-Sulamī (d. 412/1021)*, Beirut: Dār al-Mashriq, 1995, p. 17, note n. 5), Sulamī's *Sunan al-ṣūfiyya* is known to have been transmitted by Abū'l ʿAbbās Aḥmad b. Naṣr b. Aḥmad al-Khiyārijī on the authority of Abū Isḥāq b. Ḥimyār (see, ʿAbd al-Karīm b. Muḥammad al-Rafīʿī al-Qazwīnī, *Tadwīn fī akhbār Qazwīn*, 4 vols., Beirut 1408/1987, II, p. 266).

[83] Böwering, G., *op. cit.*, p. 17, note n. 6.

[84] *Ibid.*, p. 17.

[85] The text of the *Jawāmiʿ* which I have referred to in my work is that edited by Etan Kohlberg and contained in the volume *Jawāmiʿ Ādāb al-Ṣūfiyya and ʿUyūb al-Nafs wa-Mudāwātuhā by Abū ʿAbd al-Raḥmān al-Sulamī*, The Max Schloessinger Memorial Series, Texts 1, Jerusalem: Jerusalem Academic Press, 1976. Kohlberg's edition has proved extremely useful to me, as the many notes accompanying the text throughout, along with the editor's critical introduction, have helped me understand and interpret the text. In 1981 S. Ateş edited the text of the *Jawāmiʿ* along with other minor works by Sulamī (see Süleyman Ateş, *Tisʿat kutub li-Abī ʿAbd al-Raḥmān Muḥammad b. al-Ḥusayn b. Mūsā al-Sulamī*, Ankara, 1401/1981, pp. 1–212); however, as I have not been able to find this edition in Cairo, I have referred exclusively to the edition by Kohlberg.

[86] All of which are included under the term *ādāb*.

[87] Numerals within brackets refer to the appropriate section in the text as edited by Kohlberg.

[88] These same motives prompted many other Sufi authors of Sulamī's time, who composed extensive treatises intended to prove the perfect orthodoxy of Sufi tenets: see, for instance, the *Kitāb al-lumaʿ fī-'l-taṣawwuf*, a thorough exposition of Sufi doctrines written by Abū Naṣr al-Sarrāj (d. 377/988), the *Qūt al-qulūb* by Abū Ṭālib al-Makkī (d. 385/996), and the ten-volume work *Ḥilyat al-awliyā'* by Abū Nuʿaym al-Iṣfahānī (d. 428/1037). Half a century after Sulamī, two great theorists of Sufism, Qushayrī (d. 466/1074) and Hujwīrī

(d. 463/1071) wrote two of the most famous treatises on Sufi teachings and practices: the *Risāla* and the *Kashf al-maḥjūb* respectively. Of the same period is also the *Kitāb manāzil al-sā'irīn* by ʿAbd Allāh al-Anṣārī al-Harawī (d. 481/1089). Cross-references to some of these works have been made systematically and have been reported in footnotes throughout my translation of the *Jawāmiʿ*.

[89] See, for instance, the *Kitāb ādāb al-ṣuḥba*, the *Kitāb al-futuwwa*, and the *ʿUyūb al-nafs wa-mudāwātuhā*.

[90] In sections 52–53, 47–49, and 106–108 the author deals with the same issue consecutively; elsewhere, there are consecutive sections containing sayings attributed to the same person, as in the case of Sarī al-Saqaṭī (sections 88 to 99), Bishr al-Ḥāfī (sections 132 to 136) and al-Ḥusayn b. Manṣūr al-Ḥallāj (sections 83 to 87, and 155–156).

[91] Cf. *Risālat al-malāmatiyya* in G. Sassi's translation, *op. cit.*, p. 21. See also my above analysis of Sulamī's *Risāla* in the section 'The Life and Works of Sulamī'.

[92] Kohlberg, *op. cit.*, pp. 12–13, note n. 36.

[93] Sassi, *op. cit.*, p. 21.

[94] Kohlberg, *op. cit.*, p. 13.

[95] Kohlberg E., *op. cit.*, p. 10. Ibn al-Nadīm mentions a work called *al-Jāmiʿ al-ṣaghīr fī'l-adab* by ʿAlī b. Muḥammad al-Miṣrī (d. 949) (*Kitāb al-Fihrist*, Tehran, 1973, p. 237); however, since this work has been lost, its character cannot be ascertained.

[96] As does, for example, Qushayrī in his *al-Risāla al-Qushayriyya*, where he treats *adab*, intended as correct behaviour, as one of the 43 stations and states of the Sufi path and dedicates to it a separate section of his book (see, *Principles of Sufism by al-Qushayri*, translated from the Arabic by B. R. Von Schlegell, Berkeley: Mizan Press, 1990, Ch. 40: 'Correct behaviour (*Adab*)', pp. 308–315). Similarly, Hujwīrī in his *Kashf al-maḥjūb* deals with 'good manners' (*ḥusn al-adab*) and 'discipline' (*adab*) in the chapter concerning companionship (*ṣuḥba*) and the rules and principles of it (see, *The Kashf al-maḥjúb, the oldest Persian treatise on Sufiism by ʿAlī b. ʿUthmān al-Jullābī al-Hujwīrī*, translated from the text of the Lahore edition by R. A. Nicholson, London: Luzac, 1967, Ch. XXIII: 'The Uncovering of the Ninth Veil: Concerning Companionship, together with its Rules and Principles', pp. 334–366).

[97] See, for instance, *Ādāb al-ṣuḥba*, where Sulamī deals with the *ādāb* regulating the Sufi's 'companionship', i.e., his relationship with people; or the *Ādāb al-faqr*, where the author deals with the rules concerning the virtue of 'poverty' and the conduct to be observed by the 'poor'.

[98] Kohlberg, *op. cit.*, p. 13.

[99] See for instance, Sulamī's *Kitāb ādāb al-ṣuḥba*, where the author defines the

principles of social behaviour by portraying the Sufi in his relations with his family and his friends, with his servants, with the rulers, and so on.

[100] Kohlberg, *op. cit.*, p. 13.

[101] As I have already mentioned, unlike the *Ādāb al-ṣuḥba*, which is mostly a collection of Hadiths, and the *ʿUyūb al-nafs*, which contains only 39 Sufi sayings, as opposed to the many quotations from the Qur'ān and the Prophetic traditions, the *Jawāmiʿ* contains over 250 quotations of *zuhhād* and Sufis.

[102] The fact that Bayhaqī quotes Sulamī so consistently in his works is proof of that.

[103] Carl Brockelmann, in his *Geschichte der Arabischen Litteratur*, while listing Sulamī's works (GAL, I, pp. 200–201, n. 11.b; supplement, I, pp. 361–362, n. 11) does not mention any title that may be connected with the *Jawāmiʿ ādāb al-ṣūfiyya*, nor does Fuat Sezgin in his *Geschichte des Arabischen Schrifttums* (GAS, I, p. 672, n. 4).

A COLLECTION OF SUFI RULES OF CONDUCT

In the Name of God, Most Gracious, Most Merciful. His aid we seek.

1. Praise be to God first and last. God bless the Prophet Muḥammad and his people, and grant them peace! Praise be to God Who graced His friends (*awliyā'*) with rules of conduct (*ādāb*) regulating both their outward and their inward behaviour[1], at the time when He bestowed His favours on them abundantly, as He said: '... and He has made His bounties flow to you in exceeding measure, both seen and unseen.'[2] He made their external conduct modelled on the Sunna of His Prophet the Elect,[3] God bless him and grant him peace, and their innermost attitudes adorned by their vigilant attention to Him (*murāqaba*) and their contemplation of Him (*mushāhada*).[4] Their condition[5] is that of the mystical states (*al-aḥwāl*) because upon them come by inspiration (*yaridu*) and in them arise the various manifestations of spiritual growth (*al-ziyādāt*), which God accords to them in preference to others, at every moment (*waqt*) and with each breath (*nafas*). Indeed, God gives His Mercy to whom He wants of His servants (*ʿibādihi*).

2. Now, it occurred to me to collect something of the *ādāb* of those mystics[6] and friends of God (*awliyā' Allāh*) well-advanced in the spiritual path who are called Sufis (*al-ṣūfiyya*): they are those who disciplined themselves by following the example of the 'People of Purity' (*ahl al-ṣafā'*)[7] and shaped their character (*takhallaqū*) according to their morals (*akhlāq*). In this way, those

who criticise them[8] altogether without really knowing the truth (*min ghayr ḥaqīqat ʿilm*) can learn about them, their way of life and their customs, so that they may think about them as they deserve. I shall set out on this work only after seeking God's help in that and in all my affairs and after relinquishing my power and strength which I entrust to Him. God bless the Prophet Muḥammad and his people and grant them peace!

3. Among these rules of conduct[9] is the instruction that God Most High gave to His Prophet the Elect, peace and blessings upon him, with His words: 'Wert thou severe or harsh-hearted, they would have broken away from around thee: so pass over (their faults), and ask for (God's) forgiveness for them; and consult them in affairs (of moment). Then, when thou hast taken a decision, put thy trust in God. For God loves those who put their trust (in Him).'[10] God Almighty instructed the Prophet to deal outwardly with his community with the best manners and with a courteous disposition; then, in reality, He set him apart from them by making him rely on Him, as He said: 'Then, when thou hast taken a decision, put thy trust in God (*tawakkal ʿalā Allāh*).'

4. And among these rules of conduct is the instruction that God Most High gave to mankind (*al-khalq*) with His words: 'God commands justice, the doing of good (*iḥsān*), and liberality to kith and kin, and He forbids all shameful deeds, and injustice and rebellion: He instructs you, that ye may receive admonition.'[11] This injunction too belongs to the collection of *ādāb* and their virtues. The most splendid ornament in the *adab* is the type of character with which God adorned His Prophet, peace and blessings upon him, by His words: 'And you have an excellent character (*khuluq*).'[12]

5. And among these rules of conduct is the injunction given by God to the Prophet's Companions, with His words: 'O ye who believe! Raise not your voices above the voice of the Prophet, nor speak loudly to him in talk, as ye may speak loudly to one another.'[13] After that, everyone would talk as if by the expression on his face and no one would knock at his door but with his

fingernails. God Most High also said: 'If only they had patience (*ṣabarū*) until thou couldst come out to them, it would be best for them: but God is Oft-Forgiving, Most Merciful.'[14]

6. And among these rules of conduct is the instruction given to the Prophet, peace and blessings upon him, with His words: 'When those[15] come to thee who believe in Our Signs, say: 'Peace be on you'; Your Lord hath inscribed for Himself Mercy'[16] and His Words: 'When thou seest men engaged in vain discourse about Our Signs, turn away from them unless they turn to a different theme.'[17] He also said: 'Therefore treat not the orphan with harshness, nor repulse the petitioner (unheard),'[18] and: 'Send not away those who call on their Lord morning and evening, seeking His Face,'[19] and again: '... and keep thy soul content with those who call on their Lord.'[20] And so forth, many are the examples from the Book of God [and from the Sunna of the Prophet],[21] which would take us too long to mention. Indeed, for the sake of brevity, I have omitted all the chains of authorities [related to the following traditions].

7. It is related by Shaqīq that ᶜAbd Allāh said: The Prophet of God, peace and blessings upon him, said: 'Truly, God provided me with the best rules of conduct and perfected my *adab*.[22] Then, He ordered me to uphold noble traits of character, by His words: "Hold to forgiveness; command what is right; but turn away from the ignorant."'[23]

The following saying is reported by Sharīk ibn ᶜAbd Allāh, who stated: 'Indeed, people go to the man of knowledge (*ᶜālim*),[24] and what they learn from his *adab* is more important to them than what they learn from his speech.'[25]

Dhū'l-Nūn al-Miṣrī said: 'God adorned the religion of Islam with knowledge, elevated it through *adab* and gave it nobility through self-vigilance (*al-taqwā*).'

Abū Jaᶜfar said: '*Adab* is the heritage of good behaviour with God by being sincerely and faithfully devoted to Him (*ḥusn al-muᶜāmala bi'l-ikhlāṣ maᶜ Allāh*).'

Nabājī said: 'For everything there is something which serves it, and what serves religion is *adab*.' Nabājī also said: '*Adab* is the ornament of noble people. It means to keep company with the elders (*al-akābir*), to accept their words and follow their example in their conduct and morals, to guard and respect their teachings (*iltizām ḥurumātihim*), and finally to behave well with one's fellows and friends.'[26]

Abū ʿUbayd al-Nasawī said: '*Adab* is more excellent and noble for the devotees (*al-ʿubbād*) than keeping oneself thirsty for a long time in the midday heat or staying awake always at night, because *adab* confers proximity (to people and to God), while thirst and vigils confer recompense and credits (arising from pious deeds). The angels rejoice at the sight of a person in whom the *adab* of the novices (*al-murīdūn*) has become manifest and the People of Heaven glory in the vision of him.' [27]

Ṣubayḥī said: 'The way of life of God's friends consists of three things: scrupulousness (*waraʿ*),[28] *adab* and sincere devotion to God (*ʿibāda*).'[29]

Sahl ibn ʿAbd Allāh said: 'No one is free from passion (*hawā*) except the prophets and some of the righteous men—not all of them; truly, he who enjoins *adab* as a duty on himself is free from passion, as the sages said: "The most beautiful thing for the servants (*ʿabīd*)[30] is *adab*."'

Sahl ibn ʿAbd Allāh also said: 'Disregard of *adab* leads to disregard of respect (*ḥurma*),[31] and disregard of respect leads to neglect of reverence (*taʿẓīm*), and neglect of reverence leads to neglect of gratitude (*shukr*). And when gratitude is neglected, loss of faith (*īmān*) is to be feared.[32] That is because the faith of the godservant (*ʿabd*) does not prove true except through *adab*, and a bad conduct (*sū' al-adab*) shows lack of knowing (*maʿrifa*).'

Abū ʿUthmān said: 'I don't see a better condition for the godservant than a sound *adab*: that is because *adab* gives the intellect (*ʿaql*) its life and through *adab* man reaches the most sublime states and the highest ranks in both this world and the next.'[33]

It was said: '*Adab* is to guard your tongue when you speak, and your heart (*qalb*) when you are alone.'[34]

It was also said: '*Adab* is to revere those who are above you, to be compassionate to those who are below you, and to have good relations with those who are your peers.'

It was said: 'The intelligent man (*ʿāqil*) is the one who sees the consequences (of his actions)[35] and the man of *adab* is the one who takes a warning from his experiences.'[36]

It was said: '*Adab* is to hold back one's tongue and guard it, to humble one's ego-self (*dhillat al-nafs*) and keep one's heart flawless.'

It was said: 'The *adab* of the gnostic (*al-ʿārif*) is above any other *adab*, because his gnosis (*maʿrifatahu*)[37] refines his heart.'

Sarī al-Saqaṭī, may God have mercy upon him, said: 'Good *adab* is part of the mind's perfection.'

8. As a rule of conduct, the Sufi must restrain himself from his baser instincts and appetites (*shahawāt*).[38]

Abū Ḥafṣ ibn Ukht Bishr al-Ḥāfī said: 'Bishr al-Ḥāfī was craving a quince, and so my mother said: "Go and get one." Therefore, I went and brought him a quince. After he took it, he began to smell it and then he put it down in front of him. Hence, my mother said: "O Abū Naṣr, eat it!," but he replied: "How much sweeter is its smell!". And he kept smelling it, till he died without having ever tasted the quince.'

9. Among their rules of conduct is awareness of the prospect of death (*taqrīb al-ajal*) and restraint of expectation (*taqṣīr al-amal*).[39]

Sarī al-Saqaṭī said: 'Maʿrūf al-Karkhī would give the call to prayer and perform the *ṣalāh*, but he would not go before people to lead it.[40] Once he let one of his friends, whose name was Muḥammad Ibn Abī Tawba, go before the others so as to lead the ritual prayer. Muḥammad said: "If I go before you and lead you in this prayer, I won't lead you in another one." Maʿrūf replied: "And do you really believe that you will live long enough to attend another prayer? We take refuge with God from length of expectation! That, indeed, prevents us from performing the best acts." And he did not pray behind him.'

ʿAlī ibn ʿAbd al-Raḥīm al-Ṣūfī said: 'The one who restrains his expectations and carries out his work thoroughly is not anxious about his fate (and does not occupy himself with thoughts about the future).'

10. As a rule of conduct, the Sufi should see the defects of his *nafs* and always be dissatisfied with it.[41]

Abū Saʿīd al-Ziyādī said: 'The external behaviour of Abū Ḥātim al-ʿAṭṭār[42] was dissolute and licentious, while his innermost attitude was that of a pious and righteous man.[43] Sometimes he would talk with the poor (*fuqarā'*) and tell them: "Ask me anything but don't ask me about my condition, and forgive the place I am in.[44] Consider me as a wick, that I can burn myself and thus shine for you."[45] Whenever he looked at those Sufis who dressed in patched clothes (*muraqqaʿāt*) and worn wraps,[46] he would say: "O my friends! You have hoisted your flags and played your drums. I wish I knew what kind of men you really are in the engagement!"[47]

11. The Sufi must know his own worth.[48]

Junayd said: 'True knowledge is to know your own worth. To the one who knows his own worth, servanthood (*ʿubūdiyya*) becomes easy.'[49]

12. The Sufi must practise self-mortification (*mujāhada*) constantly in all circumstances.

Ibrāhīm Ibn Adham said to a man who was performing the circumambulation of the Kaʿba: 'You must know that you won't reach the stage of the virtuous ones until you overcome six difficulties. First: close the door of ease and open the door of austerity. Second: close the door of pride and open the door of humility. Third: close the door of rest and open the door of struggle (*juhd*). Fourth: close the door of sleep and open the door of wakefulness. Fifth: close the door of wealth and open the door of poverty (*faqr*). Sixth: close the door of expectation and open the door of preparedness for death.'[50]

13. The Sufi must not sit with the poor if he has any means of livelihood (*sabab*).[51]

It has been reported of Junayd that he said: 'Ibrāhīm al-Ṣayyād went to Sarī [al-Saqaṭī] wrapped in a mat; Sarī pointed to one of those with whom he was sitting, and he brought a woolen *jubba*,[52] but Ibrāhīm refused to wear it. So Sarī told him: "Take it! Indeed, I had ten dirhams with me which I gained from a good source, and I paid them in order to buy this *jubba*." Ibrāhīm replied: "Do you sit with the poor when you have ten dirhams?" And he refused to wear it.'

14. The Sufi must be a man of true piety (*waraʿ*) both in his outward and in his inward behaviour.[53]

God Most High said: 'Eschew all sin, open or secret.'[54] Yaḥyā Ibn Muʿādh al-Rāzī said: 'There are two kinds of piety: piety in one's external conduct and piety in one's innermost attitude. As for external piety, it consists in acting solely for God,[55] whereas inward piety consists in making nothing enter one's heart except God.'[56]

15. Among the Sufi's rules of conduct are those relating to his adherence to poverty (*faqr*).

Ibrāhīm ibn Fātik said: 'The qualities of the truly poor (*faqīr*) are: tranquillity in times of privation, and sacrifice and altruism (*īthār*) in times of ease.'[57]

16. The Sufi must never be pleased with his *nafs*[58] and always have a low opinion of it in every circumstance.

ʿAbd Allāh ibn Mubārak said: 'None has a good opinion of his *nafs* but the one who doesn't know its perfidy.'

Dhū'l-Nūn al-Miṣrī said: 'He who knows his *nafs* best, is the one who has the lowest opinion of it.'

17. As a rule of conduct when setting out on journeys (*safar*), the Sufi should put anxiety aside, he should be good company[59] and be helpful to his fellow travellers; finally, he should not act disloyally in his relationship with others.[60]

When asked about the *adab* of the traveller, Ruwaym said: 'That his anxiety does not go beyond each footstep and wherever his heart stops there be his abode.'

Muḥammad ibn Ismāʿīl al-Farghānī said: 'I, Abū Bakr al-Zaqqāq and Abū Bakr al-Kattānī have been travelling for twenty years without mixing with any people or being on intimate terms with anyone. Whenever we came to a village where there was a shaykh, we would greet him and stay at his place for an hour. Then we would go back to the mosque: Kattānī would go before us and pray from the beginning of the night till the early morning, reciting the entire Qur'ān. Zaqqāq would remain seated facing the *qibla*, while I would stay up all night meditating till morning. Then we would pray the morning prayer, still pure from the ablution of the beginning of the night.'[61] He said: 'And if a man had happened to be with us and he had slept all night, we would have considered him the best of us.'

Abū ʿUmrān al-Ṭabaristānī was once asked about the feeling of weakness[62] that overcomes the traveller during a journey, and he replied: 'God Most High said: "But when thou hast fears about him, cast him into the open sea,"[63] which means "Don't be concerned about what may befall you during your journey, if you turn your face toward your Lord (*baʿda an takūna mutawajjihan ilā rabbika*)."'

18. The Sufi should take whatever he takes from God Most High and leave whatever he leaves for the sake of God Most High.[64]

Aḥmad ibn Khiḍrawayh said: 'He who takes from God Most High takes with glory and he who leaves for the sake of God leaves with glory, whereas he who takes from another than God takes with humiliation and he who leaves for another than God leaves with humiliation.'

19. The Sufi must observe the proper *adab* with God Most High while in spiritual retreat (*khalwa*).

Abū Yazīd said: 'One night I got up to pray, but I felt ill and so I sat down, I stretched out my legs and I heard a voice (*hātif*) calling out to me (*yahtifu bī*) and saying: "He who sits in the company of kings should sit with proper *adab*."'[65]

Abū Muḥammad al-Jurayrī said: 'One night I was sitting in seclusion (*khalwa*) and I stretched out my legs, when sleep overwhelmed me. Then, I felt as though someone was telling me, "Not in this way does the servant sit with his Master!"'

Sarī al-Saqaṭī said: 'While coming back from a military expedition, I passed by a wall; so I lay on my back and stretched out my legs, putting them on the wall to rest a little, when suddenly I heard a voice calling out to me and saying: "O Sarī! Do the servants sit in this way in the Master's presence?"'[66]

20. The Sufi must observe the rules of poverty when with the poor.

Abū Saʿīd al-Kharrāz said: 'When I arrived at al-Ramla[67] I went to Abū Jaʿfar al-Qaṣṣāb and I spent the night at his house. Then I left al-Ramla heading for Jerusalem. Abū Jaʿfar came after me to Jerusalem, carrying with himself some small pieces of bread, and said: "Excuse me, I had this in my house and I did not even know."'[68]

21. The Sufi must not in any way place people in unpleasant situations.[69]

The following saying is reported by Anas ibn Mālik: 'The Messenger of God, God bless him and grant him peace, would not place anyone in a situation he would consider unpleasant.'

22. The Sufi should be eager to make his fellow Sufis share his acts of kindness.[70]

It is reported that ʿAlī, may God be pleased with him, said: 'To bring some of my friends to share a *ṣāʿ*[71] of food is more desirable for me than going to your market, purchasing a slave and then freeing him.' The Messenger of God, God bless him and grant him peace, said: 'There is a kind of charity which ascends[72] to Heaven faster than any other alms-giving: it is that of a man who offers some good food and brings some of his friends to share it.'

23. The Sufi must honour those senior to him (*taʿẓīm al-akābir*), be kind to novices and be on good terms with his fellow Sufis, because the Prophet, God bless him and grant him peace, said: 'He who does not show mercy to the young among us and does not respect the old among us is not one of us.'[73] The Prophet, God bless him and grant him peace, did not say: 'the young and the old'.[74] [With the expression 'the young among us'] he means 'he who accepts the advice of those senior to him and of masters, and

of those who are above him as regards spiritual state, knowledge and age.' Moreover, with the expression 'the old among us' he means 'the one who shows the young the path to integrity and gives him advice with solicitude and kindness.'

24. Among their rules of conduct there is a rule to be followed by the masters, that is to practise *adab* so that the young novice may acquire from it the master's way of behaving (*ṭarīqa*) and his virtues. Truly, the best *adab* is what is acquired through his[75] practised example rather than through his words.

25. The Sufi should be careful that every part of his body complies with God's injunctions (*awāmir*).[76]

Abū Bakr al-Warrāq said: '*Adab* is that you guard your tongue when you speak, your heart when you are alone,[77] your eye when you go out, your throat when you eat, your hand when you hold it out, your legs when you walk, and your moments (*awqāt*) when you act.[78] Truly, if a person does not guard the movements of his body and ignores his moment,[79] his body reverts to bad behaviour. In contrast, if a person guard his moment and keeps his secret (*sirr*),[80] God preserves all his moments and protects every parts of his body.'

26. Among their rules of conduct is what Muḥammad ibn ʿAlī al-Tirmidhī said: '*Adab* is to be careful how you act (*an yuḥāfiẓa fī muʿāmalatihi*) so that your masters may not reprove you; to take nothing from this world that the ascetics (*zuhhād*) would blame you for; never to prefer this world to the Hereafter, lest the men of wisdom condemn you; and to behave with your Lord during your retreat in such a way that the 'recording angels' (*al-ḥafaẓa*) need not reproach you. The basis of *adab* and its perfection consist in contemplating in your secret-heart nothing but your Lord and seeking nothing either in this world or in the Hereafter (*fī'l-dārayn*)[81] but His satisfaction.'

27. The Sufi must eat little and sleep little.

Junayd said: 'The Sufi eats like someone sick and sleeps like a drowning man.'[82]

Muḥammad ibn ʿAlī al-Tirmidhī said: 'Avoid sleep and food; indeed, if you eat you grow lazy and if you sleep you neglect (*ghafalta*)[83] your religious duties.'

28. The Sufi must choose obedience to God always, be suspicious of his *nafs*, and accept the advice of his fellow Sufis.

Abū Bakr al-Warrāq said: 'One of the rules of proper *adab* is that the servant obey his master in his secret heart as well as in public, not contradict him either with a glance or with his thoughts, return good for evil, not follow the intentions of his *nafs*, be thankful (*yashkuru*) when happy and patient (*yaṣbiru*)[84] when in adversity; finally, that he be graciously disposed towards those who are beneath him and accept the advice of those who counsel him.'

29. The Sufi should not occupy his body except in doing what his Lord consents to,[85] he should forgive his fellow Sufis when they do wrong, and not blame them except if they commit a major sin (*kabīra*) or neglect a religious duty (*farīḍa*).[86]

Muḥammad ibn Ḥāmid al-Tirmidhī said: 'The proper conduct with God consists in not moving any parts of your body except to perform what pleases Him; the proper conduct with people consists in forgiving them their faults and not reproaching them unless they disobey a divine command (*āfarīḍa*) or go against an approved practice (*sunna*). By following the example of whoever educates his ego, all can perfect their own behaviour, whereas he who opposes the people of *adab* disregards any form of respect (*ḥurumāt*)[87] and those he follows become useless to him.'[88]

Yūsuf ibn al-Ḥusayn al-Rāzī said: 'The worth of anyone who performs a deed (*ʿāmil*) lies in his *adab*; therefore, he who does not acquire *adab* is worth nothing.'

Muḥammad ibn al-Faḍl said: 'By following the external conduct of whoever practises *adab* only in the exterior (*ādāb al-ẓāhir*), his friends refine their behaviour only in the exterior, while he who practises *adab* in the interior (*ādāb al-bāṭin*) gains reverence and respect in the hearts of people.'[89]

30. The Sufi must guard his secret[90] and take care of his external conduct.

Abū ʿUthmān al-Ḥīrī said: '*Adab* consists, indeed, of two kinds of *adab*: the *adab al-sirr* and the *adab al-ẓāhir*. The *adab al-sirr* is that you purify your heart from its defects, whereas the *adab al-ẓāhir* is that you preserve your body from sins and bad morals.'[91]

31. The Sufi must always prefer others to himself.[92]

ʿAbd Allāh al-Marwāzī known as 'al-Akhawān'[93] was asked about the *adab* of this order,[94] and said: 'The basis of their *ādāb* is to prefer to act in agreement with people (*al-khalq*), as long as one acts in conformity with the Truth (*al-Ḥaqq*), rather than act in agreement with the *nafs*, always indulging it in everything great or small.'[95]

32. The Sufi should always comply with the obligations imposed by *adab*[96] on himself, lest negligence of such obligations lead him to disregard approved practices (*sunan*) and religious duties (*farā'iḍ*).[97]

ʿAbd Allāh ibn Mubārak said: 'He who neglects *adab* is precluded from the Sunna; he who neglects the Sunna is precluded from religious duties, and he who neglects religious duties is precluded from the profession of divine unity (*tawḥīd*).'

33. The Sufi must give up any thoughts about his fortunes (*tark al-ḥuẓūẓ*) and commit himself to the accomplishment of his duties towards God (*mulāzamat al-ḥuqūq*).

It is reported of ʿAbd Allāh ibn Khafīf that he said: 'Follow the *ādāb* dictated by God, for indeed he who follows the *adab* prescribed by God makes his thoughts about fortune vanish (*afnā ḥuẓūẓahu*), and commits himself totally to the accomplishing of his duties towards God.'

34. The Sufi must be aware of the significance of the moment and satisfy himself with the least.[98]

Sahl ibn ʿAbd Allāh said: 'He who is content with little, as regards food and clothes, will not be enslaved by any of (God's) creatures.' He also said: 'It was said: "The moment is the most precious thing: so, occupy it with the most precious things."'[99]

35. The Sufi must choose poverty, frugality and lowliness, so as to win in this way the love of the Prophet, peace and blessings upon him, of whom it is reported that he said: 'Poverty flows more rapidly towards the one who loves me than a torrent flowing from the top of a valley to its foot.' To those who told him how much they loved him, the Prophet, peace and blessings upon him, would reply: 'Be prepared to take poverty as your garment.'

36. The Sufi must abandon self-direction (*tadbīr*) and self-willing (*ikhtiyār*).

Sahl ibn ᶜAbd Allāh said: 'Give up self-direction and self-willing, and live a good life; for indeed, self-direction and self-willing spoil people's life.'

I heard Naṣrābādhī say about the words of God the Exalted: 'Praise be to God, Who has removed from us (all) sorrow.'[100] '[Sorrow means] the self-direction in one's life and the self's management (*siyāsatu 'l-nufūs*).'

37. The Sufi must give up his inclination to dominate others, refrain from his desire of having control over them, and endeavour to serve his fellow Sufis and his friends.[101]

Junayd said: 'One day I saw Sarī al-Saqaṭī and he seemed almost angry with me; after a while he told me: "What is this group of people which, I have heard, meet at your place?" and he said that as if it was something hateful. On hearing that, I resented his words and replied: "O Abū Ḥasan! If one of these people comes to me hungry and begs me for something to eat, and I have some leftover food with me, I feed him; if one comes to me having too much blood in his body, and says he wants to be cupped, should I refuse him that? And if one comes to me so naked that his private parts are almost bare, and I have something to dress him with, should I withhold it from him?" He replied by saying: "Don't deny them anything and be glad!" or something like that.'

38. The Sufi should roam (*wa-min ādābihim al-siyāḥa*)[102] and travel frequently (*wa'l-asfār*) at the beginning of his novitiate (*irāda*).

Yaḥyā al-Jallā' said: 'I heard Bishr al-Ḥāfī say: "Travel and wander, for indeed water is good if it runs, but if it stagnates, it alters and yellows."'

39. The Sufi must not sit with people who practise absolute poverty and isolation (*tajrīd*) if he is provided with life's necessities.[103]

Ḥassān Akhū Sinān said: 'Abū Turāb al-Nakhshabī and his friends had just gathered, when they were overcome by hunger. Thus, Abū Turāb said: "What is going on here? You gather while you are starving? Search for something to eat!" They did that, and some food was found with one of them, so Abū Turāb told him: "Give it to us! Assuming that you did not have compassion for us, why did you not have compassion for yourself?" And he took the food the man was carrying with him and fed his friends with it, and he did not let the man take any of it. Thus the man understood that he had not behaved properly.'[104]

40. The Sufi must occupy all his moments in fulfilling his duties and he must not busy himself with planning for the future.

Sahl ibn ʿAbd Allāh said: 'To be preoccupied with a past moment is to lose a second moment.' He also said: 'It was said: "Time is the most precious of all things; therefore, occupy it with the most precious things."'

Shaqīq said: 'To regret the past and plan for things to come take the blessing (*baraka*) of your life away.'[105]

41. The Sufi must look upon others with a benevolent and guiding eye.[106]

Aḥmad ibn Shāhawayh said: I heard Yaḥyā ibn Muʿādh say: 'The quest of the seeker and the deeds of the novice are not sound until they acquire three qualities: that they look upon the rich with a guiding eye, upon the poor with a humble eye,[107] and upon women with a solicitous eye.'[108]

Shāh al-Kirmānī said: 'He who looks at people with the eyes of his ego will always find himself in conflict with them, whereas he who looks at people with the eyes of the Truth will excuse them for whatever they do or say. Can they do anything other than behave as they are naturally inclined to?'[109]

42. The Sufi must train the ego (*riyāḍat al-nafs*) to be content with little.

ʿUbayd ibn 'Umar said: 'I heard Bishr al-Ḥāfī and I saw him standing at the gate of al-Ṭāq;[110] so, I asked him what he was doing in that place, and he answered: "My *nafs* has craved a cucumber for thirty years, and as I denied it, it said: 'If you won't give it to me so that I can eat it, at least show it to me so that I can content myself with looking at it instead of eating it.' For this reason, I came here to look at the cucumber and thus please my *nafs* with that."'

43. The Sufi must give up complaining.

It is reported of Abū Yazīd al-Bisṭāmī that he said: 'Since I knew God[111] I never complained of anyone, because I know that God takes care of the affairs of His servants.'

Likewise, I read in some books that God said: 'I regulated men's needs before their obligations.'

44. The Sufi must be magnanimous;[112] verily, magnanimity results from nobility of aspirations (*himma*).[113]

Sahl ibn ʿAbd Allāh said: 'Have noble aspirations, because nobility of aspirations leads to magnanimity.'

45. The Sufi must take from this world with the intention (*niyya*)[114] of getting as much sustenance as suffices him, without indulging pleasure and desire.

Sufyān said: 'If you take anything from this world, take it with the intention of getting as much sustenance as suits the way of living of a true believer. And you shall see your reward[115] for that. On the other hand, if you take anything from this world to please your *nafs* and make it live a life of comfort and ease, you shall not escape judgement on the Day of Reckoning, whether what you took was allowed (*ḥalāl*) or prohibited (*ḥarām*). You must also fear punishment whenever you indulge desire (*shahwa*). There are three kinds of desire: desire when eating, desire when speaking, and desire when looking. Therefore, watch your way of eating through intention, your tongue through sincerity (*ṣidq*), and your eye through consideration.[116] Verily, he who does not watch how he eats through intention and effort of will cannot escape greed and sin; he who does not watch his tongue through sincerity cannot avoid falsehood and slander; and he who does not watch his eye through a considerate attitude becomes blind to respect.'

46. The Sufi's apparel must suit his inward state.

[...] said: 'I heard Muḥammad ibn ʿAlī al-Kattānī of Mecca say to those dressed with patched frocks:[117] "O my friends! By God, if these garments reflect your inner thoughts, then you will enjoy disclosing them[118] to people; if, on the contrary, they are in contrast with your inner thoughts, you shall perish!"'[119]

47. The Sufi must not renounce earning his living except after he has perfected the stage of trust (*tawakkul*)[120] and he has learned how to behave accordingly.

I heard Muḥammad ibn ʿAbd Allāh say: I heard Abū ʿUthmān al-Ādamī say: I heard Ibrāhīm al-Khawwāṣ say: 'It is not necessary for a Sufi to practise abstention from gaining his living, unless that be required of him, if he happens to be in particular circumstances which prevent him from gaining his living and his condition makes him unable to earn.[121] Yet, if his needs become pressing and nothing keeps him from taking a job, then work is more appropriate for him and earning is permitted to him, because it is not right for him to refrain from working if he cannot dispense with it.'

It is reported of Abū Ḥafṣ that he said: 'I left work and I came back to it; then, it was work that left me, and I never returned to it.'

I heard Abū Bakr al-Rāzī say: I heard Abū'l-Qāsim al-Jurayrī say: I heard Junayd say: 'Every Sufi who accustomed his *nafs* to begging in order to get his living whenever he is in adversity does not free himself from bondage to his *nafs* and does not learn to endure hardship (*ṣabr*).'

48. The Sufi must be able to discern the hidden secrets of the stations (*maqāmāt*) of *tawakkul*.[122]

I heard Muḥammad ibn Shādhān say: 'Indeed, I feel ashamed before God to go into the desert to practise *tawakkul* when I am fully satiated, because being satiated is like setting out on a journey and taking along provisions.'[123]

I heard Abū'l-Qāsim al-Rāzī say: I heard Abū Bakr ibn Mumshād al-Dīnawarī say: 'He who has not discernment in the state of *tawakkul* will not be able to devote himself wholeheartedly to it and will not practise it in the right way, because *tawakkul* is a secret between God and His servant and if he fails to accomplish a part of it, God forbids him to attain its perfection.'

49. As concerns the *ādāb* of gaining one's living, I heard Abū Bakr Muḥammad ibn ʿAbd Allāh say: I heard Abū ʿAmr al-Anmāṭī say: 'Abū Jaʿfar al-Ḥaddād lived ten years earning one dinar every day, and he would give it as alms and sometimes he would spend it for the poor. Of all people he was the one who strove[124] hardest (*wa-huwa ashaddu 'l-nās ijtihādan*): he would go out at twilight and give alms through the doors, and he would not break his fast except when he came to the point that even carrion would be allowed to him.[125] He was one of the leading masters among the Sufis.'

50. The Sufi should enjoy travelling and keeping company with strangers.[126]

Abū Bakr al-Rāzī reported from Aḥmad ibn Ṣāliḥ who reported from Aḥmad ibn Muḥammad al-Makkī who reported from Bishr ibn Anas ibn Rāshid al-Bazzāz who reported from Muḥammad ibn Manṣūr who reported from Khalif ibn Tamīm who reported from Sulaymān ibn Nājya: I heard Sufyān al-Thawrī say: 'My heart thrives between Mecca and Medina in the midst of strangers wearing the *ʿabā'*.'[127]

51. The Sufi should dislike begging (*su'āl*) and he should not carry anything with himself, unless he give it to others.

I heard Jaʿfar say: I heard Junayd say: I heard Sarī al-Saqaṭī say: 'I know a short way (*ṭarīq*) to heaven.' I asked him: 'What is it?' He said: 'Don't ask anything from anyone, don't take anything from anyone, and don't carry with you anything that you might give to others.'[128]

52. The Sufi must be eager to perform religious duties and observe the principles of faith, and strive to perfect his spiritual condition (*taṣḥīḥ al-aḥwāl*) and abstain from false claims and spiritual pretensions.[129]

Dhū'l-Nūn al-Miṣrī said: 'He who rectifies [his spiritual condition] is at peace; he who draws near [to the truth] is drawn near [to the truth]; he who is sincere in his intentions purifies his heart; he who trusts is trusted; whereas he who takes upon himself what does not concern him neglects what concerns him.'[130] I heard Abū Bakr ibn Shādhān say: I heard Jaᶜfar al-Khaldī say: ᶜAlī ibn ᶜAbd al-Ḥamīd al-Ghaḍā'irī said: I heard Muḥammad ibn Abī'l-Ward say: 'The bane of man lies in two extremes: to busy oneself with works of supererogation, and thus neglect the religious duties, and to perform deeds outwardly with one's body without the intimate consent of the heart. Indeed, man is hindered from attaining the truth (*wuṣūl*) because of his negligence of the basic principles (of faith).'[131]

53. The Sufi must practise his trust in God the Maintainer, relying on Him for his sustenance (*adab al-quᶜūd ᶜalā 'l-futūḥ*).[132]

I heard Abū Bakr Muḥammad ibn ᶜAbd Allāh say: I heard Muḥammad ibn Jaᶜfar say: I heard the custodian of the mosque of al-Qulzum[133] say: 'Abū Turāb al-Nakhshabī came here—we did not know who he was—and stayed here some days, without going out of the mosque. One day, I approached him and asked: "Did you eat today?" He replied: "No." "And yesterday?" "No." "And the day before yesterday?" "No." "How long haven't you eaten?" "Seven days." So I went to the market and said: "Quick! There is a man in the mosque who hasn't eaten for seven days!" So people came and brought a lot of food, and he ate to satiety. Then he took a jar of water and he drank; finally, he took his *rakwa*[134] and went out of the mosque, without saying anything to anyone, and we thought that he probably wanted to perform the ritual ablution and would return. But he set off for the gates of the city. So we followed him for one mile and found him on his way to

Mecca, so I ran after him and said to him: "Please, may I ask you who you are?" He said: "I am Abū Turāb."

I heard Abū Bakr say: I heard Muḥammad ibn Jaᶜfar al-Farghānī say: I heard Abū Jaᶜfar al-Ḥaddād say: 'I stayed in the mosque of Qazwīn[135] for more than twenty days, keeping myself occupied by looking at some birds in front of me. It had snowed heavily and the earth around me had turned white; so the birds could not fly and were left without food, and I was like them, a stranger left without food. We stayed in front of each other for more than twenty days. Then, when the sky cleared up, each went his way.'

[Abū Jaᶜfar al-Ḥaddād] also said: I saw the following report written in the handwriting of Abū Manṣūr al-Ḥamashārī: 'I asked Muḥammad ibn al-Farrāʾ: "How do you practise the *quᶜūd ᶜalā'l-futūḥ*[136] and the *tawakkul*?" He said: "The same way as the 'People of the Bench',[137] who would follow the *ādāb* of the revealed law of Islam (*sharᶜ*) and entrust their affairs to God."'

Abū Jaᶜfar was asked: 'What is the *adab* concerning the *quᶜūd ᶜalā'l-futūḥ*?' He said: 'That you stay in a place which is not known and at a time which is not fixed, that you don't ask people for anything or importune them in any way,[138] and if anything is offered to you without your having asked for it, you should first draw back in sign of refusal and then take only as much as it suffices you.'

Yūsuf ibn al-Ḥusayn was asked: 'Is the one who practises the *quᶜūd ᶜalā 'l-futūḥ* allowed to ask others for anything?' He answered: 'No. He who asks people for something makes his condition manifest, and the aim of anyone who makes his condition manifest is merely to get his sustenance.'[139]

And it was said to one of them: 'So-and-so practises the *quᶜūd ᶜalā 'l-futūḥ*.' He replied: 'If he really practised the *quᶜūd ᶜalā 'l-futūḥ*, you wouldn't know about him; on the contrary, your knowledge of him gives him prestige by being known by you. Indeed, if his practice of the *quᶜūd ᶜalā 'l-futūḥ* were authentic, none would know his condition but the One for Whom he practises the *quʿūd*. Rather, [if he manifests his condition to people] the hearts of people cling to him,[140] and then his heart too clings to people.[141] But he who practises *quʿūd* without thinking about his own sustenance, his sustenance comes from the True Maintainer alone, and any thought about sustenance (*ru'yat al-asbāb*) completely ceases to exist for him. Indeed, the thought of one's sustenance hinders one from authentic *tawakkul* and a sincere *quʿūd ʿalā 'l-futūḥ*.' He said: 'He who occupies himself with thinking of his own subsistence is self-conceited (*muddaʿin*).'[142]

54. When setting out on a journey, the Sufi must carry with himself what is necessary for him in order to perform his religious duties properly.

I heard Abū Bakr Muḥammad ibn ʿAbd Allāh say: I heard al-Farghānī say: 'Ibrāhīm al-Khawwāṣ would practise trust in God in absolute poverty and isolation (*kāna yujarrid fi 'l-tawakkul*) and with a rigorous discipline, and, especially when travelling, he would always carry with himself a needle, some threads, a *rakwa*, and a pair of scissors. Once he was asked about that: "Why do you carry such things with you while you deprive yourself of everything else?" He replied: "The fact that I carry these things with me does not lessen my *tawakkul*, because we have religious duties towards God, and the poor man (*faqīr*) has only one garment, whether it is a *mi'zar*[143] or a shirt. Perhaps it may happen that his garment gets torn: therefore, if he does not have a needle and some threads with him, maybe his private parts would show and so he would not be able to perform the regular prayer. As for the *rakwa*, if he wants to perform an ablution for prayer, he needs to move away from people, lest they look at his private parts, and the like. Indeed, if you saw a Sufi (*faqīr*) travelling without carrying a *rakwa* with himself, you should doubt that he prays."'

55. The Sufi must observe the prescriptions of his master[144] and guard the education he received from him.[145]

Aḥmad ibn Muḥammad ibn Zakariyyā reported from Aḥmad ibn Muḥammad ibn ᶜAbd al-Wahhāb, who reported from Muḥammad ibn al-ᶜAbbās ibn al-Darqish, who reported from Aḥmad ibn Abī'l-Ḥawārī, who reported from al-Walīd ibn ᶜUtba the following saying by Ibn al-Mubārak: 'We sought the *ādāb* when the teachers were gone.'[146]

Aḥmad reported from Aḥmad who said: al-Ḥusayn ibn Aḥmad al-Qāḍī said: al-Ma'mūn said: Abū ᶜUbayd said: Muḥammad ibn al-Mubārak al-Ṣūrī said: '*Adab* for the gnostic is like repentance (*tawba*) for the novice.'[147]

Abū ᶜAbd Allāh al-Nabājī said: 'He who does not hold in reverence the teachings of those who educated him, to him are denied the blessings (*barakāt*) of that education (*adab*).'

56. The Sufi must regret the times he has failed to follow noble morals.[148]

ᶜAlī ibn Bundār told us: I heard al-Ḥusayn ibn Aḥmad al-Qāḍī say: al-Ma'mūn said: ᶜUbayd said: Wuhayb ibn al-Ward said: 'Sufyān al-Thawrī was weeping bitterly, and when asked the reason for that, he said: 'Indeed, I cry because we have grown old and our life has come to an end; yet we still don't know how to shape our character by any of the morals which lead to God's satisfaction.'

I went to see Abū ᶜAmr ibn Ḥimdān, and I found him sighing with grief, so I asked him: 'O shaykh, what's the matter with you?' He answered: 'I meditated upon my entire life and I did not find in it even one small thing[149] with which I could encounter God Almighty, and I meditated upon my self and I did not find in it any of the morals of the righteous. Hence, who should moan more than me?'

57. The Sufi must not do in private anything that he would be ashamed to do in public.

I heard Manṣūr ibn ᶜAbd Allāh say: I heard Abū ᶜAlī al-Duqqī say: Dhū'l-Nūn al-Miṣrī said: 'He who does in private what he is ashamed to do in public has no respect for himself.'[150]

I heard Manṣūr say: I heard Abū ʿAmr al-Dimashqī say: Ḥārith al-Muḥāsibī said: 'To him who strives hard in his inward heart, God bequeaths [the improvement of] his outward conduct,[151] and to him who improves his outward conduct, God bequeaths His guidance.' God the Exalted said: 'And those who strive in Our (Cause), We will certainly guide them to Our Paths.'[152]

Abū ʿUthmān al-Ḥīrī was asked: 'Who is the one who practises sincerely the spiritual path (*al-ʿāmil*)?' He said: 'He who perfects vigilance over his inward attitudes (*riʿāyat bāṭinihi*)[153] and practises the Sunna in his external conduct, and has a good opinion of people and a bad opinion of himself.'

58. About the *adab* to be observed when travelling, Muḥammad ibn Manṣūr al-Ṭūsī said: 'The least the traveller needs for his journey consists of four things: knowledge (*ʿilm*) to guide him, the invocation of God (*dhikr*)[154] to keep him company (*yu'nisuhu*), scrupulousness (*waraʿ*) to restrain him, and certitude (*yaqīn*) to sustain him. Indeed, if he has all that, he won't mind living or dying.'

59. The Sufi must not be concerned about material goods; rather, he should bestow them generously, in particular on those who render him a service.

I heard Abū'l-ʿAbbās al-Baghdādī say: I heard Abū Jaʿfar al-Farghānī say: Abū ʿAlī 'the Barber' said: 'I shaved the head of Abū Turāb al-Nakhshabī and he paid me seventy dinars.'

60. The Sufi must be patient in enduring tribulations (*balā'*).[155]

ʿAlī ibn ʿAbd Allāh of Mecca reported that Abū Bakr Aḥmad ibn ʿAbd Allāh told him: 'A poor man complained to Kattānī about what was afflicting him, and he told him: "One day Ibrāhīm ibn Adham went out to visit the poor; he looked at them and said: 'Those whom God puts to the test, they are in God's grace, and those who are in God's grace, God puts them to the test.' Verily, God made you fit for tribulation, so be fit for patience!"'[156]

61. The Sufi must despise his *nafs*, even if it orders doing good.[157]

I heard Abū Saʿīd Naṣr ibn Aḥmad say: I heard Muḥammad ibn Saʿīd al-Wāsiṭī of Baghdad say: I heard my father say: I heard Shiblī say: 'Once I found myself with one hundred dinars, so I said to myself that I would go out early in the next morning and give them to the first person I met. Thus, I went out early in the morning and I saw a blind man sitting in front of a barber who was shaving his hair off. So, I drew near to him and put the money bag in his hand, but he said: "Give it to the barber". I replied: "There is one hundred dinars in it!" He said: "Who asked you how much is inside? Pay it to the barber!" Thus, I gave it to the barber, who said: "I have decided not to take anything from him." So I felt embarrassed, I hesitated for a moment, and then I scattered those dinars on the street, saying to myself: "A beggar and a barber are more generous than you. I have decided that from now on I will no longer claim the virtues of *futuwwa*!"'[158]

62. The Sufi must accept the advice of his masters, whether he knows the reason for it or not.

I heard Aḥmad ibn Muḥammad ibn Zakariyyā say: I heard Abū ʿAbd Allāh al-Kirmānī say: 'I was performing the circumambulation of the Kaʿba, when it occurred to me (*khaṭara ʿalā qalbī*) that the matter, which Abū ʿAmr al-Zujājī had asked Junayd about, was *tawakkul*. Therefore, when I finished circumambulating the Kaʿba, I approached him and asked him about *tawakkul*. He said: "O Abū ʿAbd Allāh! Today, on your journey you won't have to practise any spiritual exercise (*riyāḍa*),[159] but just go and get married!" I replied: "O master! How could I marry, when I don't even earn what is sufficient for me!" He said: "Do you think that if you get married you will be deprived of your sustenance? Marry! Because, truly, in following the Sunna of the Prophet of God, peace and blessings upon him, there is a blessing." Indeed, when I married, I attained what I had been searching for.'

I heard the shaykh Abū Sahl Muḥammad ibn Sulaymān, may God have mercy upon him, say: 'He who asks his master "Why?" will never be successful.' He also said: 'A man said to Abū Ḥafṣ: "How did you reach these spiritual states?" He said:

"By accepting the advice of my masters without doubting in my heart or hesitating."'

63. The Sufi must strive to abate the inclinations of his *nafs* and of his nature.

I heard Abū'l-ʿAbbās al-Nasawī say: I heard Abū ʿAbd Allāh al-Kirmānī say: I heard Abū ʿAmr al-Zujājī say: 'That my human nature may decrease even by one atom only is more desirable to me than walking on water.'

64. The Sufi must be grateful for hunger and adversity.[160]

I heard Muḥammad ibn al-Ḥasan al-Baghdādī say: I heard Aḥmad ibn Muḥammad ibn Ṣāliḥ say: Muḥammad ibn ʿAbdūn said: ʿUbayd al-Warrāq said: 'One day I was at the "*qubba*[161] of the Poets" with Bishr al-Ḥāfī, when a man stood up and said: "By God! I have been starving for three days!" Bishr went to him and after talking with him the man sat down. On seeing that, I said: "I wonder what Bishr told him to make him sit." Thus, I went to him, and asked: "What did the shaykh say to you?" He answered: "He told me that God bestows hunger upon those who will thank Him for it."'[162]

65. The Sufi must be content (*wa-min ādābihim al-riḍā*) with any adversity that befalls him.

Abū'l-ʿAbbās al-Baghdādī said: I heard Jaʿfar ibn Muḥammad ibn Naṣīr say: I heard Abū ʿAbd Allāh ibn Jābir say: I heard Abū Jaʿfar al-Anbārī say: 'I was riding a donkey when I met a soldier, who made me dismount from the donkey; then, he mounted it and began to sing: "If you are angry at something, I am angry too, and if you are content with something, I am content too." So I said: "O sir! I am content." And I went back home; then, after a while, I heard someone telling me: "Your donkey is tied up at the door."'

66. Among their *ādāb* is what I heard from Abū'l-ʿAbbās al-Baghdādī who said: I heard Jaʿfar al-Khuldī say: I heard Abū Muḥammad al-Jurayrī say: I heard Sahl ibn ʿAbd Allāh say: 'Among the virtues of the righteous is that they do not swear by God, whether they are telling the truth or not, that they do not slander or let anyone utter slander in their presence, that they

never satisfy their appetite, and when they make a promise, they do not break it, that they do not talk unless they have to, by way of an exception, and, finally, that they do not jest at all.'[163]

67. Among the *ādāb* concerning the moments is what I heard from Naṣr ibn Abī Naṣr who said: I heard al-Khuldī say: I heard Junayd say: 'We founded our teachings[164] on three basic rules: that we only eat when starving, we only sleep when overpowered (by slumber) and we only speak when necessary.'

68. The Sufi must observe the *adab* of poverty, embrace it altogether, and comply with its rules both in his outward conduct and in his inward heart.

I heard ʿAlī ibn Saʿīd say: I heard Aḥmad ibn Hārūn say: I heard Abū'l-Ḥasan al-ʿAlawī say: I heard Ibrāhīm al-Khawwāṣ say: 'If you see the sign of poverty in someone's dress,[165] don't expect any good from him.'

I heard ʿAlī say: I heard Aḥmad ibn ʿAlī say: I heard Abū ʿAlī al-Kharqī say: I heard Yūsuf ibn al-Ḥusayn say: I heard Dhū'l-Nūn al-Miṣrī say, when asked about the qualities of the truly poor: 'They are: tranquillity in times of privation, and sacrifice and altruism in times of ease.'[166]

69. Among their *ādāb* is what was reported to me of Abū ʿAbd Allāh Muḥammad ibn Khafīf, who said: 'The *ādāb* proper to the Sufi way of life consists of ten qualities: to purify the heart from associating with creatures;[167] to abandon one's natural dispositions; to give up the claims and pretensions common to human nature; to avoid any despicable condition; to devote oneself to the sciences of reality (*ʿulūm al-ḥaqīqa*);[168] to conform to the attributes of spirituality (*munāzalat ṣifāt al-rūḥāniyya*), to practise what is more appropriate in [one's search for] the truth, to give constantly good advice to people and be compassionate with them, to follow the example of the Prophet of God, peace and blessings upon him, through the revealed Law of Islam (*sharīʿa*), and finally to be faithful to God for all eternity.'

70. The Sufi must practise the Sufi way of life (*taṣawwuf*) in every circumstance.

I heard Abū Bakr al-Rāzī say: I heard ʿAlī ibn ʿAbd al-Ḥamīd say: '*Taṣawwuf* is to reject hypocrisy, act with grace,[169] and discard honours.'

71. The Sufi must always oppose his *nafs* and do what is more appropriate for him in every instant.

I heard Muḥammad ibn ʿAbd Allāh al-Rāzī say: I heard Jaʿfar ibn Muḥammad ibn Naṣīr say: I heard Junayd say: 'Enduring isolation (*ʿuzla*) is more excellent than enjoying the company of the people of distinction (*khāṣṣa*), and bearing patiently one's desires is better for the hearts of the pious than pursuing them.'

72. The Sufi must tend to the highest aspirations and refrain from those aspirations which are lowly and base.

I heard Abū Bakr al-Ṭabarī say: I heard Abū'l-Ḥusayn al-Khwārizmī say: 'They were named the substitutes (*abdāl*) because for every bad disposition they would substitute a good one, and they would replace every state that kept them from God Most High with a state that would lead them to God Most High.'

I heard ʿAbd Allāh al-Rāzī say: I heard Abū Bakr al-Duqqī say: 'I asked Abū Bakr al-Maghribī about *taṣawwuf* and he said: "[It is] loftiness of aspirations."'

73. Among the *ādāb* to be observed in sickness is what I heard from Abū Bakr al-Rāzī who said: I heard al-Ḥusayn say: I heard ʿAbd Allāh al-Riḍwānī say: 'Once Bishr al-Ḥāfī and Maʿrūf al-Karkhī fell ill, and therefore the doctor began to visit them frequently. But, while Bishr would inform him about his illness, Maʿrūf would refuse to tell him anything about it. Thus, the doctor said to Maʿrūf: "Won't you tell me how you are, as Bishr does?" Maʿrūf answered: "Do you want me to complain of God to you?" So, the doctor went back to Bishr and told him what Maʿrūf had said. Bishr replied: "O doctor! We do not complain of God to you; rather, we describe to you His power over us."'

74. The Sufi must give up self-planning (*tark al-tadbīr*) and return to the state of submission (*al-taslīm*).[170]

Abū'l-Ḥusayn ibn Manṣūr said: 'If one commits his cause to God, everything is accomplished through him and for him. He who finds God does not find with Him other than Him; he who pursues God's satisfaction, God awards to him his hidden secret (*sirrihi*).'[171] God Most High said: '[If anyone does evil or wrongs his own soul] but afterwards seeks Allah's forgiveness, he will find Allah Oft-Forgiving, Most Merciful.'[172]

75. The Sufi must give up claims and pretensions (*tark al-daᶜāwā*) and return to the utmost of need and impotence (*al-iftiqār wa'l-ḍaᶜf*).[173]

I heard Muḥammad ibn ᶜAbd Allāh say: I heard Yūsuf ibn al-Ḥusayn say: I heard Aḥmad ibn Abī'l-Ḥawārī say: I heard Abū Sulaymān say: 'O my God! Whatever punishment you inflict on me, I am content with it.' Afterwards, when a toothache[174] afflicted him, he said: 'O my God! If you don't relieve me from this pain, I shall become a Jew or a Christian!'

76. The Sufi must be perseverant in performing pious deeds constantly.

God Most High said: 'And to Him is religion (*al-dīn*) due always.'[175] It was said this means: '[to Him] worship (*ᶜibāda*) is due always.'

Abū ᶜUthmān al-Ḥīrī said: 'He who savours (*dhāqa*) the taste of obedience to God does not become remiss in it, and he who becomes remiss in it, he does so because he lacks knowledge of the One Whom he obeys. Don't you know that the Prophet, peace and blessings upon him, used to pray till his feet became swollen?'

77. The Sufi must counsel and support his *nafs* while fighting it, and refrain from acting in accordance with it. Verily, the advice of the godservant to his *nafs* uplifts the soul (*min karāmati 'l-nafs*), and if someone does not give advice to his *nafs* this is because of his contempt for it.

I heard Yūsuf ibn ᶜUmar al-Zāhid ('the ascetic') of Baghdad say: I heard Jaᶜfar ibn Muḥammad ibn Naṣīr [say]: I heard Junayd say: 'The mark of those who advise their *nafs* is that they renounce its desires, shun its pleasures, avert their glances and their hearts from its charming attires, devote themselves to the life to come, and are occupied with preparing and equipping themselves for it.'

Ibrāhīm ibn Shaybān was asked: 'What is the mark of the one who advises his *nafs*?' He said: 'That he encourages the *nafs* to do what is hateful to it and what is contrary to its inclinations, and that he is always dissatisfied with it. Nobody works to bring his *nafs* into harmony and harbours opposition to his egotistical desires without God giving him success.'[176]

78. The Sufi must not occupy himself with the past and the future. He must strive to guard his moment and occupy himself with doing what is more appropriate for him in every instant, yet without attaching too much importance to it.

I heard Abū Saʿīd al-Rāzī say: I heard Jaʿfar al-Khawwāṣ say: 'When asked by one of our friends to give him some advice, Junayd said: 'I advise you not to look back at the past, because looking back at the past diverts you from what in the present is worthier of your consideration. I also advise you to avoid attaching too much importance to the present and to receive the future from the moment that comes down to you (*al-waqt al-wārid*), always remembering the One who has sent it down to you.[177] Indeed, if you do that, you will be constantly in the remembrance of the One Who is worthier of your remembrance, and the vision of things will not harm you.'[178]

I heard Abū Aḥmad al-Ḥasnuwī say: I heard ʿAbd Allāh ibn al-Mubārak say: 'He who occupies himself with the past and the future lets his time pass by in vain.'

79. The Sufi must seek the advice of his master and accept his suggestions.

It was said to a master: 'How well you conduct yourselves!' He answered: 'We are a community, and among us there are people of understanding and (mystical) knowledge, and people who have experienced the path and passed through the spiritual stations (*nāzala al-maqāmāt*). Thus, we ask them for advice and then we follow their suggestions, and that increases our correctness.'

80. The Sufi must shun this world and all that is in it,[179] abstain from worldly desires, attach no importance to this life, and, after he has done that, he must direct all his efforts to the accomplishment of his duties and religious obligations.[180]

Ḥāritha reported about himself that, when the Prophet, peace and blessings upon him, asked him what was the essence of his faith, he said: 'I have turned away from this world, to the point that its gold and its stones have become the same to me; I have made my nights sleepless and my days thirsty,[181] and it is as if I were always looking at the Throne of my Lord raised before me.'

81. The Sufi must perform his duties toward God with perseverance and he must disregard worldly prosperity and fortunes, whether they are many or few. This [rule] was founded upon the words of God Most High: 'If any do wish for the transitory things (of this life), We readily grant them such things as We will, to such persons as We will: in the end have We provided Hell for them: they will burn therein, disgraced and rejected. Those who do wish for the (things of) the Hereafter, and strive therefor with all due striving, and have faith, they are the ones whose striving is acceptable (to Allah).'[182]

82. Among the Sufis' *ādāb* is what was reported of Abū Ḥafṣ, who said, when asked about the rules of poverty and the *ādāb* related to it: '[The *ādāb* of poverty are:] to respect the prescriptions of the masters, have good relations with one's fellows, give advice to the young, abstain from quarrels when being with one's companions, always prefer others to oneself, avoid accumulating wealth, refrain from seeking the company of those who do not follow one's path, and, finally, help each other in the matters of this world and of religion.'

83. The Sufi must repent constantly what he has done and what he has not done[183] because of his negligence.

It is reported of al-Ḥusayn ibn Manṣūr that he said: 'Repentance (*tawba*) of what you don't know leads you to repentance of what you do know, and gratefulness for what you don't know leads you to gratefulness for what you do know, because the godservant is forbidden to do anything but what leads him to God Most High.'[184]

84. The Sufi must be fully aware and participating when invoking God (*waqt al-dhikr*),[185] and avoid mentioning His name in a state of negligence (*ghafla*).[186]

Thus Abū Manṣūr[187] said: 'He who invokes God and turns his eyes to something else (*yushāhidu ghayrahu*), gets more and more distant from Him,[188] his heart becomes hard, and he is lured into the wrong path[189] and led away from the path of integrity.'[190]

The following verses were recited to one of them:[191] 'No sooner had I mentioned Your name/ than I was filled with anxiety./ My longing, my thoughts, and my memory/ all partook in my remembrance of You/ and it was as if a guardian of Yours called out to me,[192] saying: /"Woe unto you! Beware of your remembrance! Beware!"'

Junayd said: 'The answer to an invocation (*dhikr*) performed in a state of negligence is cursing and rejection.'

85. The Sufi must defy his own nature and encourage the *nafs* to rectitude (*istiqāma*).[193]

It is related of al-Ḥusayn that he said: 'If someone yearns for one other than God, to him opens the door of all iniquities and sins, and if someone worships God in ignorance, he opens the door of haughtiness and pride (*ʿujb*). It is the duty of the godservants always to find their nourishment in the sustenance provided by God (*rizq Allāh*), if it is food which is allowed to them, and to make only what suffices them their food.[194] Verily, what is eaten after long starving becomes nice and sweet, and whatever food he eats, the godservant shall be called to account for it. He who withdraws from people shall wear wool, and he who lives in the midst of people shall make the mosque his shelter, that it be like a fortress, inaccessible to the enemy. The Qur'ān be your emblem, meditation your lamp, and piety your goodness. Your purity (*ṭahāra*) be repentance (*tawba*), your cleanness be like water,[195] scrupulousness (*waraʿ*) be your intention (*niyya*)[196] and God your only concern. Be perseverant in your fast[197] and to God entrust your life; let your silence be your vigilant attention to Him (*murāqabatuhu*) and your vision your contemplation of Him (*mushāhadatuhu*).[198] None will be able to do that but he whose heart God Most High has tested (*imtaḥana*) through piety.[199] God the Exalted said: "They are those whose hearts God has tested for piety."'[200]

86. The Sufi must give up self-planning, refrain from busying himself with seeking his livelihood, and trust always in the providential arrangements of the divine decree and in the assurance of the truth.

Thus said al-Ḥusayn ibn Manṣūr: 'He who wishes to taste (*yadhūq*) anything of these spiritual states, he shall bring himself to one of these three conditions: that he be as he was in his mother's womb, where everything was planned for him and he was nourished from where he did not know, that he be as he will be in his grave, or that he be as he will be on the Day of Resurrection.' He also said: 'He who relies on God unreservedly, his sustenance is bestowed on him from where he does not know, without limits or bounds,[201] and he has no need to ask for it.'

87. The Sufi must give up the words 'I', 'we', 'mine', and the like.

Thus it is reported of the Prophet, peace and blessings upon him, that he said, when a man asked permission to enter his house: 'Who is it?' The man answered: 'It is me.' And the Prophet replied: 'Me! Me!' as if he disliked him.

It is related of Abū Manṣūr[202] that he said: If the godservant says: 'I', God the Exalted says: 'You miserable wretch! I alone have the right to say "I"'. And if the servant says: 'There is nothing but "You", O my Lord!' The Lord says: 'You indeed are my servant!' And so the will of the servant becomes one with the will of God.[203]

88. The Sufi must occupy himself with the defects of his own *nafs* rather than with the defects of other people, and he must cure them with the appropriate remedy.[204]

Thus I was told by Aḥmad ibn ʿAbd Allāh ibn Yūsuf al-Qirmīsīnī that his father had been told by ʿAlī ibn ʿAbd al-Ḥamīd that Sarī said: 'He who looks at the defects of others becomes blind to the defects of his own self; he who carries out his duty does not neglect his duty, whereas he who takes upon himself a task that was not assigned to him, neglects the task that was assigned to him.'[205]

89. The Sufi must educate himself by following the instructions of his masters, and he must obey them always.

In this regard, the following saying has been attributed to Saqaṭī with the same chain of authority as that given above:[206] 'He who obeys those who are above him is obeyed by those who are below him, and he who is incapable of educating himself is even more incapable of educating others.'

90. The Sufi must guard his tongue against praising and blaming people.[207]

Sarī said: 'The best thing in religion is scrupulousness, and the best thing in scrupulousness is to guard one's tongue against praise and blame.'

91. The Sufi must take warning from the passing of time, and avoid neglecting the moment and letting it go by in vain.

Sarī said: 'Take warning from time and don't take pleasure in spending days and nights fulfilling your desires. Let the past be a guide for your future, and make up in the time left for the wrong you did in the time past.'[208]

92. The Sufi must entrust his affairs to God, so that he may find tranquillity and peace.

Sarī said: 'He who entrusts his affairs to God, gives and withholds with justice, because he knows God's good choice in giving and withholding.'[209]

93. The Sufi must renounce his desires (*tark al-shahawāt*) and turn away from them.

Sarī said: 'Fulfilling one's desires leads to lowliness and shame in this world and to contrition (*nadāma*) and sorrow in the Hereafter, it blinds the heart and veils you from God Most High.'

94. The Sufi must obey the prescriptions of the Qur'ān, so that it may guide him to doing good and lead him to the highest stages.

Sarī said: 'Make the Qur'ān your occupation, so that knowledge (*ᶜilm*) may be your guide, watchfulness (*ḥidhr*) your companion, fear (*khawf*) your spur, hope (*rajā'*) your leader, and compassion (*ishfāq*) your garment. Think of its promises and its threats[210] and yearn for that which it made you yearn for: thus, you shall attain [the stage of] proximity to the Mighty and Generous.'

95. The Sufi must review himself in relation to the Qur'ān at every instant, his states, his behaviour and his deeds, so that he may recognise in this way his own imperfection.

Sarī said: 'Review your behaviour[211] in the light of the prescriptions of the Qur'ān, so that you may detest your self, submit to your Lord, and know yourself inside out.'[212]

96. The Sufi must strive to know his *nafs* and be aware of its distance from the path of truth, so that he may recognise his own defects and abandon his vanity.[213]

Sarī said: 'Knowledge of the *nafs* brings the righteous into a state of fear, and if it were it not for that, they would display vanity and they would love singing the praises of their *nafs*.'[214]

97. The Sufi should travel frequently and he should dwell in places where he is ignored and not treated with deference or honoured.

Sarī said: 'The best for you is travelling, being far away from your homeland[215] in places where you are not known, lacking renown and reputation, eating little and wearing poor clothes, so that when death comes, you will not regret anything of this world.'

98. The Sufi must strive to demolish the conceit (*ᶜujb*) of his *nafs*, lest he may regard something of his *nafs* as good and thus be ruined because of it.

Sarī said: 'Conceit is when you despise [someone because he has caused to you] a little offense and you exaggerate the little work that you do, and by that you claim superiority over others and think little of them. That results from one's lack of knowledge of his *nafs*: truly, he who knows his *nafs* gives up vanity and pride.'

Some Sufis said: 'Conceit hinders one from knowing the worth of one's *nafs*.'

99. The Sufi must behave always in conformity with the virtues of *murūwa*.[216]

Sarī said: '*Murūwa* is to comply with the divine command and prohibition[217] and draw near to God by acquiring the loftiest and noblest traits of character.'

Junayd said: '*Murūwa* is that you do not consider yourself as superior to anyone.'

Said Abū Ḥafṣ: 'The virtue of *murūwa* is that you sacrifice your honour and your possessions in this world for the sake of your fellows, and pray to God for their salvation in the next life.'

Abū ʿUthmān said: '*Murūwa* is that you guard against violating [the Law of God].'

ʿAbd Allāh ibn al-Mubārak said: '*Murūwa* is that you do not turn away from those who have drawn near to God Almighty.'

100. The Sufi must practise poverty constantly, eat little food, wear the *khirqa*, and avoid contaminating himself with any of the vanities of this world (*fāniya*), [and he should do all that] out of his own free will and not because he is obliged to.

Thus said the Prophet, peace and blessings upon him: 'O sons of Adam! Of the things of this world, let that be sufficient for you which appeases your hunger and hides your private parts, and if it is just a small thing that hides you, let it be enough for you! Indeed, you shall be called to account for any piece of bread that you eat, for the water which is in your jar, and for what is on top of your *izār*.'[218]

101. The Sufi must dispute with his fellows on matters concerning the Sufi way of living, and then become reconciled with them, and he must warn them against neglecting any of their affairs and states.

I heard Naṣr ibn Abī Naṣr al-ʿAṭṭār say: I heard Khuldī say: I heard Ruwaym say: 'Sufism flourishes as long as the Sufis dispute with each other. Verily, if they agreed with one another, they would perish.'

102. The Sufi should speak little and perform actions instead.[219]

I heard Naṣr ibn Abī Naṣr al-ʿAṭṭār say: I heard Muḥammad ibn al-Faḍl say: I heard Muḥammad ibn al-Ḥusayn al-Naqqāsh say: I heard Ruwaym say: 'If God endowed you with the faculty of speaking and of acting and then took from you your speech and left you alone with your deeds, you should not mind, because that is a blessing from Him. But if He took from you the power of acting and left you that of speaking, it would be a misfortune, and if He took from you both the faculties of speaking and acting, it would be a real affliction.'

103. The Sufi must be benevolent and altruistic toward his fellows.

I heard Naṣr ibn Abī Naṣr say: I heard Abū'l-Ḥusayn al-Mālikī say: A Sufi master was asked about *taṣawwuf* and the *ādāb* of it, and said: '*Taṣawwuf* consists of four stations; whenever they join together in a human being, he deserves to be called a Sufi. They are: benevolence, altruism, patience, and cognisance. As to benevolence, if a rich and powerful man goes to a person and asks for something he does not have, and thinks that he is showing favour to him by making this request, that is not conferring a favour. As to altruism (*īthār*),[220] it is when a person relinquishes something in order to give it to somebody else, even if he himself needs it, while patience is the soul's ability to bear adversities. As to cognisance (*al-dirāya*), it is useful knowledge, or, otherwise, silence.'

104. The Sufi should dislike eating alone.[221]

Naṣr ibn Abī Naṣr reported to us that Aḥmad ibn ʿAbd Allāh ibn al-Nāqid reported that Ibn al-Rūdhbārī said: Ibn Aḥmad Hārūn ibn Aḥmad ibn Muḥammad al-Ḥaddād reported from Maḥfūẓ[222] from Abū Tawba from Sufyān ibn ʿUyayna from al-Zuhrī that al-Sā'ib ibn Yazīd said: 'During pre-Islamic times, if a man ate alone, his offspring would be blamed for that even after his death.'

It has been related of the Prophet, peace and blessings upon him, that he said: 'The worst of you is he who eats alone and does not let others share his food.'

105. The Sufi must shun hypocrisy (*riyā'*)[223] and pride (*ʿujb*).

Naṣr ibn Abī Naṣr said: I heard Jaʿfar al-Khuldī say: I heard Junayd say: I heard Sarī say: 'Most of the (good) deeds of the *qurrā'* [224] are cancelled by their vanity and their hidden hypocrisy.'[225]

106. The Sufi must eat little and avoid satisfying his appetite.

This [rule] was founded upon the words that the Prophet, peace and blessings upon him, said to a man, who had belched in his presence: 'Don't ever belch in our presence! Verily, the more sated you are in this world, the hungrier you will be on the Day of Final Judgement.'

I heard ʿAbd Allāh ibn ʿUthmān ibn Bakhīra say: I heard Abū ʿAmr ibn al-Sammāk say: Marwarūdhī said: 'I haven't been sated for fifty years.'

I heard ʿAlī ibn Saʿīd say: I heard Aḥmad ibn al-Bardaʿī say: I heard al-ʿAbbās ibn ʿAbd Allāh say: I heard Sahl say: 'The heart of this matter[226] is to rely on God, to eat little, and to shun people.'

107. As for the *ādāb* to be observed during spiritual exercises (*riyāḍāt*), the Sufi must endure hunger and humiliation, and as for the *ādāb* concerning the mystical states (*aḥwāl*), he must practise truthfulness (*ṣidq*) and sincerity (*ikhlāṣ*).

I heard Abū ʿAbd Allāh al-Rāzī say: I heard Muḥammad ibn ʿAlī al-Kattānī say: 'We have practised the spiritual exercises and we have not found anything that benefited our body more than hunger, mortification (*dhilla*) and the struggle against the *nafs*. We have also encountered the mystical states (*wa-nāzalnā al-aḥwāl*) and we have not found anything more proper than truthfulness and sincerity.'

108. The Sufi must eat little and drink little.

Verily, the Prophet, peace and blessings upon him, said: 'The true believer eats using only one intestine, whereas the unbeliever eats using seven.' It has also been related about the Prophet, peace and blessings upon him, that he said: 'Too much eating is a calamity [to people].'[227]

109. The Sufi must avoid greed and avidity (*al-ḥirṣ wa'l-sharah*), because in them lie suspicion and distrust. Verily, greed induces you

to pursue the things of this world, and avidity leads you to keep those worldly things through attention to worldly claims.'[228]

110. The Sufi must urge his companions to manage their own *nafs* (*siyāsat nufūsihim*) and to pursue the enhancement of their mystical states (*al-ziyāda fī aḥwālihim*).[229]

I heard ᶜAbd Allāh ibn Muḥammad al-Dimashqī say: I heard Abū ᶜAmr al-Dimashqī say, when I asked him: 'Who is the weakest of all human beings?' 'The one who is incapable of managing his *nafs*.' 'And who is the most powerful of all human beings?' 'The one who is capable of mastering his passions.' 'And who is the most intelligent of all human beings?' 'The one who renounces creation and turns to the Creator.' Then I asked him: 'How do we govern our *nafs*?' 'By practising *adab* constantly.' 'From whom can we learn *adab*, and by whom can the novice be educated?' 'By those who educate the young and the small, and those from whom *adab* is taken, namely, the masters among the Prophet's Companions (*Ṣaḥāba*), or by the traditional practices and norms that have been transmitted to us, or by the one who took his *adab* from God Most High, namely, the Prophet, peace and blessings upon him. He who keeps to the Sunna of the Prophet and lets himself be guided by it, he is the one who governs his *nafs* in the most excellent way.'

111. The Sufi must avoid the company of the wicked.

Abū'l-Ḥasan Muḥammad ibn Abī Ismāᶜīl al-ᶜAlawī al-Ṣūfī said: I heard ᶜAbd al-Raḥmān ibn Aḥmad say: I heard al-Qāsim ibn Munabbih say: I heard Bishr al-Ḥāfī say: 'Keeping company with the wicked leads to thinking ill of good people. It has been related from the Prophet, peace and blessings upon him, that he said: "Only make friends with the believer, and let nobody share your food but the God-fearing man (*taqiyy*)."'

112. The Sufi should dislike sitting in the company of the rich, because the Prophet said, peace and blessings upon him: 'Look at those who are below you and do not look at those who are above you. Verily, this is worthier of you, so that you do not disregard the blessings that God has bestowed on you.'[230]

I heard ʿAbd Allāh ibn ʿUthmān say: I heard Abū ʿAmr ibn al-Sammāk say: I heard al-Qāsim ibn Munabbih [say]: I heard Bishr ibn al-Ḥārith say: 'If you see me love the company of the rich, know that I have relapsed [into error].'

The following saying has been ascribed to Bishr ibn al-Ḥārith with the same chain of authorites: 'Your attaching importance to knowing people[231] and being friends with the rich is the beginning of love of this world. Whereas, if you renounce the company of people and the friendship of the rich, that is *zuhd*.'[232]

113. The Sufi must keep his actions and his spiritual states secret as much as he can.[233]

I heard ʿAbd Allāh ibn ʿUthmān say: I heard Abū 'l-Faḍl Aḥmad ibn ʿAbd Allāh say: I heard Muḥammad ibn Hārūn ibn al-Ḥusayn say: 'We were at Maʿrūf al-Karkhī's place at the time of the afternoon prayer, when a beggar came and she said: "Give me something to break my fast with, because I am fasting." Thus Maʿrūf called her and said: "O my sister! You have disclosed God's secret, and you hope to live till the evening?"'[234]

114. The Sufi must strive to eliminate his individual perception of things (*ru'ya*)[235] when performing deeds and acts of devotion.

I heard Abū'l-Ḥusayn Aḥmad ibn Muḥammad al-Fārisī say: I heard Abū'l-Ṭayyib al-Baṣrī say: 'The servanthood (*ʿubūdiyya*) of anyone who does not fulfil his servanthood in the glory of the lordship (*rubūbiyya*)[236] remains impure, because of his outward perception of himself, his actions and all his doings.'

115. When the Sufi experiences the stage of repentance (*tawba*), every limb of his body must participate in it, both outwardly and inwardly.

I heard Abū'l-Ḥusayn al-Fārisī [say]: I heard Fāris al-Dīnawarī say: I heard Yūsuf ibn al-Ḥusayn say: I heard Dhū'l-Nūn say: 'Every part of one's body, be it internal or external, is called to repentance. Thus, the heart is responsible for the thoughts, and the body's limbs are responsible for the movements; likewise, the innermost conscience (*sirr*) must guard the integrity of one's inner thoughts, whereas the body's limbs must guard the integrity of one's actions. That is true repentance. God Most High said: "Eschew all sin, open or secret."'[237]

116. The Sufi must begin (his path) in the right way,[238] so that he may end it in the right way.

In this regard, it was reported about Abū'l-ʿAbbās ibn ʿAṭā' that he used to say: 'He who has not strengthened the first stages of his relationship with God, will not rise to the highest stages. These first stages are: the binding religious duties (*furūḍ al-wājiba*), such extra prayers (*awrād*) as are proper, and all the acts of devotion, whether they are supererogatory (*faḍl*) or made obligatory by God (*ʿazā'im al-amr*). He who does that, God blesses him with what he will do afterwards.'[239]

117. The Sufi must abstain from talking about a state he has not encountered or telling others about a path he has not taken (*ṭarīq lam yaslukūhu*).[240]

In this regard, it has been related of Shiblī that he said: 'How impudent is the man who describes a path he has not taken and describes a state he has not encountered.'

118. The Sufi must renounce this world[241] as much as he can.

I heard Abū'l-Ḥusayn ibn Abī ʿAmr al-Balkhī say: I heard ʿAmr ibn Muḥammad say: I heard Abū'l-ʿAbbās ibn ʿAṭā' say: 'If the worldly position of anyone who lives for this world[242] is diminished, he is abased in the eyes of people; whereas the opposite happens with a Sufi, because the more he renounces this world, the greater he becomes in the esteem and in the eyes of people.'

119. Among the Sufi *ādāb* is what Abū Ḥafṣ said, when asked about the *adab* to be observed with God and the *adab* to be observed with the godservants: 'The *adab* with God consists of fulfilling His orders with the utmost sincerity (*ikhlāṣ*), and maintaining correct behaviour both outwardly and inwardly with fear (*khawf*) of God and awe (*hayba*) of Him. Moreover, *adab* is to keep company with people, showing kindness in times of tribulation and discernment[243] when making choices, to be generous and magnanimous when one's caprices and desires are feared,[244] to forgive others as much as one can, to be merciful and compassionate towards them, to

use benevolence always,[245] to establish relations with those who are rejected (by society),[246] to return good for evil, and to show reverence and respect towards all Muslims.[247] For none of the Muslims is denied the grace of God and His blessings.'

120. The Sufi must perfect his knowledge of the outward and the inward realities altogether (*ᶜilm al-ẓāhir wa'l-baṭin*).[248]

In this regard, it has been related about Yaḥyā ibn Muᶜadh that he said: 'The science of the outward realities relates to the [Sufi's] proceeding in the path (*sulūk al-ṭarīq*), whereas the science of the inward realities relates to the *ādāb* of the [Sufi's] spiritual realisation.' [249]

121. The Sufi must endure hardship and tribulations (*al-miḥan wa'l-balāyā*) as much as he can for the benefit of people.

I heard ᶜAbd al-Wāḥid ibn Bakr say: I heard Aḥmad ibn ᶜAlī say: I heard ᶜAlī ibn ᶜAbd al-Ḥamīd say: 'The Sufi is like the sun, which rises above everyone, like the earth, on which everything walks, like the water, which everything drinks, and like the fire, by which everything is illumined.'

Some Sufis said: 'The Sufi is like the earth, which puts up with harsh treatment and brings forth green pasture.'[250]

122. The Sufi must be compassionate toward his friends, have a good opinion of them and give them advice.

Abū'l-ᶜAbbās al-Baghdādī reported to us that Muḥammad ibn ᶜAbd Allāh al-Farghānī said: 'Junayd's friends spoke to him about those who stood in the *ḥalqa*[251] and asked him questions, [saying] that they were not fit to receive an answer and that they hated his dearest friends, [and asking] that he should not answer them. Junayd replied: "The way I see them is not the way you see them: yet, I prefer that they cling to only one word of mine, and that this word be the cause for their salvation."'

123. The Sufi must observe the teachings of his masters and guard the blessings (*barakāt*) of the education he receives when he stays in their company and follows their *ādāb*.

Muḥammad ibn al-Ḥasan al-Khashshāb told us: I heard Muḥammad ibn ᶜAbd Allāh al-Farghānī say: I heard Junayd say:

'I have been in the company of spiritual masters for more than ten years; they would talk about these sciences[252] and, although I didn't understand anything, I never criticised what they said. And, one week after the other, I derived much benefit from going and listening to their words, knowing that what they said was the truth, and never criticising them. No sooner had this period passed than [I saw the fruits of that, when] a question arose and people came to my house and asked me about that, saying: "Such and such an issue has been raised and we would like to hear your opinion about that," or some such words.'[253]

124. The Sufi must endeavour not to eat anything that he has not paid for.

I heard Muḥammad ibn Khālid al-Baghdādī say: I heard ʿAbd Allāh al-Fārisī say: I heard Abū'l-Ḥasan al-Rāzī say: I heard Yūsuf ibn al-Ḥusayn say: I heard Abū Turāb al-Nakhshabī say: 'I never let my *nafs* have the better of me except one time, when I felt a craving for some bread and eggs while I was travelling. So I turned off to a village, but when I arrived, a man jumped at me and seized me, and he said: "This man was one of the robbers!" So they threw me to the ground and gave me seventy lashes. Then a man recognised me and said [to them]: "Woe unto you! This is Abū Turāb!" So they lifted me up and apologised to me. Then, the man took me to his house and offered me bread and eggs. And I said to my *nafs*: "Eat them, after seventy lashes!"'[254]

125. The Sufi should [not] attempt to reach an ecstatic state (*tawājud*) during the *samāʿ* sessions,[255] but he should remain calm and keep silent, except if he is totally overcome by the emotion of the mystical ecstasy (*wajd*) in a way that his state appears as it really is.

I heard Abū Bakr al-Rāzī say: I heard al-Murtaʿish say: 'He who attempts to reach an ecstatic state by external means (*tawājada*) and whose ecstasy-inducing measures (*tawājud*)[256] are not conducive to spiritual enhancement (*ziyāda*), must feel ashamed and repent (*yatūbu*). Verily, God is worthier of man's being ashamed in front of Him.'[257]

126. The Sufi must take as much food as it is necessary for his sustenance.

Abū'l-ʿAbbās ibn ʿAṭā' said: 'If one seeks food for other than his sustenance, all that he gets out of it is sickness.'[258]

127. The Sufi must not talk about the common people,[259] unless he finds a novice that specifically requests that for the achievement of his goal. In that case, he should talk to him about that only as much as it is necessary to guide the novice, and not more than that.[260]

When Abū'l-Ḥusayn al-Nūrī entered Egypt, he was asked to talk about his fellows,[261] but he refused, saying: 'They are travelling along the path of seclusion (*waḥsha*) and the mention of this world and its creatures among them is a fault and a shame.[262] Yet, if I found a novice who has set out on the path of spiritual realisation (*murīd mutaḥaqqiq*) or anyone searching for the truth who is seeking guidance, then I will talk to him about that only as much as it can help the novice strengthen his conviction, and the one who searches for the truth to realise his intention and achieve his goal. However, I know for sure that if I talked to you now, I would do it just for pleasure, and if they listened they would do it just for fun; and I would use my words merely to satisfy my desire and make myself look good in their eyes,[263] while they would listen to my words only to claim what they actually do not know and have not experienced.'

128. The Sufi should be constantly in the two states of fear of God Most High and contemplation of Him (*mulāzamatu ḥālay al-murāqaba wa'l-mushāhada*), both in his outward and in his inward behaviour.

Thus said Abū'l-Ḥusayn al-Nūrī: 'He who does not fear God with regard to his actions, will not contemplate the vision of Him in his states, and he who does not remember that God beholds him, cannot truly fear Him.'

129. The Sufi should practise the virtues of *murūwa* in his dealing with God Most High.

In this respect, Yaḥyā ibn Muʿādh said: 'Deal with God with the virtues of *murūwa*: that you contemplate the favours He bestowed upon you in that He inspired you to serve Him, that you do not remind Him of your acts of obedience to Him and you do not ask for a reward for your actions, and that you devote your life to your gratitude to Him for enabling you to serve Him and venerate Him.'[264]

130. The Sufi should follow the rules of *adab* when asking God Most High for something; that means he should ask Him with the tongue of need and not with the tongue of command.[265] Indeed, if one asks something with the proper *adab*, his prayer will be answered soon.

131. The Sufi must advise his companions to keep company with those who guide them to the path toward God and who show them the way to draw near to Him, and who induce them to renounce pleasure in worldly things (*wa-yuzahhiduhum fī'l-dunyā*).[266]

I heard Muḥammad ibn ʿAbd Allāh ibn Shādhān say: I heard Yūsuf ibn al-Ḥusayn say: I said to Dhū'l-Nūn, when I departed from him: 'Who should I be friends with? and in the company of whom should I sit?' He said: 'You must sit in the company of those who remind you of God when you see them, inspire your heart with reverence and awe, increase your knowledge when they speak,[267] induce you to renounce pleasure in worldly things when they act, do not disobey God while you are near to them, and admonish you with their deeds and not with their words.'[268]

A man said to Junayd: 'Give me some advice!' He said: 'Be with the one who leads you to God, and keep away from the one who leads you to this world.'

A man said to Abū Ḥafṣ: 'Give me some advice!' He told him: 'Be to your Lord a true servant and to your friends a faithful brother, and know that for every Muslim there is a hidden secret (*sirr*) between him and God: therefore, guard the sacredness (*ḥurma*) of that secret and beware lest you should despise any Muslims, and thus make a slip you would never recover from.'

A man said to Muḥammad ibn al-Qaṣṣār: 'Give me some advice!' He replied: 'I will give you the advice that Fuḍayl gave to one of his friends, when he asked him for guidance, saying:

"What is better? Having many different lords or having God, the One and the Almighty?"'[269]

132. The Sufi should avoid serving the rich lest he covet their position and power.

Aḥmad ibn Naṣr al-Narsī of Baghdad reported to us that Muḥammad ibn Makhlad said: I heard ᶜAmr ibn Fayrūz [say]: I heard Bishr ibn al-Ḥārith say: 'If in your contentment (*qunūᶜ*) you found honour and glory, that would be sufficient for you.'[270]

133. The Sufi must shun all desires.

Aḥmad ibn Naṣr reported to us that [Muḥammad] ibn Makhlad said: Bishr ibn al-Ḥārith said: 'If you see a poor reciter[271] dressing like the rich because of his ambition,[272] know that he must be abhorred.'[273]

134. The Sufi must find in contentment his honour and glory (*wa-min ādābihim al-taᶜazzuz bi'l-qanāᶜa*).

Aḥmad ibn al-Naṣr reported to us that [Muḥammad] ibn Makhlad said: Muḥammad ibn Yūsuf said: Abū Naṣr Ghullām al-Bazzāz said: I heard Bishr ibn al-Ḥārith say: 'God Most High said to David, upon him be peace, in a revelation: "O David! Warn your people against being devoured by their desires. Verily, I created passions for those among my creatures who are weak: therefore, what have desires to do with the brave and strong ones?"'

135. The Sufi must avoid sating his appetite when eating lawful food, lest the goodness of his actions become doubtful and the lawful turn into the unlawful.

Aḥmad ibn Naṣr reported to us that [Muḥammad] ibn Makhlad told him that ᶜAlī ibn Khalīl said: Abū'l-ᶜAbbās al-Baghdādī of Aleppo would say: I heard Bishr ibn al-Ḥārith say: 'Don't accustom yourself to satisfying your appetite with lawful food, lest the truthfulness of your actions become doubtful and the lawful turn into the unlawful.'

136. The Sufi must make distinctions when answering people's supplications.

Aḥmad ibn Naṣr al-Narsī reported to us that [Muḥammad] ibn Makhlad said to him: Mūsā ibn Hārūn al-Ṭūsī said to me:

Muḥammad ibn Nuᶜaym ibn Hayṣam said to me: I heard Bishr say: 'The people of excellent conduct would answer the supplications only of those whose condition and circumstances they knew.'[274]

137. The Sufi must not stay too long with a sick person when visiting him.

I heard Abū'l-ᶜAbbās al-Baghdādī say: I heard Jaᶜfar al-Khuldī say: Abū'l-Qāsim ibn Bundār said: al-Sarī al-Saqaṭī said: 'During my stay in Tarsus I fell ill and I couldn't get up.[275] Therefore, some Sufis (*fuqarā'*) came to visit me and, as they protracted their stay, I told them: "Spread your hands, that we may pray to God." Hence, they spread their hands, and I said: "O God! Teach us how to behave when visiting the sick," and I wiped my face with my hands.[276] Then, they knew that they had stayed too long and so they got up and left.'

138. The Sufi must practise piety (*waraᶜ*) constantly in all moments.

I heard Muḥammad ibn al-Ḥusayn ibn Khālid say: I heard Aḥmad ibn Muḥammad ibn Ṣāliḥ [say]: I heard Muḥammad ibn ᶜAbdūn say: I heard Abū'l-Qāsim ibn Rizq Allāh say: 'One day, I walked out of the mosque and to my great surprise I saw some boys playing while some shaykhs were sitting nearby. Therefore, I told them: "You there, aren't you ashamed? There are shaykhs sitting here, and you play next to them!" One of those boys replied: "Look here! Their piety lessened and so did the awe they inspired us with."'

Sahl ibn ᶜAbd Allāh said: 'Piety is the foundation of everything: to him who practices it in his behaviour, God Most High bequeaths love in the hearts of His friends[277] and awe in the hearts of His enemies, and he always finds acceptance among those who are devoted to Him (*ahl wilāyatihi*).'

Ibn Yazdāniyār[278] was asked: 'What is piety?' He replied: 'To act in conformity with the Qur'ān and the Sunna, to follow the revealed law of Islam, and to abstain from allowing oneself any personal or misleading interpretation (*ta'wīlāt*).'[279]

139. The Sufi must guard the moments and always follow the *ādāb* when experiencing states.

Abū'l-ʿAbbās ibn Muḥammad ibn al-Ḥusayn ibn al-Khashshāb reported to us that ʿAbd Allāh ibn Aḥmad al-Naqqāsh reported to him [saying]: I heard my father say: I heard Fahdān say: 'You are between three moments: the moment that has passed and that you cannot make up for, and the moment that has not come yet and about which you do not know whether it will be counted for or against you, and whether you will master it or you will be its slave. And there is your moment, the moment that you are living in: then, beware lest you should lose your moment and not engage yourself in it.'

140. The Sufi must sit with those whose religion and piety he trusts.[280]

I heard Abū Bakr al-Rāzī say: I heard Muḥammad ibn ʿAlī al-Kattānī say: 'Sitting with people of understanding cleans hearts of the rust of sins.'

141. The Sufi must not look at the vices of his brethren for the sake of his love for them and he must always think well of them.

I heard Abū Bakr Muḥammad ibn ʿAbd Allāh al-Rāzī say: I heard Abū ʿAmr al-Zujājī say: 'I was told that a man became a friend of Ibrāhīm ibn Adham and when he decided to leave him, he asked him: "O Abū Isḥāq, did you see something of me that you disliked?" He said: "Truly, the intensity of my love for God made me oblivious of your shortcomings."'[281]

142. The Sufi must conceal the shameful deeds of his brethren and he must speak of them in good terms.[282]

I heard Abū Bakr al-Rāzī say: I heard ʿUbayda al-Ghassāl say: 'A man stole a copy of the Qur'ān from Ibrāhīm ibn Adham and went with it to the market to sell it. Then, when he was asked who knew him, he went with them to Ibrāhīm ibn Adham. They said to him: "Do you know him?" "Yes, I do," he answered. "This is the one," they replied "who stole your copy of the Qur'ān." Ibrāhīm replied: "I knew that, but I did not want to expose his hidden deeds."'[283]

He said: Ruwaym said to a man who was speaking badly of one of his brethren in his presence: 'Do you know anything good about him?' He replied: 'Yes.' He said: 'So, mention it! That, indeed, is a good thing for you and a benefit.'

143. The Sufi must keep earning and gaining his living until he reaches a state when his *tawakkul* and his total trust in God restrain him from that.

I heard Abū Bakr Muḥammad ibn ᶜAbd Allāh ibn Shādhān say: I heard Abū ᶜUthmān say: I heard Ibrāhīm al-Khawāṣṣ say: 'It is not necessary for a Sufi to practise abstention from gaining his living, unless that be required of him, because he has reached a state which detaches him from his means of livelihood and his condition makes it unnecessary for him to earn a living. Yet, if he needs to satisfy his necessities and nothing keeps him from taking a job, then work is more appropriate for him and earning is allowed to him, because it is not right for a man to refrain from working if he cannot dispense with it.'[284]

I heard Muḥammad ibn ᶜAbd Allāh al-Rāzī say: I heard Abū ᶜAlī al-Rūdhbārī say: 'If the Sufi says after five days: "I am starving", then take him to the market and order him to work and gain his living.'

144. The Sufi must refrain from begging (*su'āl*) when he finds himself in dire need.[285]

I heard Abū Bakr al-Rāzī say: I heard Abū'l-Q̱āsim al-Jawharī say: I heard Junayd say: 'Any Sufi who has become accustomed to bow[286] to get his sustenance when he is in need, will be unable to free himself from the bondage to his *nafs* and will not learn patience.'

Abū ᶜUthmān said: 'Anyone who asks when he is in need of something without being under the necessity of doing that, is truly far from the path of the pious (*wariᶜūn*).'

145. If the Sufi realises that a special blessing is manifested to him when staying in the company of one of his masters, he must keep close to him and he must never leave him for whatever reason or pretext.

I heard Muḥammad ibn ᶜAbd Allāh say: I heard Abū Bakr say: 'Upon his father's death, one of the disciples said to Jesus the son of Mary, upon him be peace: "May I have permission to go and bury my father?" He replied: "Let the dead bury the dead and follow me!"'

146. The Sufi must avoid idleness and anger.

I heard Muḥammad ibn ᶜAbd Allāh al-Ṭabarī say: I heard ᶜAlī ibn Bābawayh say: 'Beware of idleness and anger, for if you are idle, you cannot accomplish your duties toward God Most High, and if you let anger overwhelm you, you cannot bear patiently what God has set for you.'

147. The Sufi must conceal his miracles (*karāmāt*) and regard them as a temptation.

I heard Abū Bakr al-Rāzī say: I heard Abū ᶜAlī al-Rūdhbārī say: 'God enjoined the prophets to make their signs and miracles manifest; likewise, He ordered the saints (*awliyā'*) to conceal them, lest people should be led away from the right path because of them.'[287]

Abū ᶜUthmān al-Maghribī said: 'The [true] godfriend is not subject to temptations in his friendship to God nor does he subject others to temptations.'[288]

Dhū'l-Nūn said: 'The godfriend is he who is distinguished and favoured in his special friendship with God. God has charge of his every movement and his every breath.[289] God separates him from all created beings and through him He induces them to renounce pleasure in worldly things. In him He made manifest the blessings of His sight and power. The spiritual state (*karāma*) of the godfriend, if it is authentic, becomes manifest to him and to those who believe in his state.'[290]

148. The Sufi must persevere in practising poverty and act in conformity with its *ādāb*.

I heard Abū Bakr al-Rāzī say: I heard Abū ᶜAbd Allāh al-Maghribī say: 'If a poor man renounces this world,[291] even if he has not performed any excellent deed, a tiny particle of him is worth more than many of these devout men, who carry out their duties diligently but did not give up this world.'

Abū ᶜAbd Allāh ibn Khafīf said: 'The *adab* of poverty is to be happy in it, conceal one's neediness, and be content with every circumstance that comes to one because of it, knowing for a certainty that poverty is a favour bestowed by God upon those of His servants whom He loves most. Therefore, he who accepts God's favour becomes close to Him (*ānasa bihi*) and does not complain of Him, and he who complains of Him, has rejected the favour which He bestowed on him.'

149. The Sufi must seek to achieve the highest states by being perseverant in his dealings [with God] and by rectifying his dealings [with Him] through the contemplation of Him.[292]

Aḥmad ibn Abī'l-Ḥawārī said: 'Know that every godservant who is veiled from dealing with God is veiled from the true knowledge of God, and everyone who is veiled from the true knowledge of God is veiled from the contemplation of God and becomes distant from Him, and he who is distant from God is unhappy and miserable.'

150. The Sufi must conceal his states and hide them under a veil of obscurity rather than make them manifest, disguise them rather than reveal them, and allude to them rather than speak about them openly.[293]

It was related of Abū'l-Ḥusayn al-Nūrī that once a group of masters among his fellow Sufis gathered for a *samāᶜ* session when, at a certain moment, all the people present were carried away by the ardour of mystical ecstasy. Nūrī, instead, remained calm and silent. When they asked him the reason for that, he said: 'The spiritual station in which I experience the mystical ecstasy must not be told to anyone.' And they asked him: 'What is your spiritual station and how is your mystical state?' He replied: 'I express it symbolically by allusion and not with explanations, and I speak about it indirectly and not openly.'[294] Thereupon, he recited these verses:

Many a dove kept cooing in the forenoon
in grief they sang on the branch of a tree
They remembered their lovers and the good time that passed
and they cried with sorrow and awakened my sadness
Sometimes my lament would prevent them from sleeping
and sometimes their lament would make me sleepless too
Thus, when they began crying, I tried to relieve their sorrow
and when I began, they tried to relieve mine
But I could not understand their words of suffering
and they could not understand mine[295]
Yet, through my ardent love I do know them
and they too know me through their love.

After he recited these verses, all were enraptured by mystical ecstasy by his words and cried, and they understood what he meant and left him in the state in which he was.

151. The Sufi must carry the burdens of all creatures and bear with them their sufferings.

It was reported of Abū Jaʿfar that he said: 'The Sufi is not a real Sufi until he feels responsible for all mankind.'

152. The Sufi must look away from his *nafs*[296] and avoid looking into its deeds.[297]

I heard Manṣūr ibn ʿAbd Allāh say: I heard Abū ʿAmr al-Anmāṭī say: I heard Abū'l-ʿAbbās ibn ʿAṭā' say: 'The thing which is most hateful to God is the contemplation of the *nafs* and its doings, and even worse than that is to look at the compensation for its doings.'[298]

Junayd said: 'Worldly existence, mankind and the *nafs* are a veil to the hearts of the elect.'

153. The Sufi must strive constantly on the path and use knowledge (*ʿilm*) both in outward and in inward behaviour.

Al-Ḥārith al-Muḥāsibī said: 'To him who strives in his inward heart, God bequeaths good outward conduct, and to him who improves both his outward and inward conduct, God bequeaths the right way to Him.' God Most High said: 'And those who strive in Our [cause], We will certainly guide them to Our paths.'[299]

A Sufi said: 'Knowledge[300] is what makes you act, and certainty is what sustains you.'

154. The Sufi must bear patiently the humiliation of his *nafs* when begging (*tadhlīl al-nafs fī 'l-su'āl*) or in other similar circumstances.[301]

I heard one of our masters say: A man said to Shiblī: 'O Abū Bakr! Whenever we go and ask them for something, they humiliate us.' Shiblī replied: 'Woe unto you! Isn't humiliation (*dhull*) your way? And isn't your way of living only through humiliation? And doesn't your glory lie only in humiliation? And don't you get what you want only through humiliation?'[302] And he kept silent for a while. Then he said to the man: 'Now, go out to them and forget your self and them:[303] thus, you will be blameless and they will be blameless too.'

Ḥamdūn al-Qaṣṣār said: 'He who did not taste the humiliation of a disdainful refusal when asking for something shall not be successful.'

Abū ʿAbd Allāh ibn al-Jallā' said: 'If one looks at himself with the eye of pride[304] and haughtiness, verily he deserves that God humiliates him by making others refuse his requests.'

Fāris al-Baghdādī said: 'One day, I saw Shiblī in the mosque while he was saying: "Whoever has brought something with him for charity[305] shall give it to me: indeed, my present circumstances have put me in need of you." So a man offered to him some money.[306] Then he said: "Give it to the greengrocer!" And he cried. Then, he said: "There is no profession that is more miserable than begging. Indeed, how can we know God, when we practise the most despicable profession of all?"'[307]

155. The Sufi must endeavour to devote himself totally to any state that comes upon him and to any thing that passes before him in his moments. He must also avoid neglecting (*ighfāl*) his states and he must be fully aware of the moment, because that is the most precious thing of all, and it is incumbent upon the gnostic, above all else, not to neglect it. Verily, once the moment has passed, you cannot make up for it.

It has been reported of al-Ḥusayn ibn Manṣūr that he said: 'Guard your breaths,[308] your moments and your hours, and guard what has passed before you and what you are in. Indeed, he who knows whence he comes, knows whither he is going; and he who knows what he does, knows what is done to him;[309] and he who knows what is done to him, knows what is expected of him; and he who knows what is expected of him, knows what he has a right to; and he who knows his right, knows his duty; and he who knows his duty, knows what he has with him.[310] He who does not know whence he came, nor where he is, nor how he exists and for Whom, that one is of those who have no knowledge, yet he is not aware of his not knowing and, therefore, he thinks that he does know.'

156. The Sufi must strive to recognise the inner voices inspiring his heart (*dawāʿī*) and pursue in every moment the *ādāb* of what the inner voice of that moment inspires him to.

Al-Ḥusayn ibn Manṣūr said: 'The voice of faith (*īmān*) calls to integrity, the voice of submission (*islām*) calls to morality, the voice of virtue (*iḥsān*) calls to the contemplation of God, the voice of discernment (*fahm*) calls to spiritual enhancement, the voice of reason (*ʿaql*) calls to 'tasting' (the spiritual realities, *madhāq*), the voice of knowledge (*ʿilm*) calls to the mystical audition, the voice of gnosis (*maʿrifa*) calls to repose (*rawḥ*), to peace of mind and to heavenly fragrance,[311] the voice of the soul (*nafs*)[312] calls to worship, the voice of trust (*tawakkul*) calls to reliance [on God], the voice of fear (*khawf*) calls to disquiet,[313] the voice of hope (*rajāʾ*) calls to reassurance, the voice of love (*maḥabba*) calls to longing, the voice of longing (*shawq*) calls to passion, and the voice of passion[314] (*walah*) calls to God. He who in his inward being is not urged by any of these voices, he shall fail; he is of those who were forsaken in the desert of bewilderment and whom God does not care for.'

157. The Sufi must give good counsel to his brethren when they set out on journeys and always advise them.

I heard Abū'l-Qāsim al-Dimashqī say to a man, while giving him some advice about a journey he wanted to make: 'O my brother! God alone should be your companion: verily, He is the one who protects you from adversities, rewards you for your good deeds, and forgives you your evil ones; He is the one who will never abandon you along the path.'[315]

158. The Sufi must not occupy himself with this world, as he knows its harm and its ephemeral nature.

I heard ʿAbd Allāh ibn Muḥammad ibn al-Faḍl say: 'Attaching importance to this world and occupying oneself with it will make you lose both this world and the next.'

159. The Sufi must occupy himself with the present moment and take it up totally, without thinking about the past or the future.

I heard Muḥammad ibn ʿAbd Allāh ibn Shādhān [say]: I heard Muḥammad ibn ʿAlī say: I heard Abū Saʿīd al-Kharrāz say: 'To be preoccupied with a past moment is to lose a second moment.'

160. Upon mentioning the name of God (*dhikr*), the Sufi must purify his mouth both outwardly, by cleaning it with the *siwāk*[316] and some water, and inwardly, through repentance, contrition (*nadam*), and the asking of God's forgiveness.

It has been related of the Prophet, peace and blessings upon him, that he said: 'The *siwāk* is a tool for cleaning one's mouth and a means of winning God's approval.' It has also been related of the Prophet, peace and blessings upon him, that he said: 'Clean your mouths, because they are the paths of the Qur'ān.'[317] It has been reported of Abū Yazīd al-Bisṭāmī that he said: 'For thirty years, whenever I intended to invoke God Most High, I would rinse my mouth and clean my teeth out of reverence for God the Exalted and Mighty.'

161. The Sufi must strive with perseverance till he reaches the station of union (*maqām al-wuṣla*).

God Most High said: 'While he was standing in prayer in the niche (*fī 'l-miḥrāb*), the angels called unto him.'[318] Abū Ḥafṣ said: 'The *miḥrāb* is the gate to all good.'

A man came to Abū'l-Khayr al-Aqṭaʿ and said: 'What is the way to God Most High?' He answered: 'Water and the *miḥrāb*.'

The man replied: 'I asked you about the way to God.' He said: 'The ways are many and different, but from here[319] we found the way that leads to union (*wuṣūl*) with Him.'

162. The Sufi must always occupy himself with what is incumbent upon him to do in every moment, in every time and in every breath, and he must avoid leisure.

Thus Sahl ibn ʿAbd Allāh said: 'The idler abounds with defects because the one who is busy always tries to achieve more, whereas the idle, and not the busy one, is concerned with trivialities.'

163. The Sufi must prevent his heart from thinking about his subsistence through the contemplation of the True Sustainer.

Sahl ibn ʿAbd Allāh said: 'Anyone who believes that means of subsistence is what makes it possible for him to live doubts the promise which God Most High has made to him and attributes falsehood to Him. The obedience of the godservant is not authentic until God becomes his nourishment and he becomes content and satisfied with Him.'

Abū Bakr al-Warrāq said: 'There is no servant who is more despicable than the one who, when his master calls for him, is too occupied with what belongs to his master to answer his master's call.'

Sahl was asked: 'What is nourishment?' He said: 'True nourishment is God. Verily, in Him everything finds its sustenance: he whose sustenance is in other than Him is powerless, and he whose life is in other than Him is dead.' In this regard, he recited to me the following verses: 'If you were the nourishment of the soul and then you abandoned it/ the soul, whose nourishment you are, would not survive/[320] it would be left like a lizard in the water/ or like a fish living in an endless desert.'

164. The Sufi must find his strength and honour in devoting himself totally to God, knowing that anyone other than Him is in need of Him, that He is the Supreme Being Who needs none, and that he who glories in any other than Him is ever despicable and lowly. Therefore, he who finds strength and honour in Him, God fortifies him in this world and the next and protects him

from the worries of this world and the next, and none can do that but He.

God Most High said: 'But honour belongs to Allah and His Messenger, and to the Believers.'[321] The Sufi must occupy himself in every moment with what is more appropriate for him, as regards his spiritual states, his knowledge, his discipline, and his striving [along the path]. The *adab* of knowledge (*ʿilm*) is that he must make his self an ornament of his knowledge and not his knowledge an ornament of his self; he must know that his heart cannot hold all the sciences and, therefore, entrust to it only those sciences which can be for him the right provisions [for the journey] to his Lord and can guide him to carrying out His orders; he must know that what he owns[322] cannot satisfy the needs of all people, and, therefore, he must give it to the people of God and to those who pursue the truth[323] in preference to others; he must know that he should not reveal his true character to everyone,[324] and, therefore, he should disclose it only to those who follow his same mode of living (*tarīqa*) and belief and who have a close relationship with him, and in particular to the people of his same order,[325] for whom he shall reserve the authentic and peculiar traits of his character, while to all others with whom he associates, he shall show a joyful and cheerful face, and he shall use piety with true and consistent behaviour.[326] [The proper *adab* is] that his devotion to knowledge be without pause, his renunciation without desires, his vigilance without negligence, his certitude without doubts, and his gratitude without conditions.[327] He must be forbearing and steady, in such a way that he will be gentle with the one who behaves foolishly toward him, he will not return wrong if someone wrongs him, he will not get angry if someone lies to him, and he will not be delighted if someone praises him, because his compassion, his mercy and the integrity of his heart will have come to perfection. He keeps away from greed, pride and avarice, because they are the sources of all evil, and from them come[328] the satisfaction of one's appetites,[329] abundance of sleep and leisure, the love of leadership and the pursuit of pleasures. All that leads to the love of this world: the love of this world brings on these calamities and all of them derive from this worldly existence. God Most High described this world and told us about it when He said: 'Know ye (all), that the life of this world is but play and amusement, pomp and mutual boasting and multiplying, (in rivalry) among yourselves, riches and children. Here is a similitude: how rain and the plants, which it brings forth, delight (the hearts of) the unbelievers'[330] till the end of the verse.[331] He who loves any of the things mentioned above,[332] loves them for the sake of this world,[333] and he who loves this world, loves what is hateful to God. It has been related about the Prophet, peace and blessings upon him, that he said: 'Truly, God Most High has never looked at this world after He created it, because of His hatred for it.' Four qualities keep you away from this world and bring you close to the Hereafter: avoiding this world and the comfort it brings and regarding it as transient and ephemeral. Junayd said: 'He who lives in the transient (*fanā'*) is himself transient (*fānin*).' Refrain from anything about which you are doubtful, desist from all that desire drives you to, bear the difficulty of assiduous devoutness, and be content in misfortunes.

165. The Sufi must love seclusion (*khalwa*),[334] because in that are God's blessings for the one who secludes himself with knowledge.[335]

I heard Abū ʿUthmān al-Maghribī say: 'Seclusion and mystical audition are appropriate only for the one who knows God.'

Sarī al-Saqaṭī said: 'Five are the things which spiritual retreat bequeaths: respite from evil company, renunciation of this world, silence, experiencing the pleasure of practising [the Sufi path][336] when hidden from the eyes of people and, finally, giving up finding fault with people, as you do not see anyone disobey God.'[337]

166. The Sufi must be in a constant state of repentance in every instant. For in every instant there are duties towards God Most High which he fails to accomplish, and grace from God continually renewed for which he forgets to be grateful, and therefore it becomes necessary for him to repent and ask God's forgiveness.

167. The Sufi must conceal the signs that God manifested in him[338] and he must keep them secret.

A Sufi reported this saying: 'Miracles are the most subtle thing by which godfriends are led astray, along with the manifestation of the signs of divine favour.'

168. The Sufi must conceal the secrets of God's favour to him[339] and he must not divulge them except among those who have knowledge of these secrets, lest people should be misled by them. He must not behave with affectation because of the secrets he knows and he must not speak of them or use them in any way when being with the common people.

169. The Sufi must remain silent whenever he has a strong desire to speak, and speak whenever he has a strong desire to remain silent.

Thus Bishr al-Ḥāfī is reported to have said: 'Whenever you feel like speaking, keep silent, and whenever you feel like remaining silent, speak!'

170. The Sufi must doubt his *nafs* in all moments, and never be pleased with it in any way, nor let it speak about a science he has not practised or a state he has not experienced. His knowledge must not induce him to transgress the revealed law of Islam and the *ādāb* of it, or to neglect it. Rather, he must endeavour to revere the divine law (*taʿẓīm al-sharʿ*) and the outward manifestation of the [divine] science[340] in every moment that comes down to him (*fī kull wārid*).

The Sufi must give up all pretensions and claims, whether they are small or big; he must not make false claims about any of his actions and states and must not find pleasure in his own statements and words. He must enjoin on himself a service of total obedience to his master, whatever effort it takes. He must be content with the divine decree, rely totally on God, entrust to Him all his affairs, guard his moments, his states and his breaths, and never omit anything of them, unless he is ordered to do that. He must endeavour also to show his brethren a cheerful face and always treat them with kindness, even though in truth he has his Lord as his only companion and he feels no liking for people (*istawḥasha*).

He should watch his outward conduct and preserve his inward heart, he should guard his tongue and have a good opinion of his brethren and a poor opinion of himself.

Nobody can practise *adab* properly unless he follows the example of a guide of great knowledge and experience,[341] who may show him his shortcomings, his errors, and his missteps. In fact, he who consumes himself with struggle (along the mystical path, *man qatala nafsahu fī 'l-mujāhada*) and devotes his moments to the renunciation [of this world], (*wa-afnā awqātahu fī 'l-zuhd*), is constantly accompanied by his own *nafs*[342] and thus becomes proud of it. Such a person cannot be aware of the flaws in his behaviour unless they are shown to him by someone who has gone through the mystical stations and has experienced the spiritual states (*man salaka al-maqāmāt wa-nāzala al-aḥwāl*), and upon whom has been bestowed the blessings of his masters and the lights of their kindness. He[343] shall lead the novice on his path and teach him how to distinguish his right moments from his bad ones, and he shall tell him what is good for him and what is not.

Then, if God grants him success in that, he[344] shall be guided to the path of integrity. And if such a guide (*sālik*),[345] who has gone through the mystical stations and experienced the spiritual states, leaves him, the novice shall turn to a learned mentor (*ʿālim nāṣiḥ*), whose science can benefit him and who shuns the things and concerns of this world. To him the novice shall show his state and from him he shall receive advice and suggestions: if he does so, his integrity shall not be lost. And if the novice's willingness to learn is firm and sincere, God will send him a fellow mystic or a learned mentor. Truly, he who turns to God totally, God will be responsible for all his intentions and He will never abandon him. In the absence of a learned mentor or of a close companion on the way, the novice shall turn totally to his Lord, so that He may take charge of his education and training, if He sees in him a genuine willingness and determination.

As for me, I ask God the Almighty to make me one of those who follow the *adab* of His Book, who learn from the Sunna of

His Prophet, peace and blessings upon him, and act in accordance with His Book and the Sunna of the Prophet. And I ask Him not to make me one of those who are precluded from the blessings of both,[346] and not to make me deviate from the path which they have instructed people to follow. I ask God to inspire me with guidance on the Day of Judgement and to suggest to me the argument which I shall advance, when the two angels Munkar and Nakīr, peace be upon them, will come and question me [in my grave]. I ask God to reassure me on the Day of the Greatest Fear and bless me with His water on the Day of the Greatest Thirst, and to keep me company in my grave on the Night of my solitude. I ask Him that for me, for my beloved ones, my father, and all the believers, men and women, and the Muslims, men and women, by His blessing and His generosity, by His grace, His magnanimity, and His mercy: truly, He is the All-hearing and the Near. Praise be to God, the Cherisher and Sustainer of the worlds,[347] and blessings and peace be on the seal of the prophets, Muḥammad, and on his family, and his companions altogether.

Praise be to God, the Cherisher and Sustainer of the Worlds.

Notes

[1] *Ādāb al-ẓawāhir wa'l-bawāṭin*: 'the discipline of the outward conduct and the inward heart.' The concept of harmonising one's outward and inward conduct as an essential step towards attaining self-realisation recurs frequently in the *Jawāmiʿ* as well as in other works by Sulamī: see, for instance, Sulamī's *Kitāb ādāb al-ṣuḥba wa-ḥusn al-ʿishra*, pp. 86–87 (Kister's edition, *op. cit.*) and Sulamī's *Kitāb al-futuwwa* (Sassi's translation, *op. cit.*), III, 3; IV, 28; V, 6.

[2] Qur'ān, 31:20. For the Qur'ānic quotations I have referred mostly to ʿAbd Allāh Yūsuf ʿAlī's translation: ʿAbd Allāh Yūsuf ʿAlī, *The Holy Qur'ān*, text, translation and commentary, Cairo: Al-Zahrā' li'l-Iʿlām al-ʿArabī, 1990.

[3] *Al-Muṣṭafā*: 'The Elect', 'The Chosen', one of the epithets of the Prophet Muḥammad.

[4] In his *Kitāb al-futuwwa*, Sulamī speaks of *mushāhada* as the state of God's lovers, who contemplate the truth and its unveiled secrets: 'È prerogativa della cavalleria ... che nello svelamento [il servitore] ricerchi la contemplazione con la realizzazione ... An-Nūrī ha detto: Allāh Altissimo ha rivelato la scienza alle creature, mentre ha dato in particolare ai Suoi intimi la conoscenza, ai puri lo svelamento, e ai Suoi amati la contemplazione [*al-mushāhada*]' (II, 32, p. 39; all my cross-references to Sulamī's *Kitāb al-futuwwa* refer to the Italian translation by G. Sassi mentioned above in 'The Life and Works of Sulamī', n. 35. The Roman numerals refer to the chapter's number in Sassi's work, while the number placed after the comma refers to the section, as numbered by Sassi in her translation.

[5] *Munāzalatuhum*: 'encounter'. *Munāzala*, more often in the plural form *munāzalāt*, 'encounters', cf. Sells, Michael A., *Early Islamic Mysticism*, New York: Paulist Press, 1996, p. 113. However, I have preferred to follow in my translation the suggestion of Etan Kohlberg, who considers it to be more plausible to interpret *munāzala* as a mistake of the copist for *manāzil* (pl. of *manzil*, condition, status). See, Kohlberg, E., *op. cit.*, p. 1 Arabic, note 15.

[6] *Arbāb al-aḥwāl:* lit. 'those endowed with the mystical states' or 'those who possess states.'

[7] A probable reference to the *Ahl al-ṣuffa*. *Al-ṣuffa*: 'of a mosque: a bench placed near a veranda' (*al-Munjid*, p. 425). The 'People of the Bench' were a group among

the Prophet's Companions who 'abode in his mosque and engaged in devotion, renouncing the world and refusing to seek a livelihood' (Hujwīrī, *op. cit.*, pp. 81–82). Some identified them with the first Sufis, whose name they believed derived from *ṣuffa* (cf. Schimmel, Annemarie, *Mystical Dimensions of Islam*, Chapel Hill: The University of North Carolina Press, 1975, p. 14; on *Ahl al-ṣuffa*, cf. also Molé, Marijan, *I Mistici Musulmani*, Milan: Adelphi, 1992, p. 47).

[8] Referring to the Sufis.

[9] Meaning the *ādāb Allāh*, or the rules of conduct with which God graced His friends, as said in the opening section.

[10] Qur'ān, 3:159.

[11] Qur'ān, 16:90.

[12] Qur'ān, 68:4. On the Prophet's character taken as a model for correct behaviour, cf. *K. ādāb al-ṣuḥba*, Kister, *op. cit.*, pp. 22–23 Arabic.

[13] Qur'ān, 49:2.

[14] Qur'ān, 49:5.

[15] Meaning the lowly and humble disciples.

[16] Qur'ān, 6:54.

[17] Qur'ān, 6:68.

[18] Qur'ān, 93:9,10.

[19] Qur'ān, 6:52.

[20] Qur'ān, 18:28.

[21] *Wa-ghayra dhalika min kitābi 'Llāh mā yaṭūlu dhikruhu wa-qad ḥudhifat* (or: *ḥadhaftu*) *al-asānīd kullahā ṭalaban li'l-ikhtiṣār.* It seems that the text is corrupted, because Sulamī's mention of the chains of authorities (*al-asānīd*) obviously cannot be meant as referring to the Qur'ān. Therefore, I am suggesting to read the passage as '*wa-ghayra dhalika min kitābi 'Llāh wa-min sunnati rasūlihi ...*'

[22] '*Inna 'Llāha addabanī fa-aḥsana adabī* (or *ta'dībī*)': this Hadith (see also *K. ādāb al-ṣuḥba*, Kister, *op. cit.*, p. 86 Arabic) gained wide popularity in Sufi circles, and they based on it their belief in the excellence of the Prophet's *adab*, seen as exemplary for all believers. Later on, it was cited as proof of the superiority of Muḥammad over other prophets (see al-Sarrāj, Abū Naṣr, *op. cit.*, p. 142). This tradition was probably in circulation more than a century before Sulamī's time: M. J. Kister has pointed out (cf. Kohlberg, *op. cit.*, p. 11, note 26) that it appears, although in a different form, in al-Mubarrad's *Kitāb al-fāḍil* (see, al-Mubarrad, Muḥammad b. Yazīd, *Kitāb al-fāḍil*, Cairo, 1375, p. 14).

[23] Qur'ān, 7:199.

[24] On *ʿilm* and the *ādāb* of it, see below, section 164.

[25] Sulamī indicates the importance of *adab* to the mystics by quoting utterances of early Sufi masters: here, for example, the acquisition of *adab* is described as preferable to the accumulation of knowledge (*ʿilm*). A similar idea is attributed

to ʿAbd Allāh ibn ʿAbd al-Raḥmān ibn al-Mubārak (d. 181/797) in Qushayrī's *Risāla*: 'We stand more in need of a small amount of correct behaviour (*adab*) than a great deal of knowledge' (Qushayrī, *Principles of Sufism: Selections from al-Risāla al-Qushayriyya*, translated from the Arabic by B. R. Von Schlegell, Berkeley: Mizan Press, 1990, p. 311; this same saying is quoted in Sarrāj, *op. cit.*, p. 142: '*naḥnu ilā qalīl min al-adab aḥwaju minnā ilā kathīr min al-ʿilm*'). Further on in this same section, Sulamī reports another saying, wherein *adab* is described as more important to the Sufi than prolonged engagement in ascetic exercises.

26 On behaving well (*ḥusn al-khuluq*), cf. *Kitāb al-futuwwa*, III, 22, 36; V, 10.

27 Meaning in contemplating him.

28 On *al-waraʿ*, see ʿAbd Allāh al-Anṣārī al-Harawī, *Les Étapes des Itinérants vers Dieu*, S. De Laugier De Beaurecueil O. P., Cairo: Imprimerie De L'Institut Français d'Archéologie Orientale, 1962, p. 66.

29 A description of the *ʿibāda* of the godservant is found in the *Kitāb al-futuwwa*: 'È un atteggiamento del cavaliere essere contento, felice e gioioso di avere l'abitudine di servire il proprio Signore ...Yahyā ben Muʿādh, che Allāh gli usi misericordia, ha detto: "Chi è contento di servire Allāh, le cose sono contente di servirlo. Chi si rallegra a causa di Allāh, ogni cosa si rallegra di vederlo"' (*K. al-futuwwa*, G. Sassi, *op. cit.*, p. 37). We read also in Sulamī's *Risālat al-malāmatiyya*: '*Wa-samaʿtu Abā ʿUthmān yaqūlu: qāla rajulun li-Abī Ḥafṣ: awṣinī. Qāla: lā takun ʿibādatuka li-rabbika sabīlan li-an takūna maʿbūdan. Wa-'jʿal ʿibādataka lahu iẓhāra rasm al-ʿubūdiyya wa'l-khidma ʿalayka fa-inna man naẓara ilā ʿibādatihi fa-innamā yaʿbudu nafsahu*' (al-Fāwī, ʿAbd al-Fattāḥ Aḥmad, *op. cit.*, p. 311).

30 *al-ʿabīd*, pl. of *ʿabd*, 'the servant', 'the slave', here interpreted in the literal meaning of the term.

31 On 'respect', cf. ʿAbd Allāh al-Anṣārī al-Harawī, *op. cit.*, p. 71.

32 Any disregard of *adab* is said to lead ultimately to loss of faith in God. Cf. the saying of al-Julājulī al-Baṣrī in Qushayrī's *Risāla*: '[...] Obeying the divine law requires correct behaviour (*adab*). So one who does not observe correct behaviour cannot obey the divine law (*sharīʿa*), have faith (*īmān*), nor assert the divine unity (*tawḥīd*)' (Qushayrī, *op. cit.*, pp. 309–310).

33 *Fī'l-ḥālayn*: lit. 'in both states (of being)': i.e., the physical existence in this world and the spiritual being in the Afterlife.

34 'When you are alone': *idhā khalawta*. Also: 'when you are in spiritual retreat.'

35 *Man abṣara al-ʿawāqib*: the one who *ponders* the consequences. The verb *abṣara* properly means 'to see with the eyes of the *baṣīra*', which is the 'inner vision', 'the faculty of the intellect (*ʿaql*).'

36 *Man aḥkama al-tajārib*: lit. 'he who evaluates his experiences, who goes through his experiences carefully and learns from them.'

37 According to the var. in MS Laleli 1516 (Kohlberg, *op. cit.*, p. 5 Arabic, section 7, note 46): *'lianna* maʿrifatahu *mu'addib qalbihi.'* In text (MS Berlin 3081): *'lianna* maʿrūfahu *mu'addib qalbihi.'*

38 Cf. *Kitāb al-futuwwa*, III, 49; III, 5, 10.

39 See below, sections 34, 40, 78, 91, 159; cf. also Muḥāsibī's discourse on 'preparedness for death and restraint of expectation' in Sells, *op. cit.*, pp. 179–183. On *taqṣīr al-amal*, cf. Ibn Abī'l-Dunyā's *Kitāb al-manām*: Kinberg, Leah, *op. cit.*, section 28.

40 *Kāna yu'adhdhinu wa-yuqīmu wa-lā yataqaddamu.*

41 *Ru'yat ʿuyūb anfusihim wa-qillat al-riḍā ʿanhā*: I have interpreted the pronominal suffix *hā* as referring to *anfusihim* rather than to *ʿuyūb*, hence: 'to see the defects of the *nafs* and be dissatisfied with it (i.e., the *nafs*)'. See below, section 16.

42 Abū Ḥātim al-ʿAṭṭār al-Baṣrī was a contemporary of Abū Turāb al-Nakhshabī (d. 245/860).

43 In this paragraph, there is an evident allusion to the attitude of the *Malāmatiyya* or the 'People of Blame' (*ahl al-malāma*), which consisted, as in the case of Abū Ḥātim al-ʿAṭṭār, in dissimulating one's spiritual states (*talbīs al-ḥāl*) by sometimes assuming an outward behaviour that would draw the blame and indignation of the common people (see *Risālat al-malāmatiyya*, in my survey of Sulamī's works). Cf. Sulamī's *Risālat al-malāmatiyya*, tr. by G. Sassi, *op. cit.*, pp. 21–23 and p. 38.

44 The (bad) places he would attend and the licentious conduct he would show were just a means for the *malāmatī* mystic to hide his real interior condition, especially when his spiritual achievements were too great to be showed to people.

45 One of the basic principles of the *Malāmatiyya* was to have a low opinion of oneself (so as not to yield to the inclinations of the ego), while having a good opinion of people and showing respect for them. The *Malāmatī*s would not expect anything from others, as much as they would not expect God to reward them for their good deeds. Cf. *Risālat al-malāmatiyya*, tr. by G. Sassi, *op. cit.*, pp. 24, 31; *ibid.*, p. 33 (n. 3) and p. 45 (n. 16).

46 *Aṣḥāb al-muraqqaʿāt wa'l-fuwaṭ min al-ṣūfiyya*: it was the practice of some ascetics to walk among people wearing patched frocks (*muraqqaʿāt*) and worn clothes (*fuwaṭ*) as if to proclaim their poverty and their vow of renunciation of the world.

47 Sometimes, the habit of wearing patched frocks as a sign of one's poverty might result in an attitude of arrogance and conceit on the part of the ascetic, who would find a sort of self-satisfaction in displaying poverty (seen as an exterior mark of his status as an ascetic) and thus gaining people's respect. In the last

passage, by quoting the words of Abū Ḥātim al-ᶜAṭṭār, Sulamī clearly expresses his disapproval of such behaviour, which he believes to be a mere ostentation of outward appearances: patches and worn clothes are just the surface, while the inward achievements of the soul are hidden, and prove true only in the engagement, i.e., the mystic's encounter with God. We find a mention of the *aṣḥāb al-muraqqaᶜāt* in a passage of the *Kitāb al-futuwwa* as well, where Sulamī denounces once again the hypocrisy of those who would claim the badges of chivalry '*al-futuwwa*' and wear the dress '*muraqqaᶜa*' of the chivalrous, without fulfilling in their inward heart the duties of chivalry. 'È proprio della cavalleria che un servitore non si attribuisca le insegne del cavaliere se non dopo aver sopportato gli oneri della cavalleria e averne assunto le qualità. Hanno chiesto ad ᶜAbd Allāh as-Sajazī: 'Perché non indossi la *muraqqaᶜa* ..?' Egli ha risposto: 'Sarebbe ipocrita indossare gli abiti del cavaliere, senza aver adempiuto i doveri della cavalleria. Solo chi sopporta con pazienza gli oneri della cavalleria può indossarne gli abiti' (*K. al-futuwwa*, *op. cit.*, p. 75). In the last passage of this section, we can see as well an implicit criticism of the *malāmatī* attitude. In fact, the hypocritical behaviour which the words of Abū Ḥātim al-ᶜAṭṭār denounce might be seen also in some *Malāmatī*s, who would indulge in blameworthy habits only for the sake of drawing upon themselves the attention of people and their reproval. On the Sufis' criticism of the *malāmatī* attitude, see my discussion of *Risālat al-malāmatiyya* in the chapter 'The life and works of Sulamī'. Cf. also Hujwīrī's *Kashf al-maḥjūb*: 'Purity (*ṣafā*) is a gift from God, whereas wool (*ṣūf*) is the clothing of animals. [...] In short, the *muraqqaᶜa* is the garb of God's saints. The vulgar use it merely as a means of gaining worldly reputation and fortune, but the elect prefer contumely to honour, and affliction to prosperity. [...] You must seek what is spiritual, and shun what is external. [...] How can he who has gained it (i.e., annihilation) choose one garment rather than another, or take pains to adorn himself at all? How should he care whether people call him a Sufi or by some other name?' (Hujwīrī, *op. cit.*, p. 48).

[48] *Aqdār anfusihim*. Also: 'the worth of his self', meaning by 'self' the *nafs* or the ego. *Aqdār*, as the plural of *qadr*, means 'worth', 'value'. As plural of *qadar*, *aqdār* means also 'destiny', or the 'predestined Decrees' as settled by Divine Will; hence, the phrase could be interpreted as well as meaning: 'The Sufi must know his own destiny.' Whatever might be one's ambitions or intentions, they cannot set aside what Destiny has decreed must take place. The person who knows that is detached towards his own actions, and does not attach any importance to their positive or negative results: he does not rely on his own deeds, but trusts totally in God's Will, and he humbles himself before Him.

[49] The mystic, who is aware of the imperfect nature of his self and of the transitoriness of the human condition, acknowledges the lordship of God and

easily submits himself to Him. In the same way, the mystic who recognises his destiny as decreed by God's Will abandons any claims and pretensions of his ego and humbles himself before the Divinity's omnipotence. In his *Kitāb al-futuwwa*, Sulamī describes the condition of servanthood by quoting Junayd's words: 'La servitù è l'abbandono del proprio libero arbitrio (*ikhtiyār*) e l'inseparabilità dall'atteggiamento modesto e dalla condizione di bisogno (*iftiqār*)' (*Kitāb al-futuwwa, op. cit.*, p. 37). We also read in *Risālat al-malāmatiyya*: '*Wa-min uṣūlihim anna aṣl al-ʿubūdiyya shay'āni: ḥusn al-iftiqār ilā Allāh taʿālā, wa-huwa min bāṭin al-aḥwāl, wa-ḥusn al-qudwa bi-rasūl Allāh ṣallā 'Llāhu ʿalayhi wa-sallama wa-huwa alladhī laysa li'l-nafs fīhi nafas wa-lā rāḥa*' (Fāwī, *op. cit.*, p. 313).

[50] The concepts of restraint of expectation and preparedness for death have already appeared (see above, section 9), and are mentioned elsewhere in Sulamī's collection. The author's meditation on expectation and death serves as an antidote to all the forms of egoism. Egoistic impulse is, as Sells puts it, a 'forgetfulness of mortality': human beings tend toward the assumption that death will be indefinitely deferred, and this implicit denial of mortality leads them to egoism. The Sufi must therefore cut such expectations by his constant remembrance and contemplation of the uncertainty of the appointed time, 'for the spirit of the godservant is something borrowed and does not know when the owner will send for its return' (from Ḥārith al-Muḥāsibī's *Kitāb al-riʿāya li-ḥuqūq Allāh*, 'The Book on the Observance of the Rights of God', in M. A. Sells, *op. cit.*, p. 179 and p. 181). The themes of expectation and death are leitmotifs in Islamic spirituality since its beginnings. ʿAlī's is the saying: 'Two things bring ruin: desire and length of expectation. Desire blocks access to the Real (*al-Ḥaqq*), while length of expectation brings forgetfulness of the finality (*al-akhira*)' (*ibid.*, p. 182).

[51] According to Sulamī, the Sufi can engage in activites in order to gain his living (begging is frowned upon in the *Jawāmiʿ*) and carry on his contemplative life within society, the one doing so being called a *mutasabbib*. On the other hand, the Sufi can also choose to live a life of isolation, totally depriving himself of any possessions and dedicating himself to the contemplation of God (cf. below, section 39).

[52] A long outer garment, open in front, with wide sleeves.

[53] On *waraʿ*, cf. Ibn Abī'l-Dunyā, *op. cit.*, section 279.

[54] Qur'ān, 6:120.

[55] Lit. 'moving only for God', 'directing one's deeds only towards God': *fa-lā yataḥarraku illā li'Llāh*.

[56] *Fa-lā yudkhilu qalbahu shay'an siwā Allāh*. Cf. *Kitāb al-futuwwa*, II, I.

[57] *Naʿt al-faqīr al-sukūn ʿinda 'l-ʿadam wa'l-badhl wa'l-īthār ʿinda 'l-wujūd*. Cf. Hujwīrī, *op. cit.*, p. 26.

[58] *Qillat al-riḍā ʿan al-nafs*. On the Sufi's struggle against self-satisfaction and his exercise of rigorous and unflinching self-criticism, see above, section 10.

[59] In the *Jawāmiʿ*, Sulamī stresses the importance of having a pleasant attitude with people and being good company with them (*ḥusn al-ṣuḥba*). The Sufi should be cheerful when staying with his fellows, following the example of the Prophet, who would make people feel comfortable with him and show a happy face, lest his excessive seriousness might make them feel uneasy in his presence. In his *Risāla*, Sulamī speaks of *al-ṣuḥba* as one of the principles of the *Malāmatiyya*: '*Wa-min uṣūlihim fi'l-ṣuḥbati mā samaʿtu Abā ʿUthmān Saʿīd ibn Ismāʿīl yaqūlu lamma su'ila ʿan al-ṣuḥba: ḥusn al-ṣuḥba ẓāhiruhu an tuwassiʿa ʿalā akhīka min māli nafsika wa-lā taṭmaʿa fī mālihi wa-tunṣifahu wa-lā taṭluba minhu al-inṣāf wa-takūna tabaʿan lahu wa-lā taṭluba an yakūna tabaʿan laka wa-tataḥammala minhu al-jafwata wa-lā tajfūwahu wa-tastakthira qalīla birrihi wa-tastaqilla mā yattaṣilu minka ilayhi min dhalika*' (Fāwī, *op. cit.*, p. 322). Cf. also *Kitāb al-futuwwa*, I, 29, where the following hadith on *ḥusn al-ṣuḥba* is quoted by Sulamī: 'God Almighty detests the one who shows an unsmiling face when staying with his brethren.'

[60] *Wa-tark al-khiyāna fi'l-asbāb*. Also: 'he should not be disloyal when dealing with provisions (for the journey) and means of subsistence.' On *sabab*, see above, section 13.

[61] *Bi-wuḍū' al-ʿatama*; i.e., not yet having done anything to make another *wuḍū'* necessary, like, for example, going to sleep.

[62] *Al-ʿajz*: the kind of feeling which may befall the traveller, making him feel weak and impotent to face the difficulties and the adversities of the journey.

[63] Qur'ān, 28:7 (the Qur'ānic passage refers to Moses' mother and the baby Moses).

[64] *Wa-min ādābihim akhdh al-rafaq min Allāh taʿālā wa-tark mā yutrak li'Llāh taʿālā*. I have used the reading of *rafaq* as meaning 'to take possession of something', 'to take somthing with oneself'. If it is read as *rifq* (i.e., *akhdh al-rifq min Allāh*), then it would mean: 'The Sufi should take [the quality of] compassion from God Most High and leave what must be left to Him.' The Sufi's virtues and good qualities find their source and cause in God's Excellence and Beauty. Good deeds and acts of kindness are therefore inspired by God and by the mystic's meditation on Him (on *rifq* and the importance of dealing gently with one's brethren, cf. below, sections 22, 23 and *Kitāb al-futuwwa*, I, 1, 14; II, 15). Moreover, as he finds in God alone his inspiration and goal, the sincere Sufi does not seek reward for his good deeds: he acts unconditionally and not out of fear of punishment or hope for recompense. Hence the expression 'to leave to God what must be left to Him' (*tark mā yutrak li'Llāh taʿālā*) would mean that the consequences or merits of our actions are left to God and to His Will, and nothing must be expected from people.

[65] Cf. *Kitāb al-futuwwa*, III, 45.

[66] Here, where sitting on the ground is customary, one is expected to sit cross-legged or with folded legs, not with legs stretched out, especially in the presence of superiors. Sitting with legs stretched out indicates ease and informality, and is not proper except in very private situations. Cf. Hujwīrī's *Kashf al-maḥjūb*: 'Rules of discipline (*ādāb*) are of three kinds. Firstly, those which are observed towards God in unification (*tawḥīd*). Here the rule is that one must guard one's self in public and private from any disrespectful act, and behave as though one were in the presence of a king. [...] Ḥārith Muḥāsibī is said never to have leaned his back against a wall, by day or night for forty years, and never to have sat except on his knees. On being asked why he gave himself so much trouble he replied: "I am ashamed to sit otherwise than as a servant while I am contemplating God"' (Hujwīrī, *op. cit.*, p. 335).

[67] Al-Ramla: a city in Palestine to the north-east of Jerusalem.

[68] If he had known that he had some bread in his house, Abū Jaʿfar would have deprived himself of it in order to give it to Abū Saʿīd. For this reason, he followed Abū Saʿīd to Jerusalem, driven by the natural attitude of generosity, which is the virtue of the truly poor (see above, section 15). At the same time, while staying at Abū Jaʿfar's place, Abū Saʿīd followed thoroughly the *adab* of poverty, as he did not ask for food or anything else but his hospitality. Yet, if we compare this saying with that of section 13 on the *adab* to be observed when staying with the poor, we can suggest a different intepretation of this passage. Aware of the rule of poverty, according to which a person must not sit with the poor while having any means of livelihood with himself, Abū Jaʿfar went after the poor ascetic Abū Saʿīd to ask him for forgiveness: in fact, he had broken that rule, as, without knowing, he had kept food in his house while Abū Saʿīd was present.

[69] *Wa-min ādābihim an lā yuwājihū aḥadan bi-makrūhin bi-ḥāl*. Lit. 'The Sufi must not face anyone with what he dislikes.' Cf. *K. ādāb al-ṣuḥba*: '*Wa-min ādābihā* [i.e., *ādāb al-ṣuḥba*] *an lā yuwājiha akhan min ikhwānihi bi-mā yakrahu*' [Kister, *op. cit.*, p. 31 Arabic].

[70] *An yajmaʿū ikhwānahum ʿalā 'l-rifq*. Lit. 'to gather his fellow Sufis in a gathering of kindness'. As he practises poverty, the Sufi shuns any idea of ownership and possession, which result from those selfish and egotistic inclinations that he struggles to fight. Therefore, the sincere mystic is altruistic with his friends and enjoys making them join with one another in sharing his acts of kindness and generosity.

[71] A cubic measure of varying magnitude.

[72] In the text: *taṣdaʿu*. Correct reading: *taṣʿadu*.

[73] *Laysa minnā man lam yarḥam ṣaghīranā wa-yuwaqqir kabīranā*. Cf. *Kitāb ādāb al-ṣuḥba*: '*Laysa minnā man lam yuwaqqir kabīranā wa-yarḥam ṣaghīranā*' (Kister, *op. cit.*, p. 75 Arabic).

[74] Rather he said: 'the young and the old among us.'

[75] Meaning of the master.

[76] *Ḥifẓ al-jawāriḥ ʿalā 'ttibāʿ al-awāmir*. Cf. *Kitāb al-futuwwa*, II, 6: 'È caratteristico della cavalleria mirare all'integrità del cuore, sorvegliando e occupando i propri organi con ciò che è loro competenza..', and IV, 26: 'La cavalleria consiste nel dominare quattro cose: la vista, la lingua, il cuore e la passione. L'occhio non deve guardare ciò che non gli è lecito; bisogna controllare che la lingua non dica che ciò che è giusto e vero, che il cuore non sia soggetto a falsità e astio, e che la passione non aneli a qualcosa di cattivo.' Cf. also *K. ādāb al-ṣuḥba*, Kister, *op. cit.*, pp. 85–86 Arabic.

[77] Cf. above, section 7.

[78] *Wa-ḥifẓ awqātika fī jamīʿ taṣarrufātika* (*corr.*). This concept recurs frequently in the *Jawāmiʿ* (see below, sections 34, 40, 78, 91). The mystic must be constantly aware of the significance of the present moment and, therefore, he must make good use of any instant of his life: his *waqt* should not be wasted but wholly taken up by pious deeds, in the performance of which every part of the mystic's body must be totally involved.

[79] That is to say: 'he disregards the significance of the present instant'.

[80] *Ḥafaẓa waqtahu wa-rāqaba sirrahu*. On 'guarding one's interior moments and keeping one's secret,' cf. Sulamī's *Uṣūl al-malāmatiyya*: '*Wa-min uṣūlihim ḥifẓ al-qalb maʿa Allāh subḥānahu bi-ḥusn al-mushāhada wa-ḥifẓ al-waqt maʿa Allāh bi-ḥusn al-adab wa-kitmān mā yaẓharu ʿalayhi min al-muwāfaqāt illā mā lā budda min iẓhārihi*' (Fāwī, *op. cit.*, p. 313). Cf. also *Risālat al-malāmatiyya*, Sassi, *op. cit.*, pp. 22–23, and pp. 46–47, 51 and 54 ('Principi e regole fondamentali dei Malāmatiyya', n. 21, 37, 45).

[81] Cf. *K. al-futuwwa*, II, 5.

[82] Lit. 'The food of the Sufi is that of the sick and his sleep is that of someone dead from drowning.' Here, the expression is probably used by Junayd to mean that, as the mystic sleeps only when it is inevitable and for a very short time, his sleep is deep and sound. See below, section 67: *wa-lā nanāmu illā ʿan ghalaba* ('and we only sleep when overpowered by slumber'). Cf. also Hujwīrī's *Kashf al-maḥjūb*: 'The Shaykhs have said, describing the Sufis: "They eat like sick men, and sleep like shipwrecked men (*al-gharqā*), and speak like one whose children have died"' (Hujwīrī, *op. cit.*, p. 348). On the Sufi's sleep, cf. also *Risālat al-malāmatiyya*, *Uṣūl*, n. 30 (Sassi, *I custodi del segreto*, p. 49). As for the necessity of eating little, Hujwīrī says: 'Men cannot dispense with nourishment, but moral

virtue requires that they should not eat or drink in excess [...]. Nothing is more hurtful to a novice in Sufism than eating too much' (Hujwīrī, *op. cit.*, p. 347).

[83] From the verb *ghafala*, 'to neglect, ignore'. On the mystic's *ghafla*, we read in the *Risālat al-malāmatiyya*: '*Wa-min uṣūlihim anna al-ghaflata hiya allatī aṭlaqat li'l-khalq al-naẓara fī afᶜālihim wa-aḥwālihim wa-law ᶜāyanū amānan min al-ḥaqq la-'staḥqarū mā yabdū minhum fī jamīᶜ al-aḥwāl wa-'staṣgharū mā lahum fī janbi mā ᶜalayhim*' (Fāwī, *op. cit.*, p. 298). Strangely enough, in his *Risālat al-malāmatiyya* Sulamī uses also the term *ghafla* with a second and totally different meaning: in fact, he talks about *ghafla* as the 'recreation' or 'break', which God allows the servant who occupies all his moments with spiritual exercises and with fighting against the *nafs* (ᶜAfīfī, *op. cit.*, p. 115, n. 30; see also, G. Sassi, *op. cit.*, *Uṣūl* n. 30, p. 49). On *ghafla* during the performance of *dhikr*, see below, section 84.

[84] On the Sufi's virtue of patience (*ṣabr*), cf. al-Ḥasan al-Baṣrī's saying reported by Hujwīrī: 'Patience is of two sorts: firstly, patience in misfortune and affliction; and secondly, patience to refrain from the things which God has commanded us to renounce and has forbidden us to pursue' (Hujwīrī, *op. cit.*, p. 86).

[85] *Illā fī muwāfaqat mawlāhum.* The word *mawlāhum* could also be interpreted as meaning the Sufi master or shaykh, i.e., the Sufi who has achieved a higher spiritual stage and therefore guides the novice along the mystical path. In this case, the phrase would mean that every act of the mystic must be in conformity with his master's instructions and teachings. I would prefer this interpretation if we accepted the variant reported in MS Leiden Or. 1842, which suggests the version '*bi-muwāfaqat mawlāhum*' instead of '*fī muwāfaqat mawlāhum*', hence: 'The Sufi should not occupy his body but *with the consent of his master*'. However, I believe that the term *mawlā* is used here by Sulamī to refer to God, the Master and Lord of creatures, rather than to the Sufi teacher; the sincere mystic must wholly occupy his body in performing acts of worship, remembering constantly his Lord, and doing whatever pleases Him and satisfies His expectations.

[86] On forgiving one's brethren and abstaining from reproaching them when they are wrong, cf. *Kitāb al-futuwwa*, I, 33; II, 11, 40; *Kitāb ādāb al-ṣuḥba*, Kister, *op. cit.*, pp. 28, 29, 38, 49 Arabic.

[87] *Takhaṭṭā 'l-ḥurumāt.* Also: 'he disregards the sacred things of God'. On respect (*ḥurma*), see above, section 7. The one who neglects *adab* inevitably lacks respect for religious laws and transgresses the divine commandments and prohibitions.

[88] In text: *wa-ṣāra matbūᶜu-hu* (sing.) *baṭṭālīn*; corr. *matbūᶜū-hu* (pl.). However, I believe the text is corrupted, and I suggest to read it as '*wa-ṣāra* tābiᶜū-*hu baṭṭālīn*', i.e., 'and *those who follow him* become idle'.

[89] On *ādāb al-bāṭin*, cf. below, section 30.

[90] *Ḥifẓ al-sirr*: cf. above, section 25.

[91] In the *Jawāmiʿ* Sulamī uses the two expressions *adab al-bāṭin* and *adab al-sirr* interchangeably to refer to the inward *adab*.

[92] *Īthār al-khalq ʿalā anfusihim*. On preferring others to oneself, cf. *Kitāb al-futuwwa*, III, 12. Cf. also Hujwīrī's *Kashf al-maḥjūb*: 'The true nature of preference (*īthār*) consists in maintaining the rights of the person with whom one associates, and in subordinating one's own interest to the interest of one's friend, and in taking trouble upon one's self for the sake of promoting his happiness, because preference is the rendering of help to others, and the putting into practice of that which God commanded to His apostle: "Use indulgence and command what is just and turn away from the ignorant"' (Hujwīrī, *op. cit.*, p. 190).

[93] ʿAbd Allāh *al-maʿrūf bi'*l-Akhawaynī al-Marwāzī: we find a mention of a Sufi called ʿAbd Allāh al-Marwāzī (yet without any reference to the nickname al-Akhawānī) in Qushayrī's *Risāla* Qushayrī, *al-Risāla al-Qushayriyya*, Cairo: Dār al-Kutub al-Ḥadītha, 1966, vol. 2, p. 569).

[94] Reference to the Sufis.

[95] *Īthār muwāfaqat al-khalq fī-mā wāfaqa 'l-Ḥaqq ʿalā muwāfaqat anfusihim fī-mā daqqa wa-jalla*. The mystic should prefer to please people, in doing what is consistent with God's commandments, rather than please his *nafs*, by indulging its whims and satisfying its fickle and capricious nature. In translating this passage, I have interpreted the two genitives *al-khalq* and *anfusihim* (respectively in the two expressions: *muwāfaqat al-khalq* and *muwāfaqat anfusihim*) as objective genitives. If we considered them as subjective genitives, the meaning of the phrase would be instead: 'to prefer *the approval of* people, in what is consistent with the Truth, to *the approval of* the *nafs*.' *Fī-mā wāfaqa 'l-Ḥaqq*: pleasing people and acting in accordance with their interests is desirable for the Sufi, as long as he does not disobey God and his acts are consistent with His prescriptions. Cf. *Kitāb al-futuwwa*, I, 12; II, 10.

[96] *Ḥifẓ sharā'iṭ al-adab*: lit. 'observe the conditions of *adab*'.

[97] It is interesting to note that Sulamī's application of *adab* closely resembles here that of *mandūb* in Islamic jurisprudence or *fiqh* (indeed, the terms *adab* and *mandūb* have been often used interchangeably by the jurists to refer to the same category of acts; cf. Ḥasan, Aḥmad, *Principles of Islamic Jurisprudence*, Islamabad: Islamic Research Institute, 1993, p. 91). In *fiqhī* language, the word *mandūb* designates a recommended act (as opposed to *makrūh*, the disapproved act), which one is demanded to perform in a non-peremptory manner, that is to say 'if he performs it, he is praised and rewarded, and if he omits it, he is neither blamed nor punished' (Ḥasan, Aḥmad, *op. cit.*, p. 79). Although they are not compulsory, performance of the *mandūb* and abstention from the *makrūh* are meritorious as they secure the qualities of *wājib* (the obligatory) and *ḥarām* (the forbidden). In the same way, as Sulamī states in the above passage, complying

with the obligations imposed by *adab* protects the observance of the obligatory religious duties and of the Sunna, while the neglect of *adab* leads 'to disregard the approved practices and the religious duties.'

[98] See below, section 42. On being content with little, cf. also *Kitāb al-futuwwa*, III, 19.

[99] Cf. *Uṣūl al-malāmatiyya*: '...*Wa-qāla Abū ʿAbd Allāh al-Mazanī: laysa fī'l-dunyā shay'un aʿazzu min qalbika wa-waqtika fa-in ḍayyaʿtahumā fa-qad ḍayyaʿta aʿazza al-ashyā' ʿalayka*' (Fāwī, *op. cit.*, p. 313). Cf. also *K. al-futuwwa*, III, 13: 'È proprio della cavalleria che il servitore non si preoccupi che dell'istante (*waqt*) in cui si trova. Chiesero a Sahl ben ʿAbd Allāh at-Tustarī, ..: "Quando il discepolo si sbarazza della sua anima? " Egli rispose: "Quando non vede per sé altro oltre all'istante in cui si trova."'

[100] Qur'ān, 35:34.

[101] In a word, he should give up what Muḥāsibī calls *al-ri'āsa* or power-lust, which is 'the love of aggrandisement and exercising power over creatures and looking down on them—that not a single word of his be rejected, that not a single person equal him in knowledge, that no one be put before him' (from Muḥāsibī's discourse on *riyā'*, in Sells, *op. cit.*, p. 189).

[102] Cf. above, section 17.

[103] See above, section 13.

[104] *Fa-futiḥa ʿalayhi*: lit. 'the door of understanding was opened to him', or 'the truth was disclosed to him'.

[105] Cf. *K. al-futuwwa*, III, 38.

[106] Lit. 'with the eye of compassion and advice (i.e., the eye of one who is disposed to give sincere advice). On the Sufi's compassion (*shafaqa*) and his solicitude for his brethren, cf. *K. al-futuwwa*, I, 20; II, 42.

[107] *Bi-ʿayn tawāḍuʿ*: lit. 'With the eye of modesty'. Cf. Qur'ān, 25:63: 'And the servants of Allah Most Gracious are those who walk on the earth in humility.' On *al-tawāḍuʿ*, cf. ʿAbd Allāh al-Anṣārī al-Harawī, *op. cit.*, p. 84.

[108] *Bi-ʿayn al-shafaqa*: lit. 'with the eye of solicitude.' Cf. *K. al-futuwwa*, III, 39.

[109] See *Risālat al-malāmatiyya*: *uṣūl al-malāmatiyya*, n.16, in Sassi's translation, *op. cit.*, p. 45. See also above, section 29. The Sufi who sees the reality not with his own eyes but with the eyes of the Truth is ready to forgive people and excuse them for their faults, because he knows that they cannot do any other than behave as they are naturally disposed to do.

[110] *Al-Ṭāq*: a famous stopping place in the eastern quarter of Baghdad, also known as *Ṭāq al-asmā'*.

[111] *ʿAraftu 'Llāh*, i.e., the mystical knowing achieved by the *ʿārif*, the gnostic.

[112] *Tawsiʿat al-ṣadr*: the Arabic expression, which literally means 'to widen one's breast, or heart', is used as a synonym of both 'generosity, magnanimity' and 'open-mindedness, liberality'. Cf. *Kitāb ādāb al-ṣuḥba*: '*Wa-min ādābihā … saʿatu 'l-qalb*' (Kister, *op. cit.*, p. 33 Arabic).

[113] On nobility of aspirations (*sharaf al-himma*), see Thaqafī's saying, quoted in Sulamī's *K. al-futuwwa*, IV, 12: 'Ho udito Abū Ahmed al-Hīrī dire che avesse sentito Abū ʿAlī ath-Thaqafī dire: "Abbi aspirazioni nobili, perché le aspirazioni possono spostare le cose, non soltanto le anime, e recitò: Fate sopportare al cuore ciò che il corpo non può sopportare, perché il cuore sopporta ciò che il corpo non ha la capacità [di fare]."'

[114] René Guénon explains the importance of *niyya* in these terms: 'As regards action, it is important to observe that it is the intention (*niyyah*) which counts for most, for this alone depends wholly on man himself, without being affected or modified by outward contingencies as the results of actions always are.' *Symbolism of the Cross*, London: Luzac & Co., 1958, p. 44.

[115] *Al-thawāb*, according to the variant reading in MS Laleli 1516 (Kohlberg, *op. cit.*, p. 18 Arabic, section 45, note n. 3). In the text (MS Berlin 3081): *al-qiwām*.

[116] Or: 'Watch how you eat by being determined (*bi'l-niyya:* through determination and effort of will), how you speak by being sincere, and how you look by being considerate.'

[117] *Aṣḥāb al-muraqqaʿāt*: see above, section 10.

[118] Meaning your inner thoughts.

[119] Cf. Hujwīrī's *Kashf al-maḥjūb*: 'If, by wearing this garb (i.e., the *muraqqaʿa*), you wish to make known to God that you are one of the elect, God knows that already; and if you wish to show to the people that you belong to God, should your claim be true, you are guilty of ostentation; and should it be false, of hypocrisy' (Hujwīrī, *op. cit.*, p. 48).

[120] Cf. above, section 3, and below, sections 48, 53; *Kitāb al-futuwwa*, II, 41; III, 6; IV, 24.

[121] On this saying of Ibrāhīm al-Khawwāṣ, cf. *K. al-futuwwa*, I, 34. The particular circumstances which may prevent the Sufi from working may be of physical nature, such as any disease which makes him unable to perform a job, or of a spiritual kind, as in the case of a mystic who, having achieved a high stage in the path, is required to leave any activities so as to dedicate himself totally to spiritual practices.

[122] We read in Sulamī's *Risālat al-malāmatiyya*: '*Wa-min uṣūlihim fī'l-tawakkul mā samaʿtu Manṣūr ibn ʿAbd Allāh yaqūlu: samaʿtu … Abā Yazīd yaqūlu: ḥasbuka min al-tawakkul allā tarā nāẓiran ghayrahu wa-lā li-rizqika jāliban ghayrahu wa-lā li-ʿamalika shāhidan ghayrahu*' (Fāwī, *op. cit.*, p. 319). See also Ibn Abī'l-Dunyā, *op. cit.*, sections 21 and 28.

123 Cf. *K. al-futuwwa*, I, 35.

124 On *ijtihād*, cf. *mujāhada*: above, section 12.

125 *Wa-lā yafṭur illā fī waqt mā uḥilla lahu 'l-mayta*. The term *al-mayta* designates in Islamic law the meat of an animal not slaughtered in accordance with ritual requirements; it refers especially to animals which died without being slaughtered, i.e., diseased or old. In case of prolonged lack of food, the Muslim would be allowed to eat whatever kind of food was available to him, be it permitted (*ḥalāl*) or forbidden (*ḥarām*), lest he might die of starvation.

126 *Al-ghurabā'*, pl. of *gharīb*: I have rendered the term *gharīb* with the English 'stranger'. However, I would also like to mention G. Sassi's interpretation of the word as 'the outcast', 'the destitute', and also 'the emigré', 'the exile' (cf. Sassi's translation of *K. al-futuwwa*, p. 24: 'Fa parte della cavalleria l'amore per gli emarginati e i diseredati (*ghurabā'*) e badare a essi con sollecitudine'; see also the translator's note, *ibid.*, p. 24).

127 *ʿAbā'*: a cloak-like woolen wrap, occasionally striped; a garment which is open in front and is usually worn on top of one's clothes. According to Hujwīrī, it was the 'religious habit', usually a mantle, worn by mystics, distinguished from the coat (*qabā'*) which was worn by ordinary people (Hujwīrī, *op. cit.*, pp. 48, 52 and 133).

128 See below, sections 53, 144, 154. We read in Sulamī's *Risālat al-malāmatiyya*: '*Wa-min uṣūlihim tark al-rujūʿi ilā aḥadin min al-makhlūqīna wa'l-istiʿānati bihim li-ʿilmihim anna man istaʿāna bi-makhlūqin fa-qad istaʿāna bi-muḥtājin muḍṭarrin mithlahu wa-laʿallahu ashaddu ḥājatan wa-iḍṭirāran minhu wa-huwa lā yashʿur*' (Fāwī, *op. cit.*, p. 321). On begging, see also G. Sassi's translation of the *Risāla*, *op. cit.*, p. 27, and *Kitāb al-futuwwa*, in G. Sassi's translation, *op. cit.*, II, 44; III, 4, 47.

129 *Taṣḥīḥ al-aḥwāl wa-tark al-ishtighāl bi'l-daʿāwā*. Cf. Sulamī's *Risālat al-malāmatiyya* (G. Sassi, *op. cit.*, p. 21) and *K. al-futuwwa*, II, 25.

130 This same saying by Dhū'l-Nūn al-Miṣrī is also reported in *K. al-futuwwa*, III, 21. Cf. also *ibid.*, II, 23: 'È una qualità della cavalleria che il servo si occupi di ciò che lo riguarda ... Abū Bakr as-Ṣiddīq .. ha riferito che l'Inviato di Allāh .. abbia detto: "Una qualità che rende l'Islām integro è che l'uomo lasci stare ciò che non lo riguarda."'

131 *Wa-innamā muniʿū 'l-wuṣūl li-taḍyīʿ al-uṣūl*: see the wordplay between the term *wuṣūl*, which means 'arriving at God', 'attaining the Truth through union with the Divinity', and the term *uṣūl*, which refers to the basic principles of Islamic faith (i.e., the five *arkān* of Islam).

132 *Al-futūḥ*, pl. of *al-fatḥ*: 'the nourishment which is bestowed by God' (*al-Munjid*, Beirut: Dar el-Machreq, 1994, *al-fatḥ*, I., p. 567). On the Sufi's absolute trust in God the Maintainer, cf. *K. al-futuwwa*, I, 41: 'Chi si preoccupa del suo nutrimento dopo che Allāh gliel'ha assicurato, non ha nessun valore presso

Allāh'; II, 4: 'Non preoccuparti del nutrimento che ti è già stato garantito, ma preoccupati di compiere le azioni che ti sono state assegnate, perché questo è il modo di agire dei nobili e dei cavalieri'; and III, 6.

[133] Al-Qulzum: 'Medieval town at the site of modern Suez' (*al-Munjid*, p. 441).

[134] *Rakwa*: a leather water-bottle used by Sufis when travelling (see R. A. Nicholson, *The Kashf al-maḥjūb*, p. 69).

[135] Qazwīn: city in Iran (*al-Munjid,* pp. 437–438).

[136] On *qu'ūd ʿalā 'l-futūḥ*, see the Glossary.

[137] *Aṣḥāb al-ṣuffa*, also known as *Ahl al-ṣuffa*. See note 7.

[138] Lit. 'that you don't get in their way': i.e., he should not bother others or importune them with begging them persistently for food.

[139] Cf. Sulamī's *Risālat al-malāmatiyya*: '*Wa-min uṣūlihim anna al-faqr sirr Allāh ʿinda ʿabdihi idh al-ʿabdu amīnun ʿalayhi fa-idhā ẓahara faqruhu aw ashyā'un minhu fa-qad kharaja min al-umanā', wa'l-faqīr ʿindahum faqīrun mā lam yaʿlam bi-faqrihi aḥadun illā man yakūnu iftiqāruhu ilayhi fa-idhā ʿalima bihi ghayruhu fa-qad kharaja min ḥadd al-fuqarā' ilā ḥadd al-ḥāja. Wa'l-muḥtājūna kathīrun wa'l-faqru ʿazīzun*' (Fāwī, *op. cit.*, pp. 314–315).

[140] *Wa-innamā yataʿallaqu qulūbu 'l-khalqi bihim*: the suffix *-him* in the Arabic text is probably a printing mistake for *-hi* (*bihi*).

[141] Meaning that if he manifests his state to people and asks them for help or food, people feel compassion for him and thus help him, and in this way he becomes dependent on them for his sustenance.

[142] He is arrogant because he believes that his nourishment comes from him alone and depends on him alone: in this way he cannot trust in God unreservedly and he cannot free himself from the bondage to his own self.

[143] *Mi'zar*: waist-wrapper. Still worn in Arabia, Yemen and Oman; it is like a sarong.

[144] *Ḥifẓ ḥurumāt man addabahum*: cf. below, section 123. 'His master': lit. 'the one who educated him,' 'the one who taught him *adab*.'

[145] The presence of a spiritual master and the observance of his teachings are essential for the Sufi's realisation along the Path; cf. *Risālat al-malāmatiyya*: '*Wa-min uṣūlihim al-ta'addubu bi-imāmin min a'immati 'l-qawmi wa'l-rujūʿu fī jamīʿi mā yaqaʿu lahu min al-maʿlūmi wa'l-aḥwāli ilayhi. Wa-samaʿtu … Ibrāhīm ibn Shaybān yaqūlu: man lam yata'addab bi-ustādhin fa-huwa baṭṭāl*' (Fāwī, *op. cit.*, p. 311).

[146] This same saying by Ibn al-Mubārak is reported in Qushayrī's *Risāla*: 'We sought the knowledge of correct behaviour after those who taught it had passed away' (Qushayrī, *Principles of Sufism*, p. 311).

[147] *Al-adab li'l-ʿārifīn bi-manzilati 'l-tawba li'l-murīdīn*. On *tawba*, see below, section 83. Cf. *K. al-futuwwa*: 'Il pentimento consiste in tre cose: il rimorso

di ciò che è avvenuto, la ferma decisione di non ricaderci e il timore interiore a questo proposito, perché si è certi della propria colpa, mentre non si sa se il proprio pentimento verrà accettato o no' (*K. al-futuwwa*, *op. cit.*, p. 39; see also: I, 31). The Sufis usually considered *tawba* the very beginning on the spiritual path, as Hujwīrī explains: 'You must know that repentance (*tawbat*) is the first station of pilgrims on the way to the truth, just as purification (*ṭahārat*) is the first step of those who desire to serve God' (Hujwīrī, *op. cit.*, p. 294).

148 Cf. *Kitāb al-futuwwa*: I, 46.

149 *Fa-lam ajid fīhi* shay'an: var. MS Leiden (Kohlberg, *op. cit.*, p. 24 Arabic, section 56, note 17). In text (MS Berlin): *Fa-lam ajid fīhi* nafasan: 'And I did not find in it not even one *breath*.'

150 Cf. *K. al-futuwwa*, IV, 28.

151 *Man ijtahada fī bāṭinihi warrathahu 'Llāh muʿāmalata ẓāhirihi*: if someone strives hard to improve his inward attitudes and behaviour, God rewards him by improving his external conduct.

152 Qur'ān, 29:69.

153 On *riʿāya*, cf. *K. al-futuwwa*, *op. cit.*, p. 20; Anṣārī, *op. cit.*, p. 70.

154 On *dhikr*, cf. below, section 84. In his *K. al-futuwwa* (II, 9), Sulamī says that the godservant must vivify his inwardness with the remembrance of God (*dhikr*), and he must bear the mark of *dhikr* both in the outward conduct and in the inward heart: the external mark is humility and submission (to God's will), while the interior mark is satisfaction (*riḍā*) (*K. al-futuwwa*, II, 3). On the remembrance of God, cf. also Ibn Abī'l-Dunyā, *op. cit.*, sections 42, 52, 72, 82, 150, 217.

155 On the Sufi's virtue of patience (*ṣabr*) in enduring tribulation (*balā'*), cf. *K. al-futuwwa*, II, 18. See also Ibn Abī'l-Dunyā, *op. cit.*, sections 62, 79, 150, 189, 190, 274.

156 Cf. Hujwīrī's *Kashf al-maḥjūb*: 'Again, it is glorious for a man to bear the burden of trouble laid upon him by his Beloved, for in truth, misfortune is glory, and prosperity is humiliation' (Hujwīrī, *op. cit.*, p. 27).

157 Cf. *Risālat al-malāmatiyya*: '*Wa-min uṣūlihim ittihāmu 'l-nafsi fī jamīʿi 'l-aḥwāl, aqbalat am adbarat aṭāʿat am ʿaṣat, wa-tarku madḥihā wa'l-mayli ilayhā bi-ḥāl*' (Fāwī, *op. cit.*, p. 299).

158 On *futuwwa*, see the Glossary. A description of the virtue of *futuwwa* is found in the *Risālat al-malāmatiyya*: '*Wa-su'ila baʿḍu mashā'ikhihim man yastaḥaqqu ism al-futuwwa ʿindakum fa-qāla: Man kāna fīhi iʿtidhāru Ādām wa-ṣalāḥu Nūḥ wa-wafā'u Ibrāhīm wa-ṣidqu Ismāʿīl wa-ikhlāṣu Mūsā wa-ṣabru Ayyūb wa-bukā'u Dāwūd wa-sakhā'u Muḥammad,* [...] *wa-ra'fatu Abī Bakr wa-ḥamiyyatu ʿUmar wa-ḥayā'u ʿUthmān wa-ʿilmu ʿAlī,* [...]. *Thumma maʿa hadhā kullihi yazdarī nafsahu wa-yaḥtaqiru mā huwa fīhi wa-lā yaqaʿu fī qalbihi khāṭirun min mā huwa fīhi annahu*

shay'un aw annahu ḥālun murḍin. Bal yarā ʿuyūba afʿālihi wa-nuqṣāna nafsihi wa-faḍla ikhwānihi ʿalayhi fī jamīʿi hadhihi 'l-aḥwāl' (Fāwī, *op. cit.*, p. 302).

[159] On *riyāḍa*, cf. Anṣārī, *op. cit.*, p. 61.

[160] Lit. 'be grateful for hunger and harm' (*ḍarr*). Cf. Ibn Abī'l-Dunyā, *op. cit.*, section 217. Related to *shukr* is the mystical station of *riḍā*, which is described by Sulamī in the next paragraph (see below, section 65).

[161] *Qubba*: domed shrine, memorial shrine.

[162] *Add.* in MS Laleli 1516 (Kohlberg, *op. cit.*, p. 28 Arabic, section 64, note 8): 'and He does not give it to those who will complain to Him about it.' On hunger, cf. Hujwīrī's *Kashf al-maḥjūb*: 'Hunger sharpens the intelligence and improves the mind and health [...]. Although hunger is an affliction to the body, it illumines the heart and purifies the soul, and leads the spirit into the presence of God [...]. The more the natural humours are nourished by food, the stronger does the lower soul [*nafs*] become ... and in every vein a different kind of veil (*ḥijāb*) is produced. But when food is withheld from the lower soul it grows weak, and the reason gains strength, and the mysteries and evidences of God become more visible' (Hujwīrī, *op. cit.*, pp. 324–325).

[163] *Wa-lā yamzaḥūna aṣlan*. Var. reading in MS Laleli 1516 (Kohlberg, *op. cit.*, p. 29 Arabic, section 66, note 7): *wa-lā yamzujūna* ('and that they do not set people against each other': on the meaning of *mazaja*, see *al-Munjid*, II, p. 759).

[164] Lit. 'we founded what we founded'.

[165] Lit. 'if you see the *light* of the poor man in his dress', i.e., 'if someone shows his poverty in his dress.' On the Sufi's duty to conceal his state, cf. above, section 53, and *K. al-futuwwa*, III, 47.

[166] Cf. above, section 15.

[167] Also, 'to purify the heart from following one's innate disposition (*khalīqa*).'

[168] Cf. below, section 116.

[169] *Istiʿmāl al-taẓarruf*: to show grace, wittiness and esprit. Cf. above, 17 on *ḥusn al-ṣuḥba*. Cf. also *K. al-futuwwa*, I, 7; III, 14.

[170] Cf. above, section 36. Cf. also *Kashf al-maḥjūb*: '[...] because knowledge of God requires abandonment of forethought (*tadbīr*), and abandonment of forethought is resignation (*taslīm*), whereas perseverance in forethought arises from ignorance of predestination' (Hujwīrī, *op. cit.*, p. 140).

[171] *Ḥabāhu 'Llāh bi'l-maknūn min sirrihi*: God discloses to him what is concealed of his secret. *Sirr* can mean here both the secret heart of man and the hidden secret or mystery of God, which is revealed to those who submit totally to the Divinity. *Ḥabāhu*: in MS Berlin 3081: *ḥayyāhu* ('God *vivifies* him').

[172] Qur'ān, 4:110.

[173] Cf. above, section 52.

[174] Lit. 'a pain in his molar tooth'.

[175] Qur'ān, 16:52.

[176] The Arabic sentence is confusing because a mistake was probably made by the copyist (see Kohlberg, *op. cit.*, p. 32 Arabic, section 77, note 6). I suggest that the *illā* was misplaced, which, I believe, makes better sense than Kohlberg's suggestion in the text's footnote.

[177] *Wa-ūṣīka bi-talaqqī 'l-mustaqbal min al-waqt al-wārid bi-dhikr mawridihi*. The Sufi must give himself totally to the moment and accept what God sends down to him (*wārid*), without thinking about present, past and future, but always recollecting (*dhikr*) the One Who is the source and origin where his moments come from (*mawrid*).

[178] That is, the vision of created things will not distract you from the Creator.

[179] Lit. 'he must shun this world and its people (*ahlihā*)'. Cf. al-Ḥasan al-Baṣrī's saying in *al-Risāla al-Qushayriyya*: '*Zuhd* in this world is to hate its people and all that is in it and to leave what is in this world to those who dwell in it' (Smith, Margaret, *Rābiʿa The Mystic and Her Fellow-Saints*, Cambridge: Cambridge University Press, 1984, p. 77).

[180] Cf. Sarrāj's statement in *Kitāb al-lumaʿ*, according to which 'love of the world is the root of all sin, and renunciation of the world is the root of all good and obedience (to God)' (see Smith, M., *op. cit.*, p. 76).

[181] Meaning: 'I spend the night awake and the day being thirsty'. Keeping oneself thirsty during the day and spending the night awake were some of the most common ascetic exercises of the *riyāḍa*, or the mystic's self-training on the path (cf. above, section 7).

[182] Qur'ān, 17:18–9.

[183] Variant reading in MS Laleli 1516 (see Kohlberg, *op. cit.*, p. 35 Arabic, section 83, note 2): *dawām al-tawba mimmā ʿamalū wa-mimmā lam* yaʿlamū: 'The Sufi must repent constantly of what he did and what he did not know.'

[184] Lit. 'because everything is prohibited (*ḥarām*) to the godservant unless it follows a commandment that leads him to the commandment of God.'

[185] On *dhikr*, cf. *Risālat al-malāmatiyya*: '*Wa-min uṣūlihim ayḍan anna al-adhkāra arbaʿatun: dhikr bi'l-lisān wa-dhikr bi'l-qalb wa-dhikr bi'l-sirr wa-dhikr bi'l-rūḥ. Fa-idhā ṣaḥḥa dhikru 'l-rūḥi ... wa-dhalika dhikru 'l-mushāhada; wa-idhā ṣaḥḥa dhikru 'l-sirri ... wa-dhalika dhikru 'l-ālā' wa-'l-naʿmā'; wa-idhā ṣaḥḥa dhikru 'l-qalbi ... wa-dhalika dhikru 'l-ḥuḍūri wa'l-qurb. Wa-idhā sakata al-qalbu ʿan al-dhikri aqbala al-lisānu ʿalā al-dhikri wa-dhalika dhikru 'l-ʿāda*' (Fāwī, *op. cit.*, p. 294).

[186] Cf. Ibn ʿAṭā'llāh's *Kitāb al-ḥikam*: 'Do not abandon the invocation (*al-dhikr*) because you do not feel the presence of God therein. For your forgetfulness of the invocation of Him is worse than your forgetfulness in the invocation of

Him. Perhaps He will take you from an invocation with forgetfulness (*ghafla*) to one with vigilance (*yaqaẓa*), and from one with vigilance to one with the presence of God (*ḥuḍūr*), and from one with the presence of God to one wherein everything but the Invoked (*al-Madhkūr*) is absent' (Ibn ʿAṭā'llāh al-Iskandarī, *Ṣūfī Aphorisms* (*Kitāb al-Ḥikam*), translated with an introduction and notes by Victor Danner, Leiden: E. J. Brill, 1984; p. 32).

[187] Massignon regards the 'Abū' as an error and identifies Ibn Manṣūr al-Ḥallāj as the source of the reported saying (Massignon, Louis, *Essai sur les origines du lexique technique de la mystique musulmane*, Paris: J. Vrin, 1954, p. 428).

[188] Lit. 'he does not increase in anything but in his distance from God.'

[189] Lit. 'he is deceived, misled'.

[190] Cf. Hujwīrī: '[...] because if anyone forgets the praise, it is no matter; but it does matter if he remembers the praise and forgets God. [...] The fundamental principle of remembrance of God (*dhikr*) is either in absence (*ghaybat*) or in presence (*ḥuḍūr*). [...] When anyone is absent from God and present with himself, that state is not remembrance of God (*dhikr*), but absence; and absence is the result of heedlessness (*ghaflat*)' (Hujwīrī, *op. cit.*, p. 155).

[191] 'One of them', i.e., one of the Sufis.

[192] *Ḥattā ka'anna raqīban minka yahtifu bī*. The figure of the *raqīb*, the guardian who reproaches the lover and instructs him how to behave properly, recurs frequently in Sufi poetry. The character of the *raqīb* was taken from the literary tradition of the pre-Islamic *nasīb* (the love prelude of the *qaṣīda*) and from the Umayyad traditions of the *ḥijāzī* and *ʿudhrī* poetry of love (on the Arabic *ghazal*, cf. Gabrieli, F., *La letteratura araba*, Florence: Sansoni/Accademia, 1967, ch. I, IV; *The Cambridge History of Arabic Literature: ʿAbbasid belles-lettres*, Cambridge: Cambridge University Press, 1990, ch. XII). In the above mentioned verses, the *raqīb* takes the place of the mystical hidden voice (*hātif*), which would call out to the Sufi to reproach him or give him advice (cf. above, section 19).

[193] On *istiqāma*, cf. *K. al-futuwwa*, I, 13; Anṣārī, *op. cit.*, p. 73.

[194] 'Their food', *idām*: lit. 'anything eaten with bread'.

[195] 'Your cleanness be like water': *naẓāfatukum al-mā'*. Cf. Hujwīrī: 'Purification (*ṭahāra*) is of two kinds: outward and inward. Thus prayer requires purification of the body, and gnosis requires purification of the heart. As, in the former case, the water must be clean, so in the latter case unification must be pure and belief undefiled' (Hujwīrī, *op. cit.*, p. 291).

[196] Purity (*ṭahāra*) and intention (*niyya*) are the ritual acts which precede the *ṣalāh*, the official Islamic ritual prayer. As no prayer can be performed but after ritual purity and formulation of intention, in the same way no spiritual achievement can be attained by the Sufi unless he first repents his sins (*tawba*) and is scrupulous (*wariʿ*) in following God's prescriptions.

[197] *Wa-ṣawmukum ilā 'l-mamāt*: also: 'fast till death' or 'fast until the time of your death'. The expression 'fast till death' means that the Sufi must not break his fast unless he comes to the point that 'even the (meat of) carrions would be allowed to him' (see above, section 49), whereas the expression 'fast until the time of your death' means that he must be perseverant in his fast throughout his life and live always in abstinence and poverty. The phrase could be also interpreted as meaning implicitly that the Sufi should fast while being aware of the prospect of death, and therefore he should fast not for this world but for the life to come.

[198] This means that the Sufi's eyes should be only for his contemplation of God, and also that he should look at things as if he were watching God.

[199] *Illā man imtaḥana 'Llāh qalbahu bi'l-taqwā*. Var. in MS Laleli 1516 (Kohlberg, *op. cit.*, p. 36 Arabic, section 85, note 6): *illā man ʿamara 'Llāh qalbahu bi'l-taqwā*: 'but he whose heart God has *vivified* through piety,' and also 'but he whose heart God has *provided* with piety.'

[200] Qur'ān, 49:3.

[201] *Bi-ghayr ḥisāb*: 'without limits'; also 'without his expecting it'. I have preferred the first interpretation, following the explanation in *al-Munjid*: 'God provides with the means of subsistence those whom He wills *bi-ghayr ḥisāb*, i.e., without parsimony or limitation' (*al-Munjid*, *ḥasaba*, 1., p. 132).

[202] Probably an error for Ibn Manṣūr (Ḥallāj).

[203] Cf. Hujwīrī on *fanā'*: 'Whoever is annihilated from his own will subsists in the will of God, because thy will is perishable and the will of God is everlasting' (Hujwīrī, *op. cit.*, p. 245).

[204] Cf. *K. al-futuwwa*, II, 8, and the saying attibuted to Dhū'l-Nūn al-Miṣrī; cf. also *Risālat al-malāmatiyya*: '*Wa-min uṣūlihim tarku 'l-ishtighāli bi-ʿuyūbi 'l-nās shughlan bi-mā yalzamuhum min ʿuyūbi anfusihim, wa-muḥādharatu sharrihā. Wa-aṣluhum fī dhalika* [...] *mā yurwā ʿan al-nabī, ṣallā 'llāhu ʿalayhi wa sallama, annahu qāla: ṭūbā li-man shaghalahu ʿaybuhu ʿan ʿuyūbi 'l-nās*' (Fāwī, *op. cit.*, pp. 315–316).

[205] Cf. above, section 52.

[206] *Wa-bi-hadhā 'l-isnād ʿan al-Saqaṭī annahu qāla*. Sulamī repeats this formula (from section 89 to section 99) to introduce the following sayings, which are all attributed to al-Sarī al-Saqaṭī with the same chain of authorities (*bi-hadhā 'l-isnād*) as that mentioned in section 88. To avoid repetition, I have translated the formula only in this section and I have omitted it in the following ones.

[207] *Ḥifẓ al-lisān* ʿan *ḥamd al-nās wa-dhammihim*. Cf. var. in MS Laleli 1516 (Kohlberg, *op. cit.*, p. 38 Arabic, section 90, note 2): *ḥifẓ al-lisān* ʿinda *ḥamd al-nās wa-dhammihim*, 'to guard his tongue *when* praising and blaming people.'

[208] Lit. 'and put right in the time left to you what you have spoiled in the time that has passed.'

[209] He who is sincere in his path, God opens up his understanding of deprivation (*manʿ*) and gift (*ʿaṭā'*), and he recognises the divine justice in giving and taking away. God's justice becomes, therefore, his model and he learns how to give and take from people with moderation and temperance.

[210] Reference to the Qur'ān's promises and threats.

[211] Lit. 'your morals' (*akhlāq*).

[212] In the text: *naqṣaka wa-ibrāmaka*. The word *naqṣ* is most probably a printing mistake for *naqḍ* since *naqḍ* and *ibrām* always go together: lit. 'twisting and untwisting'.

[213] Lit. *mawāqif al-ʿujb*: 'the attitudes of vanity and pride'. On *ʿujb*, cf. below, section 98.

[214] He who does not know the limited value of his ego-self falls into vanity and enjoys praising himself (cf. above, section 11). Compare this saying by Sarī with the following one by Muḥāsibī: '[The person who falls into vanity] becomes blind to most of his sins so that he overrates his actions, deludes himself about them, loses his fear of doing wrong, and increases his self-delusion concerning God Most High' (Sells, *op. cit.*, p. 172). Cf. also *Risālat al-malāmatiyya*: '*Wa-min uṣūlihim anna 'l-iftikhāra bi'l-ʿamali wa'l-ʿujba bihi wa'l-naẓara ilayhi qillatu 'l-ʿaqli wa-ruʿūnatu 'l-ṭabʿi: kayfa taftakhiru bi-mā laysa laka fīhi shay'un wa-huwa yajrī min al-ghayr ʿalayka*' (Fāwī, *op. cit.*, p. 314).

[215] *Khayr al-ashyā' laka ʿalā 'l-sayr wa'l-ightirāb*, according to the edited text MS Berlin 3081. The var. in MS Laleli 1516 (Kohlberg, *op. cit.*, p. 39 Arabic, section 97, note 5) reads instead: *khayr al-ashyā' laka ʿalā 'l-sayr al-ightirāb*.

[216] Or 'Sufi chivalry'. On *murūwa*, see the Glossary.

[217] *Bi-amr Allāh wa-nahyihi*: the orders, commandments of God and His prohibitions as laid down in the Qur'ān.

[218] *Izār*: 'waist-wrapper' (see above, section 54: *mi'zar*), that is, the least the Sufi needs to cover himself, and beyond which anything else is considered to be superfluous.

[219] On the Sufi's rules in speech and silence, cf. Hujwīrī: 'In short, speech is like wine: it intoxicates the mind, and those who begin to have a taste for it cannot abstain from it. Accordingly, the Sufis, knowing that speech is harmful, never spoke except when it was necessary, i.e., they considered the beginning and end of their discourse' (Hujwīrī, *op. cit.*, p. 355).

[220] On *īthār*, cf. above, sections 15, 31.

[221] Cf. Hujwīrī: 'It is an obligatory rule that they should not eat alone, but should unselfishly share their food with one another' (Hujwīrī, *op. cit.*, p. 348).

[222] The 'ibn' before Muḥammad al-Ḥaddād is probably a mistake. *Corr.*, *qāla Ibn Aḥmad Hārūn ibn Aḥmad*: samaʿtu *Muḥammad al-Ḥaddād ʿan Maḥfūẓ...*: '... Hārūn ibn Aḥmad said: I heard Muḥammad al-Ḥaddād report from Maḥfūẓ...'.

[223] On shunning hypocrisy, cf. *Risālat al-malāmatiyya*: '... *samaʿtu Abā ʿAmr ibn Najīd wa-sa'altuhu: Hal li'l-malāmatī ṣifa? Fa-qāla: Naʿm. Allā yakūna lahu fī'l-ẓāhiri riyā'un wa-lā fī'l-bāṭini daʿwan wa-lā yaskuna ilā shay'in wa-lā yaskuna ilayhi shay'un*' (Fāwī, *op. cit.*, p. 299).

[224] *Al-qurrā'*, plural of *al-qāri'*: lit. 'the reciter of the Qur'ān'. The term here probably refers to a particular group in early Islam, noted for their strictness and ostensible piety (among whom the first Kharijis arose): see, T. Nagel's article 'Kurrā'', in *The Encyclopaedia of Islam*, new edition, vol. V, pp. 499–500. Cf. also *Lisān al-ʿArab*, Beirut: Dār Iḥyā' al-Turāth al-ʿArabī, 1988, vol. XI, *qara'*, p. 79.

[225] *Khafiyy al-riyā'*: they act as though pious but are not really, although it is extremely difficult to detect their hypocrisy.

[226] Probably: Sufism and its true realisation.

[227] Also, 'too much eating is a bad sign (in people).'

[228] Avidity leads you to view created things as essential and to satisfy the claims of this worldly existence in order to get and keep those worldly things.

[229] Cf. below, section 125.

[230] Cf. below, section 132. Cf. also Hujwīrī: 'Dervishes ought not to go to the houses of rich men or beg anything of them: such conduct is demoralising for ṣūfīs, because worldlings are not on confidential terms (*maḥram*) with the dervish' (Hujwīrī, *op. cit.*, p. 349).

[231] *Ḥasbuka bi-maʿrifati 'l-nās*. Var. reading in MS Leiden Or. 1842 (Kohlberg, *op. cit.*, p. 45 Arabic, section 112, note 10): *ḥubbuka li-maʿrifati 'l-nās*'.

[232] On *zuhd*, cf. above, section 26.

[233] On concealing one's condition, cf. above, sections 10, 53; on *sirr*, cf. above, section 25. The idea of guarding one's secret and concealing one's actions and states is one of the basic rules of conduct of the 'People of Blame' and the basic theme of Sulamī's *Risālat al-malāmatiyya*. There, it is said that showing off one's acts of devotion is a form of 'associationism' (*shirk*), and disclosing one's interior states is the equivalent of apostasy (*irtidād*): '*Wa-min uṣūlihim annahum ra'ū al-tazayyuna bi-shay'in min al-ʿibādāti fī'l-ẓāhiri shirkan wa 'l-tazayyuna bi-shay'in min al-aḥwāli fī'l-bāṭini irtidādan*' (Fāwī, *op. cit.*, p. 297).

[234] *Wa-ta'mulīna an taʿīshī ilā 'l-layl*. Var. reading in MS Leiden Or. 1842 (Kohlberg, *op. cit.*, p. 46 Arabic, section 113, note 15): *wa-ta'mulīna an taʿīshī ilā 'Llāh*.

[235] Cf. above, 41. See also *Risālat al-malāmatiyya*: '*Wa-min uṣūlihim anna kulla ʿamalin wa-ṭāʿatin waqaʿat ʿalayhi ru'yatuka wa-'staḥsantahu min nafsika fa-iʿlam annahu bāṭil. Wa-aṣluhum fī dhalika mā ḥaddathanā Abū ʿAbd Allāh ibn Ḥasan qāla: qāla al-Ḥusayn ibn ʿAlī: kullu shay'in min afʿālika ittaṣalat bihi ru'yatuka fa-dhāka dalīlun ʿalā annahu lam yuqbal minka wa-mā inqaṭaʿa ʿanhu naẓaruka min afʿālika fa-dhāka dalīlun ʿalā qubūlihi*' (Fāwī, *op. cit.*, p. 312).

[236] Only if it is embraced by the lordship of God, is man's servanthood totally realised: deeds and acts of devotion come, in fact, from God, and on Him alone they depend. The vision of things with the eyes of the self pollutes man's servanthood: the godservant who thinks of himself as the actor of everything takes pride in his good acts and easily yields to vanity and self-conceit. Cf. below, section 129.

[237] Qur'ān, 6:120.

[238] *Taṣḥīḥ al-ibtidā'*: lit. 'the Sufi must *rectify the beginning* (of his path)'.

[239] Cf. above, section 69.

[240] Cf. above, sections 52 and 75, on *tark al-daᶜāwā*.

[241] *Al-tajarrud min al-dunyā*: cf. also *tajrīd*, above, section 39.

[242] Lit.: 'anyone who *takes from* this world'.

[243] *Al-ḥilm*. Var. reading in MS Laleli 1516 (Kohlberg, *op. cit.*, p. 47 Arabic, section 119, note 8): *al-ḥukm,* 'judgment'.

[244] *ᶜIndamā yukhāfu hawāhu*. When someone has position and power, he can easily subject others and use them as a means to satisfy his caprices and desires. Yet, if he is a man of *adab*, he should not abuse his power and people's fear of him, but rather be generous toward them and deal with them with magnanimity.

[245] On *al-faḍl*, see above, section 103.

[246] *Ṣilat al-qāṭiᶜ*. *Al-qāṭiᶜ*: the outcast, those who are marginalised and excluded from society.

[247] Cf. *Kitāb ādāb al-ṣuḥba*: '*Fa min dhalika an taᶜlama anna 'l-muslimīna ka 'l-jasadi 'l-wāḥidi wa-anna ᶜalā baᶜḍihim an yuᶜīna 'l-baᶜḍa ᶜalā 'l-khayrāti wa-yadfaᶜa ᶜanhu 'l-makārih*' (Kister, *op. cit.*, p. 24 Arabic).

[248] On *ᶜilm al-baṭin*, see also *ᶜulūm al-ḥaqīqa*: above, section 69.

[249] *Adāb al-manzila*, according to var. reading in MS Leiden Or. 1842. *Al-manzila*: lit. 'status, position', i.e., the Sufi's spiritual status, his stage in the mystical path, and the mystical stations and states related to it.

[250] A similar idea is attributed to Junayd: 'The Sufi is like the earth—every kind of abomination is thrown upon it, but naught but every kind of goodness grows from it;' and also: 'The Sufi is like the earth—both the righteous man and the sinner walk upon it. He is like the clouds—they give shade to all things. He is like the raindrop—it waters all things' (Qushayrī, *Principles of Sufism*, p. 304).

[251] The Sufi circle (see Glossary).

[252] Reference to the mystical sciences.

[253] Cf. *Kitāb al-futuwwa*, II, 14.

[254] Meaning after he got seventy lashes as a payment for it.

[255] In the text: *Wa-min ādābihim al-tawājud fi'l-samāᶜ*. It seems to me that the Arabic text is corrupted here and I would suggest the reading of the passage as '*Wa-min ādābihim tark al-tawājud fi'l-samāᶜ*'. Cf. *Risālat al-malāmatiyya*: '*Wa-min*

uṣūlihim tarku 'l-bukā'i ʿinda 'l-samāʿi wa'l-ʿilmi wa-ghayra dhalika wa-mulāzamatu 'l-kamdi fa-innahu aḥmadu li 'l-badan.' Also: '*Wa-min uṣūlihim anna 'l-samāʿa idhā ʿamala, ʿamala fī man yataḥaqqaqu fīhi anna haybatahu tamnaʿu 'l-ḥāḍirīna ʿan al-ḥarakati wa'l-qiyāmi li-tamāmi haybatihi ʿalayhim. Samaʿtu ... ʿAlī ibn Hārūna 'l-Ḥiṣrī yaqūlu: Al-samāʿu 'l-ḥaqīqiyyu idhā ḥalla makānan min qalbin mutaḥaqqiqin zayyanahu bi-anwāʿi 'l-karāmāti, wa-ḥaqīqatu muṣāḥabati 'l-samāʿi minhu an yaghliba waqtuhu awqāta 'l-ḥāḍirīna wa-yaqharahum fa-humma taḥta qahrihi wa-asrihi*' (Fāwī, *op. cit.*, p. 320 and p. 314). On *samāʿ*, see also *Uṣūl al-malāmatiyya* n. 8, G. Sassi, *op. cit.*, pp. 38–39.

256 Or, according to Sells' interpretation of *tawājud* (Sells, *op. cit.*, pp. 111–112): 'whose *making-ecstatic* is not conducive ...' (see Glossary: *tawājud*).

257 On *ziyāda*, cf. above, section 110.

258 *Man ṭalaba 'l-ṭaʿāma li-ghayri 'l-qiwām kāna intifāʿuhu saqām* (corr. *al-saqāmu* or *saqāman*).

259 *ʿAwāmm al-nās*: lit., 'the common people', i.e., the non-Sufis. However, the passage on Nūrī reported in the next paragraph seems to suggest a different interpretation of the heading, i.e., 'the Sufi must not talk about *other Sufis*.'

260 Cf. Hujwīrī: 'The Sufis, knowing that speech is harmful, never spoke except when it was necessary, i.e., they considered the beginning and end of their discourse; if the whole was for God's sake, they spoke; otherwise they kept silence, because they firmly believed that God knows our secret thoughts' (Hujwīrī, *op. cit.*, p. 355).

261 Reference to the Sufis.

262 *Humma fī safar al-waḥsha wa-dhikr al-khalq baynahum ʿaybah*. The path of the Sufi is a path of solitude and alienation from the ephimeral things of this world; therefore, the mention of the creatures is for him a fault and a sin. *Dhikr al-khalq*: it can be interpreted as both a subjective genitive and an objective genitive, i.e., 'mentioning people and being mentioned by them.'

263 *Fa-fā'idatī fī kalāmī qaḍā' waṭarī fīhi wa'l-tazayyun bihi*: lit. 'And the benefit of my words would be just the satisfaction of my desire and the adorning of myself with them.'

264 Cf. above, section 114. Cf. also *Risālat al-malāmatiyya*: '*Wa-min uṣūlihim anna aqalla 'l-ʿabīd maʿrifatan bi-rabbihi ʿabdun ẓanna anna fiʿlahu aw ṭāʿatahu tastajlibu 'l-ʿaṭā'a wa-anna ṭāʿatahu taqbalu faḍlahu, wa-lā yaṣiḥḥu li'l-ʿabdi ʿindahum shay'un min maqāmi 'l-maʿrifati ḥatta yaʿlamu anna kulla mā yaridu ʿalayhi min rabbihi min jamīʿi 'l-wujūhi faḍlun min ghayr istiḥqāq*' (Fāwī, *op. cit.*, pp. 316–317). Man must acknowledge that his serving God is a Grace from God Himself, and he must love Him with unconditional love, that is without expectations and not out of fear of punishment or hope for reward. Finally, man should constantly be grateful to God for making him worthy of serving Him and

venerating Him, because the obedience of the godservants is a gift of Grace from the Lord.

265 Meaning that he should ask God in a pleading tone and not in a commanding one.

266 *Man yadulluhum ʿalā 'l-sabīli ilā 'Llāh wa'l-iqbāli ʿalayhi wa-yuzahhiduhum fī 'l-dunyā*. Cf. *Kitāb ādāb al-ṣuḥba*: '*Wa-wājibun ʿalā 'l-mu'min an yajtaniba ʿishrata ṭullāba 'l-dunyā* [...] *wa-yajtahida fī muʿāshirati ahli 'l-khayr wa-man yadulluhu ʿalā ṭalabi 'l-ākhirati wa-ṭāʿati mawlāhu*' (Kister, *op. cit.*, p. 30 Arabic).

267 Cf. Ibn ʿAṭā'illāh's saying in *Kitāb al-ḥikam*: 'Do not keep company with anyone whose state does not inspire you and whose speech does not lead you to God' (Ibn ʿAṭā'illāh, *op. cit.*, p. 31).

268 Lit. ' who admonish you with the tongue of their deeds and not with the tongue of their words.'

269 Qur'ān, 12:39.

270 *Law lam yakun fī 'l-qunūʿ illā 'l-tamattuʿ bi'l-ʿizz la-kafā ṣāḥibahu*: lit. 'if in contentment there were just the enjoyment of glory, that (i.e., the contentment) would be sufficient for the one who is content (*ṣāḥibahu*).' Cf. below, section 134: *wa-min ādābihim al-taʿazzuz bi'l-qanāʿa*. *Al-qunūʿ*: 'man's being satisfied with what has been foreordained and assigned to him (by God)' (*al-Munjid, qana'*, 1. p. 657).

271 *Al-qāri' al-faqīr*. *Al-qāri'*: see above, section 105.

272 *Ṭamaʿ*: the ambition, the desire of the man who covets the possessions and power of the rich and aspires after their position (cf. above, section 132).

273 A similar idea is attributed to Junayd: 'If you see a Sufi caring for his outer appearance, then know that his inward being is corrupt' (Qushayrī, *Principles of Sufism*, p. 304).

274 Lit. 'they would answer only the supplications of those people of whom they knew what they ate and where they lived.'

275 *Iʿtalaltu ʿillata qiyām* (Kohlberg, *op. cit*, p. 53 Arabic, section 137, note 5: *tamnaʿunī al-qiyām*): lit. 'I was taken ill with a disease that would keep me from getting up.'

276 Passing one's hands over one's face is the sign of finishing a prayer.

277 Cf. *Kitāb al-futuwwa*: 'È un procedimento della cavalleria quello di ottenere l'amore di Allāh facendosi amare dai Suoi intimi ... Allāh guarda nel cuore dei Suoi intimi ogni giorno e ogni notte settanta volte, cosicché può darsi che scorga il tuo nome nel cuore di un Suo amico intimo e che per questo ti ami e ti perdoni' (G. Sassi, *op. cit.*, p. 27).

278 In MS Laleli 1516 (Kohlberg, *op. cit.*, p. 54 Arabic, section 138, note 12): Ibn Yazāniyār.

279 On *ta'wīl*, see Glossary.

[280] Cf. *Kitāb ādāb al-ṣuḥba*: '*Wa-min ādābihā muʿāsharatu man yathiqu bi-dīnihi wa-amānatihi fī ẓāhirihi wa-bāṭinihi*' (Kister, *op. cit.*, p. 29 Arabic).

[281] *Masāwīka*; corr. reading: *masāwi'ika, al-masāwi'* pl. of *masā'a*. In MS Laleli 1516 (Kohlberg, *op. cit.*, p. 55 Arabic, section 141, note 5): *mā sa'alta ʿanhu*, 'the intensity of my love for God hid me from seeing *what you have asked me about*.'

[282] Cf. *Kitāb ādāb al-ṣuḥba*: '*Wa-min ādābihā an yajtahida fī sitri ʿawrāti ikhwānihi wa-iẓhāri manāqibihim wa-kitmāni qabā'iḥihim*' (Kister, *op. cit.*, p. 61 Arabic).

[283] *Lam uḥibb an ahtika sitrahu. Hataka Allāhu sitrahu*: 'God showed his shortcomings' (*al-Munjid, satara*, 1., p. 320). In MS Berlin 3081 (Kohlberg, *op. cit.*, p. 55 Arabic, section 142, note 9): *sirrahu*: 'I did not want to disclose *his secret*.'

[284] See above, section 47.

[285] Lit. 'the Sufi must refrain from *asking*': on *su'āl*, see sections 51, 53.

[286] Meaning to beg.

[287] Cf. *Risālat al-malāmatiyya*: '*Wa-min uṣūlihim kitmānu 'l-āyāti wa'l-karāmāti wa'l-naẓaru ilayhā bi-ʿayni 'l-istidrāji wa'l-buʿdi ʿan sabīli 'l-ḥaqq. Ka-dhalika samaʿtu ... Abā ʿAmra al-Dimashqī yaqūlu: kamā faraḍa 'llāhu taʿālā ʿalā 'l-anbiyā'i iẓhāra 'l-karāmāti wa'l-muʿjizāti ka-dhalika faraḍa ʿalā 'l-awliyā'i kitmāna karāmātihim li'allā yaghtarra bihā 'l-nās*' (Fāwī, *op. cit.*, pp. 319–20). Cf. also Hujwīrī: 'So long as a disciple's eye is obscured by a single atom of the miracles of the Shaykhs, from the standpoint of perfection that atom is a potential veil (between him and God)' (Hujwīrī, *op. cit.*, p. 291).

[288] The sober mystics considered miracles as obstacles along the path of spiritual training. Junayd, for example, spoke of miracles as one of the three veils which can cover the hearts of the high-ranking Sufi, along with excessive attention to acts of worship and hope for reward (cf. Schimmel, *op. cit.*, p. 211).

[289] *Al-walī man tawālat wilāyatuhu wa-tawallā Allāhu ʿalayhi ḥarakātihi wa-anfāsahu. Tawālā*: *tamayyaza* (*al-Munjid, walā*, p. 919). Cf. *Kitāb al-ḥikam:* 'Not a breath do you expire but a decree of destiny has made it go forth' (Ibn ʿAṭā' illāh al-Iskandarī, *op. cit.*, p. 27).

[290] Also 'becomes manifest *in* (or *through*) him and *in* (or *through*) those who believe in his nobility.'

[291] *Al-faqīr al-mujarrid min al-dunyā*. On *tajrīd*, cf. above, section 39.

[292] *Bi-mushāhadati man yaʿmalu*: lit., 'through the contemplation of the One *with whom he is dealing*.' Var. in MS Laleli 1516 (Kohlberg, *op. cit.*, p. 58 Arabic, section 149, note 2): *man yaʿmalu lahu*, 'the One *for whom he strives*.'

[293] *Wa-min ādābihim kitmān al-aḥwāl bi'l-ishkāl ʿan al-iẓhār wa-bi'l-satr ʿan al-kashf wa-bi'l-kināya ʿan al-ifṣāḥ.*

[294] Cf. Junayd's saying: 'Expressions are wholly pretensions, and where realities are established pretensions are idle' (Hujwīrī, *op. cit.*, p. 355).

[295] I have translated this verse according to the variant reading reported in note by E. Kohlberg (Kohlberg, *op. cit.*, p. 58 Arabic, section 150, notes 13 and 16): *wa-la-qad tashkū fa-mā afhamuhā/ wa-la-qad ashkū fa-mā tafhamunī.*

[296] Lit. 'to be blind to the vision of his *nafs*.'

[297] *Wa-min ādābihim al-ʿamā ʿan ru'yat al-nafs wa-muṭālaʿat al-afʿāl.* I have read the passage as: *wa-min ādābihim al-ʿamā ʿan ru'yat al-nafs wa-muṭālaʿati al-afʿāl*, i.e., 'the Sufi must look away from his *nafs* and avoid looking into *its* deeds'. The saying by Abū'l-ʿAbbās ibn ʿAṭā', reported in this section of the *Jawāmiʿ*, seems to confirm this interpretation. However, the reading in MS Leiden (see Kohlberg, *op. cit.*, p. 59 Arabic, section 152, note 1), adding the word *al-aḥwāl* (read. *wa-muṭālaʿat al-afʿāl wa al-aḥwāl*), seems to suggest that the term *al-afʿāl* refers to the deeds of the Sufi, rather than to the deeds of the *nafs*. In this case, the phrase would read: *wa-min ādābihim al-ʿamā ʿan ru'yat al-nafs wa-muṭālaʿatu al-afʿāl*, 'the Sufi must look away from his *nafs* and look instead into his own deeds.'

[298] Trying to compensate for the shortcomings of the *nafs* by performing other deeds, which come also from the *nafs*, is as wrong as looking at the *nafs* itself and being satisfied with it: indeed the *nafs* must be shunned altogether and no attention must be paid to its actions.

[299] Qur'ān, 29:69.

[300] *Al-ʿilm*, according to the reading in MS Laleli 1516 (Kohlberg, *op. cit.*, p. 60 Arabic, section 153, note 5).

[301] Cf. Hujwīrī: 'It is permissible to beg with the object of training the lower soul. The Sufis beg in order that they may endure the humiliation of begging, and may perceive what is their worth in the eyes of other men, and may not be proud' (Hujwīrī, *op. cit.*, p. 359).

[302] The particular stress that Shiblī's words lay on the humiliation of the self is typical of the *malāmatī* attitude. Cf. *Risālat al-malāmatiyya*: '*Wa-min uṣūlihim allā yaqbalū mā yuftaḥu lahum bi-ʿizzin wa-yas'alū bi-dhullin ḥattā anna aḥadahum su'ila ʿan dhalika fa-qāla: fī 'l-su'āli dhullun wa-fī 'l-futūḥi ʿizzun wa-anā lā ākulu illā bi-dhullin liannahu laysa fī 'l-ʿubūdiyyati taʿazzuz*' (Fāwī, *op. cit.*, p. 297).

[303] *Lā tarā nafsaka wa-lā tarāhum.* Only if he forgets his self and does not care for the opinion of people, can the mystic practise humiliation in the proper way.

[304] *Bi-ʿayn al-ʿizza*, according to the reading in MS Laleli 1516 (Kohlberg, *op. cit.*, p. 60 Arabic, section 154, note 9).

[305] *Man maʿahu li-'Llāh shay'un*: lit. 'whoever has something with him *for God*.'

[306] *Fa-aʿṭāhu rajulun jumlatan. Jumla*: lit. 'something, a little of everything,' be it money or anything else.

[307] *Wa-naḥnu na'khudhu bi-akhass al-ḥiraf.* MS Berlin 3081 (Kohlberg, *op. cit.*, p. 60 Arabic, section 154, note 17): *bi-aḥsan al-ḥiraf.* As E. Kohlberg observes (see

Kohlberg, *op. cit.*, p. 13, note 41), the variant reading in MS Berlin, according to which begging is 'the best profession' rather than 'the most despicable profession', is characteristic of the *malāmatī* attitude, and is not representative of Sulamī's attitude toward begging, as depicted in the *Jawāmiʿ* (cf. above, sections 51, 53, 144).

[308] Cf. below, section 170. Cf. also *Kitāb al-futuwwa*: 'È dovere della cavalleria che il servitore vigili sui suoi stati e i suoi respiri (*anfās*), senza lasciarsene sfuggire nessuno' (G. Sassi, *op. cit.*, p. 38).

[309] *Wa-man ʿalima mā yaṣnaʿu ʿalima mā yuṣnaʿu bihi*: he who knows and ponders his actions when dealing with people, knows people's response to his actions and how they deal with him. Also: 'he who knows what he does, knows what is done through him,' i.e., the one who is aware of his deeds knows the reason and purpose which is beyond them and beyond his whole existence.

[310] *ʿAlima mā maʿahu*: i.e., he knows the reality and understands the nature of everything that surrounds him.

[311] *Yadʿū ilā 'l-rawḥ wa'l-rāḥa wa'l-rā'iḥa*. The reference to the *rawḥ*, or the 'respose' in the innermost secret, along with the mention of the *rā'iḥa*, or 'the fragrance', is found elsewhere in Sulamī's works, probably recalling the Qur'ānic verses: "Thus if he be of those brought nigh,/ then (he shall find) rest (*rawḥ*), heavenly fragrance (*rayḥān*) and a garden of bounty" (56:88-89). Therefore, I have given preference here to the reading of *rawḥ* over *rūḥ* and interpreted *rā'iḥa* as equivalent to the Qur'ānic *rayḥān*.

[312] Al-Ḥusayn ibn Manṣūr (al-Ḥallāj) uses the term *nafs* with a different connotation from that of Sulamī in the *Jawāmiʿ*, as *nafs* designates here not the ego-self but the soul at peace, which has found tranquillity in belief.

[313] *Al-inziʿāj*: disturbance, upset, which results from the servant's awe towards his Lord and the fear of His punishment.

[314] *Al-walah*: passionate love, amorous rapture, proper of the mystic who has achieved spiritual realisation and whose self is totally enraptured in the contemplation of the Beloved.

[315] *Wa-lā yufāriquka fī khaṭra min al-khaṭarāt*; corr. reading: *wa-lā yufāriquka fī khaṭwa min al-khaṭawāt* (see Kohlberg, *op. cit.*, p. 62 Arabic, section 157, notes 2 and 3): lit. 'and He is the one who will never abandon you in every step you take.'

[316] 'A small stick (the tip of which is softened by chewing or beating) used for cleaning and polishing the teeth' (H. Wehr, *A Dictionary of Modern Written Arabic*, Beirut: Librairie du Liban, 1980, p. 443).

[317] *Fa-innahā ṭuruq al-Qur'ān*; i.e., they are the instrument through which the Qur'ān is recited and proclaimed.

[318] Qur'ān, 3:39.

[319] Meaning from the *miḥrāb*.

[320] *Fa-lam talbath*. Variant reading in MS Berlin 3081 (Kohlberg, *op. cit.*, p. 63 Arabic, section 163, note 7): *fa-lam tathbut*.

[321] Qur'ān, 63:8.

[322] *Al-māl*: whatever he is in possession of, be it money or goods.

[323] *Ahl al-ḥaqq wa-muttabiᶜīhi*: also 'to the people of the truth and their followers,' i.e., the Sufis and their brethren.

[324] *Wa-yaᶜlamu anna akhlāqahu lā yasaᶜu ishtighāluhā maᶜa 'l-khalā'iq kullihim*. Variant reading in MS Laleli 1516 (Kohlberg, *op. cit.*, p. 64 Arabic, section 164, note 9): *istiᶜmāluhā*. Lit., he knows that 'he cannot *use* his (true) behaviour ...'

[325] *Ahl niḥlatihi*. Variant reading in MS Laleli 1516 (Kohlberg, *op. cit.*, p. 64 Arabic, section 164, note 13): *ahl najlatihi*: his descendants (?).

[326] Lit. 'he shall practise the *adab* of piety truly and follow all its conditions.'

[327] *Wa-shukruhu bilā kufrān* (*bi'l-niᶜma?*): lit. 'his gratitude without ungratefulness'.

[328] Lit. 'because they are the trunks (of the trees) of evil, whose branches are ....'

[329] Lit. 'and from them come satiety and the quenching of one's thirst.'

[330] Qur'ān, 57:20.

[331] '... soon it withers; thou will see it grow yellow; then it becomes dry and crumbles away. But in the Hereafter is a penalty severe (for the devotees of wrong). And forgiveness from Allah and (His) Good Pleasure (for the devotees of Allah). And what is the life of this world, but goods and chattels of deception?'

[332] *Fa-man aḥabba shay'an min hadhihi 'l-muqaddimāt*. Var. read. in MS Laleli 1516 (Kohlberg, *op. cit.*, p. 64 Arabic, section 164, note 27): *fa-man aḥabba shay'an min hadhihi 'l-maqāmāt*: 'he who loves any of these *stations*.'

[333] *Fa-qad aḥabbahā li'l-dunyā*. Var. read. in MS Laleli 1516 (Kohlberg, *op. cit.*, p. 64 Arabic, section 164, notes 28 and 29): *fa-qad aḥabba 'l-dunyā*: 'he loves this world'.

[334] Cf. *Kitāb al-futuwwa*: 'È caratteristico della cavalleria preferire l'isolamento e la solitudine all'allegria e alla compagnia. Yahyā ben Muᶜādh, che Allāh gli usi misericordia, ha detto: "Ogni cosa ha una salvaguardia. La salvaguardia dell'anima è l'isolamento (*al-khalwa*) e l'abbandono della frequentazione delle creature, perchè chi non è con te è contro di te"' (*Kitāb al-futuwwa,* III, 7; cf. also V, 23). See also above, section 106.

[335] *Li-man khalā bi-ᶜilm*: for the one who chooses seclusion with full awareness and cognition of the significance and purpose of his choice.

[336] *Ḥalāwat* al-ᶜamal. Var. read. in MS Leiden Or. 1842 (Kohlberg, *op. cit.*, p. 65 Arabic, section 165, note 13): *ḥalāwat* al-ᶜilm, 'the pleasure of knowledge'.

[337] On *khalwa*, cf. Ibn ʿArabī's *Risālatu 'l-anwār fī-mā yumnaḥu ṣāḥibu 'l-khalwati min al-asrār*, where it is said that the Sufi retreat is 'l'acte de renoncement total inspiré par le désir de la présence divine. Celui qui entreprend le *khalwa*, comme un mort, abandonne toutes les affaires religieuses et profanes extérieures, ce qui est le premier pas vers l'abandon de sa propre existence' (Ibn ʿArabī, *Voyage vers le Maître de la Puissance*, tr. by Rabia Terri Harris and Corine Derblum, Monaco: Le Rocher, 1987, p. 138).

[338] *Wa-min ādābihim ikhfā' mā yuẓhiru Allāh ʿalayhim min karāmātihi. Al-karāmāt*: signs of the divine favour, miracles; cf. above, section 147. *Mā yuẓhiru Allāh ʿalayhim*: 'in them'. Var. read. in MS Berlin 3081 (Kohlberg, *op. cit.*, p. 66 Arabic, section 167, note 1): *mā yuẓhiru Allāh* ʿalayhi, 'in him'.

[339] *Asrār maʿrūfihim*: the secrets of the special favour that God has bestowed on him and the mysteries of what has been manifested to him by divine Grace.

[340] *Ẓāhir al-ʿilm*: the outward application of the divine knowledge as put down in the Qur'ān, which is revered by following the literal meaning of God's commandments and prohibitions.

[341] *Bi-imām min a'immati 'l-qawm*: lit. 'a guide chosen among those who guide people (i.e., the Sufis)'.

[342] *Yakūnu maṣḥūb nafsihi*: his self becomes his companion and his master.

[343] Meaning the spiritual guide.

[344] Referring to the novice (*al-murīd*).

[345] Although the term *sālik* is commonly used to refer to the novice or the training Sufi who travels along the way and follows the path methodically, in this last section of the *Jawāmiʿ* Sulamī gives it a connotation which is very close to that of *shaykh*, as he uses it to designate the novice's guide or master (elsewhere referred to also as *imām*, or *ʿālim nāṣiḥ*).

[346] Reference to the Qur'ān and the Sunna.

[347] *Rabb al-ʿālamīn*: instead of the usual translation as 'Lord', I have preferred here ʿAbd Allāh Yūsuf ʿAlī's translation as 'the Cherisher and Sustainer (of the Worlds)' (see, Yūsuf ʿAlī, ʿAbd Allāh, *op. cit.*, p. 14, note 20) because it renders the Arabic word *rabb* well, whose root has the meaning of 'raising, bringing up (a child), sustaining, cherishing.'

A Glossary of Sufi Technical Terms in the *Jawāmiʿ Ādāb al-Ṣūfiyya*

ʿabd (pl. *ʿibād*): servant; godservant. The term is used in the *Jawāmiʿ* to mean the creature dependent on his Creator and also the worshipper of God. Therefore, in my translation I have usually rendered it as 'godservant' or 'the servant of God'.

ʿabd (pl. *ʿabīd*): servant, slave.

ʿābid (pl. *ʿubbād*): the devotee, one who is occupied with the external acts of devotion (*ʿibāda*, *q.v.*).

akbar: *al-akbar* (pl. *al-akābir*). The term properly means 'elder', as regards age, but it can also be used, in a wider sense, to refer to those among the Sufis who are on a higher stage in the spiritual path. In my translation I have usually interpreted the word as meaning, using Sulamī's words, 'those who are above him (i.e. the mystic in the middle of the path) as regards spiritual state, knowledge and age' [*Jawāmiʿ*, 23]. In this sense, I have rendered the Arabic word sometimes with the English 'elder' or 'senior' and other times with the term 'master'.

ʿālim: learned man, scholar, man who possesses *ʿilm* (*q.v.*). In the *Jawāmiʿ* the term appears also in the two expressions *ʿālim rabbānī*, 'the divinely learned man', i.e., he who knows God and the mystical sciences (*ʿulūm al-ḥaqīqa*, *q.v.*), and *ʿālim nāṣiḥ*, the guide or mentor of great knowledge, who can lead the novice on the right course.

ʿamal (pl. *aʿmāl*): deed, action; meritorious act.

ʿāmil (*ʿāmilūn*): the one who performs an *ʿamal* (*q.v.*), i.e., he who performs meritorious acts and strives on the path to God with fervour and genuine effort.

amr (pl. *awāmir*): the divine command (God's injunctions and prohibitions) as embodied in the Qur'ān.

ʿāqil (pl. *ʿuqalā'*): the man of understanding, who possesses *al-ʿaql* (*q.v.*).

ʿaql: mind; the 'discursive knowledge', which is the faculty of the intellect.

ʿārif (pl. *ʿārifūn*): gnostic; realised knower; he who possesses *maʿrifa* (*q.v.*).

badal (pl. *abdāl*): the 'substitutes'. They belonged to the hierarchy of saints who, according to the Sufi theories on saintship (*wilāya*, *q.v.*), were believed to constitute the *wilāya khāṣṣa*, the saintship of the advanced mystics. They were forty in number and had special prominence in Islam, where they were objects of great devotion. The word *abdāl* was frequently used also to designate a saint who would be substituted for (*badal*) by another person after his death.

balā': tribulation, affliction. It designates a tribulation, which descends on a mystic. Hujwīrī explains it as 'the probation of the bodies of God's friends by diverse troubles and sicknesses and tribulations' [Hujwīrī, *op. cit.*, p. 388]. The degree of *balā'* is usually considered as more honourable than that of *imtiḥān* (*q.v.*), 'for *imtiḥán* affects the heart only, whereas *balá* affects both the heart and the body and is thus more powerful' [*ibid.*, p. 389]. In the *Jawāmiʿ*, *balā'* is viewed as a means of approaching God, and therefore it is considered as a blessing for the Sufi. From the same root, we find also in the *Jawāmiʿ* the word *baliyya*, used in the plural *balāyā*, with the same meaning of *balā'*.

baraka (pl. *barakāt*): benediction, blessing. It designates the special power that the disciple would acquire during the investiture with the patched frock (*khirqa*, *muraqqaʿa*, *q.v.*) by putting his hand into the shaykh's hand and by dressing in a garment, which had been worn or touched by a master. In the *Jawāmiʿ*, the term is often used in such expressions as *barakāt al-ta'addub*, *barakāt al-adab*, to indicate the special blessing that the novice would acquire through his master's teachings (see also *ḥurumāt al-mashāyikh*). The term is also used to refer to God's blessings and His favour.

bāṭin (pl. *bawāṭin*): the interior; the opposite of *ẓāhir* (pl. *ẓawāhir*): the exterior, the outer. These two terms recur frequently in Sufi literature to indicate the exterior appearance of things (*ẓāhir*), which is indicative of their interior realities (*bāṭin*). In his process of interiorisation, the mystic must look beyond the visible world of phenomena and be attentive towards the Real, of which the Creation is only a manifestation. In the *Jawāmiʿ*, Sulamī often uses the two terms in connection with *adab*: the Sufi, he says, aspires to attain complete harmony between his external conduct (*adab al-ẓāhir*) and his innermost attitudes and beliefs (*adab al-bāṭin*, which is referred to also as *adab al-sirr*. See *sirr*, *q.v.*), because 'he who does in private what he is ashamed to do in public has no respect for himself' [*Jawāmiʿ*, 57]. Only by disciplining his outward behaviour, can he perfect his interior states and thus achieve true spiritual realisation.

dāʿin, *dāʿiya* (pl. *dawāʿin*): the inner voices inspiring the Sufi and guiding him to right behaviour; cf. *hātif* (*q.v.*).

dārān: *al-dārān*: 'the two abodes: this world and the Hereafter' [*al-Munjid*, Beirut: Dar el-Machreq, 1994, *dār*, 4., p. 229].

daʿwā (pl. *daʿāwā*): claim; pretension, allegation. The Sufi must strive for absolute integrity towards himself and towards others and give up false claims and spiritual pretensions (*tark al-daʿāwā*): thus, for instance, he should abstain from claiming to have experienced mystical illumination if he has not, or to have reached ecstasy during a mystical audition, and he should avoid talking about states which he has not experienced.

dhawq: taste; intuition; mystical experience, or rapture and immediate tasting of the ineffable joy of ecstasy. The Sufis often speak of the experience of the mystical states in terms of 'drunkenness' (*sukr*) and 'tasting' (*dhawq*, *madhāq*), as Qushayrī explains: 'Two frequently used terms among them are taste and drink. Through these terms they expressed what they find or experience of the fruits of self-manifestation, the results of unveilings, and the sudden thoughts and emotions of oncomings' [Sells, Michael A., *op. cit.*, pp. 126–127].

dhikr: invocation, remembrance of God; mention of the Lord's name. The distinctive worship of the Sufi is the practice of *dhikr*, the remembrance or recollection of God, which was founded upon a Qur'ānic order: 'And recollect God often' (Qur'ān, 33:40), because 'the recollection of God makes the heart calm' (Qur'ān, 13:28). According to Sulamī [see, al-Fāwī, ᶜAbd al-Fattāḥ Aḥmad, *op. cit.*, p. 294], *dhikr* can be performed aloud (*dhikr bi'l-lisān*: recollection with the tongue); silently (*dhikr bi'l-qalb*: recollection in the heart); in one's innermost being (*dhikr bi'l-sirr*: pronounced in intimacy with God), or with the spirit (*dhikr bi'l-rūḥ*). In its highly developed phase, *dhikr* was performed during the Sufi ritual session (*ḥaḍra*) and was usually accompanied by music (*samāᶜ*, *q.v.*). However, in its primary form, *dhikr* can be performed at any time and in any place: in fact, '*dhikr* is the first step in the way of love; for when somebody loves someone, he likes to repeat his name and constantly remember him. Therefore the heart of him in whom the love of God has been implanted will become a dwelling place of constant *dhikr*' [Schimmel, Annemarie, *op. cit.*, p. 168].

dhilla: mortification; humiliation. The practice of mortifying the senses and repressing one's physical needs.

fanā': annihilation. It is one of the leitmotifs of Sufi literature. At the highest stage on the path, the mystic attains his complete realisation in the 'finding' of God (*wujūd Allāh*) and in unity with Him, when he annihilates the attributes of his limited self (the 'I' of man's individuality) and takes on the attributes of the Divinity. This theme finds its best expression in the Sufi literature of love, and in particular in Sufi poetry. At the utmost limit of mystical love, the lover no longer sees himself as a separated individuality from his Beloved, but becomes one with Him, to the point that the mystic can say: '*Anā man ahwāhu wa-man ahwāhu anā*', 'I am the One I love, and the One I love is me' [al-Ḥallāj, Ibn Manṣūr, *Diwān*, *muqaṭṭaᶜa* n. 57, in Massignon, Louis, *Le Dīwān d'al-Ḥallāj*, Paris, 1995]. At this stage, the ego-consciousness is completely nullified, and any distinction between creature and Creator—'I' and 'You', subject and object—is lost in the union of absolute love, and there remains only the unity of reality in its purity [see *Jawāmiᶜ*, 87]. In the *Jawāmiᶜ* we also find from the same root: *fānin*, 'transient, ephemeral'; *al-fāniya*, 'this world, worldly existence'; *afnā*, verb in the fourth form, used in such expressions as *afnā al-awqāt*, 'to completely devote one's moments (to something).'

faqīr (pl. *fuqarā'*): poor man, possessed of the quality of *al-faqr* (*q.v.*); the 'needy'. This term is often used by Sulamī as a synonym of mystic, especially to designate the initiate on the spiritual path, who has chosen poverty (of life and of spirit) as his way of life.

faqr: poverty; need in a spiritual sense. There are many passages in Sulamī's *Jawāmiᶜ* dealing with the Sufi's duty of poverty and the rules of *adab* to be followed when staying with the poor. Indigence is an innate condition of human beings, who are always in need of something and as creatures they are always in need of their Creator: 'O mankind! It is you who stand in need of God' (Qur'ān, 35:15). In Sufi language the term *faqr* means both the condition of someone who has renounced all possessions and the state of spiritual indigence of the mystic who has effaced his self before God. Many a Sufi treatise speaks of poverty as one of the stations (*maqāmāt*) of the Sufi path: in the *Kitāb al-lumaᶜ*, Sarrāj distinguishes between the physical poverty of the novice and the poverty of the gnostic (*al-ᶜārif*), which is 'the absence of everything that is and the entering into things for others, not for oneself' [Sells, *op. cit.*, p. 205]. Need is essential to human nature, which is totally dependent for its existence on God: with the achievement of this life in poverty, without consciousness of the self's own poverty, the claims of the ego are abandoned and the *nafs* is extinguished before the Divinity. Yet, Sulamī says, true poverty is a secret between God and His servant [*La Cavalleria spirituale: Kitāb-ul-Futuwwa*, translated by Giuditta Sassi, *op. cit.*, II, 19, p. 36] and the truly poor must strive to conceal his condition: therefore, he should be tranquil when in adversity [*Jawāmiᶜ*, 15], always refrain from asking people for anything [*Jawāmiᶜ*, 51] lest he make his state manifest [*Jawāmiᶜ*, 53], and behave outwardly like a rich person, even if he is in indigence [*Kitāb al-futuwwa*, *op. cit.*, III, 47, p. 56].

futuwwa: 'the totality of the noble, chivalrous qualities of a man, noble manliness, magnanimity, generosity, noble-heartedness, chivalry' [Wehr, Hans, *op. cit.*, p. 696]. The idea of *futuwwa* was adopted by early Sufism. The *fatā* is the young man, the brave youth, faithful and magnanimous. The Qur'ān (18:10–15) calls the Seven Sleepers of the Cave *fityān* (plural of *fatā*), and also Abraham, who destroyed the idols (21:53–67), is called *fatā*: both Qur'ānic examples identify the virtues of the *futuwwa* with those of faithfulness and courage, and with the pure and total devotion to a Supreme Principle. Generally, the term *fatā* was connected with ʿAlī ibn Abī Ṭālib, as the saying goes: 'There is no *fatā* but ʿAlī, and no sword but Dhū'l-Fiqār' [see, *First Encyclopaedia of Islam*, *op. cit.*, vol. III, *futuwwa*, pp. 123–124]. Sulamī wrote a whole treatise on *futuwwa*, where he described the virtues of spiritual chivalry and the rules of conduct to be followed by the *fityān*. For Sulamī, the *fatā* is anyone who strives to destroy the idols of his own individuality (*nafs*), fights his passions and acts solely for God.

ghafla: the negligence of the mystic who forgets, for a moment, to perform his religious duties; also the 'ritual lapse' or 'moment of forgetfulness' which can happen to the Sufi during the performance of exterior duties. Later poets liked to call this state 'the sleep of heedlessness', which entrances the adept who lacks concentration and convinction.

ḥāfiẓ (pl. *ḥafaẓa*): the 'recording angels', i.e., 'the angels who are responsible for writing people's merits and bad deeds' [*al-Munjid*, *ḥafaẓa*, 1, p. 143].

ḥāl (pl. *aḥwāl*): spiritual state; condition. The technical meaning of this word in Sufi terminology is that of 'something that descends from God into a man's heart, without his being able to repel it when it comes, or to attract it when it goes, by his own effort' [Hujwīrī, *op. cit.*, p. 181]. Therefore, a mystical state usually comes upon someone independent of his intention or will, and is distinguished from the station (*maqām*, *q.v.*), which is attained through self-discipline and willed human effort. The Sufis often emphasised the ephemerality of the states: Junayd, for instance, described them as 'sudden gleams of light/ when they appear, apparitions,/ revealing a secret,/ telling of union' [Sells, *op. cit.*, p. 105]. After tasting the experience of union with the Divinity in a previous state, the mystic rises up to a higher and subtler state, his consciousness being continually intensified. Sulamī uses the term both in its technical meaning and to mean an individual state (such as delight, anxiety, fear) or a condition, a situation in the more general sense of the word. In the *Jawāmiʿ*, when used in its first meaning (i.e., mystical state), the term *ḥāl* appears often with the verb *nāzala* (*q.v.*), in the expression *nāzala al-aḥwāl*, 'to experience a spiritual state'.

ḥalqa: the Sufi circle. The Sufis used to join in a circle formed around a pivot (*quṭb*): they would put their right hands on the left hands of their neighbours and repeat the formulae of *dhikr* (*q.v.*), with increasing rhythmical movements.

ḥaqīqa (pl. *ḥaqāʾiq*): truth; esoteric truth; reality of something in an inner sense; the divine Reality. Mystics have described the way leading to God as developing on three different levels, the *sharīʿa*, the *ṭarīqa*, and the *ḥaqīqa*, which, according to a tradition attributed to the Prophet, are thus explained: 'The *sharīʿa* are my words (*aqwālī*), the *ṭarīqa* are my actions (*aʿmālī*), and the *ḥaqīqa* is my interior states (*aḥwālī*)' [Schimmel, *op. cit.*, p. 99]. The *sharīʿa* is the revealed, or canonical, law of Islam, while the *ḥaqīqa* is the true Reality, i.e., what is witnessed by the mystic at the highest stages of his spiritual realisation. In Hujwīrī's words 'the Law is one of the acts acquired by Man, but the Truth is one of the gifts bestowed by God' [Hujwīrī, *op. cit.*, p.384]. *Sharīʿa, ṭarīqa,* and *ḥaqīqa* are mutually interdependent, as 'the Law without the Truth is ostentation, and the Truth without the Law is hypocrisy' [*ibid.*, p. 384]. No mystical experience can be realised, and no truth can be attained, if the binding injunctions of the divine law are not followed faithfully first, as it is said in Qushayrī's *Risāla*: 'No divine law unsupported by *ḥaqīqa* is acceptable./ No reality unbound by divine law is acceptable./ Divine law is performed through the efforts of creatures./ Reality is a report from the disposition of the real./ Divine law is that you worship it./ Reality is that you witness it' [Sells, *op. cit.*, p. 141].

ḥaqq (pl. *ḥuqūq*): right, claim; the duties of the godservant and his obligations towards his Lord. Also, the Lord's rights which He demands from His servants.

al-Ḥaqq: the term, which means properly the truth, the real, is used usually to refer to the Truth, the Real, as a substitute for 'Allah' or 'God'. More often in Sufi literature, and at times in Sulamī's *Jawāmiʿ* as well, the term refers to what in English has come to be called the absolute, or the ultimate reality. In his preface to *Early Islamic Mysticism*, Michael A. Sells explains the meaning of the term *al-Ḥaqq* and its implications: 'To collapse the two words ('the real' and 'the ultimate Reality') into a single translation such as 'God' would be to lose a key tension in early Islamic writings between the personal deity that speaks through the Qur'an and the concept of ultimate truth or reality. To say there is a tension between these two terms is not, of course, to say that the two terms refer to two different things; such a notion would be absurd in early Islam. The two terms represent different ways of referring, however, and those different ways of referring create much of the richness and texture of the early writings' [Sells, *op. cit.*, pp. 7–8]. Trying to maintain the 'richness and texture' of Sulamī's work, I have variously rendered the term *al-ḥaqq* as 'God', or 'the Truth', or 'the Real', according to the connotations the word assumed in the different contexts. In the *Jawāmiʿ*, the term is also used in the expression *ahl al-ḥaqq* to designate 'the people of the Truth', i.e., the Sufis.

hātif: The term was used in earlier Sufism to refer to an 'invisible voice' or 'invisible caller', which would call out to the ascetic mystic, usually at night and during a spiritual retreat (*khalwa*, *q.v.*). This voice would reproach the Sufi when being negligent, inspire him to speak or behave in a particular way, and reveal to him the innermost secrets of the Unknown (*al-Ghayb*).

hawā: passion; caprice. It includes false desires for the things of the material world and also wrong ideas. Cf. Qushayrī: 'They recite: 'The *nūn* of *hawan* [abasement] has been stolen from *hawā* [passion]. Succumbing to every passion is falling victim to abasement' [al-Qushayrī, Abū'l-Qāsim, translated from the Arabic by B. R. Von Schlegell, *op. cit.*, p. 100].

hayba: reverence; awe before God's grandeur. *Hayba* represents one of the two modes of consciousness (the other one being *uns*, *q.v.*) which characterise man's experience of the Divine and it arises from contemplating greatness, which is an attribute of God. *Hayba* awakens in the heart of the mystic when he meditates on God's majesty and power (*al-jalāl*), whereas *uns* is experienced at the manifestation of God's loving attributes and beauty (*al-jamāl*). On *hayba* and *uns*, Hujwīrī says: 'God annihilates the souls of those who love Him by revealing His majesty and endows their hearts with everlasting life by revealing His beauty' [Hujwīrī, *op. cit.*, p. 377].

himma (pl. *himam*): resolution, determination, spiritual aspiration; also, fervour. The term indicates the ardour of the mystic, who concentrates totally on his spiritual goal and strives to achieve his aims. In this sense, it is also used to refer to the preoccupation of the Sufi, who directs his thoughts and his intentions only towards his objective, and remains fixed on it, like the gaze of the Prophet, which (Qur'ān, 53:17) 'did not turn aside nor did it turn elsewhere.'

ḥirṣ: greed. Greed and avidity (*sharah*, *q.v.*) represent in Sufi literature the negative counterpart of *zuhd* (*q.v.*), as they are the qualities of those who are not able to renounce the world, who worship the ephemeral things of this life and have enslaved themsleves to the power of the *nafs* (*q.v.*).

ḥurma: respect; holiness, sacredness, inviolability. The Sufi concept of respect consists of abstaining from any act of disobedience and observing God's commandments and prohibitions unconditionally, and not out of fear of chastisement or hope for reward. Like *al-wara*ᶜ (*q.v.*), at the highest Sufi stages respect means to avoid anything that distracts the mystic from concentrating on God. In the singular, the term is also used with the meaning of 'inviolability, holiness', especially in the expression *ḥifẓ ḥurmata 'l-sirr*, 'to guard the sacredness of the secret (between man and God).' The term is used in the plural (*ḥurumāt*) as meaning 'that which is holy, sacred, or worthy of reverence and respect'. Thus it appears in Qur'ān 22:30: 'Whoever honours the *sacred things* of God (*man yuʿaẓẓim ḥurumāt Allāh*) then that is better for him with his Lord.' In the *Jawāmiʿ* it is mostly used in expressions such as *ḥifẓ ḥurumāt al-mashāyikh*, meaning 'to guard and respect the teachings of the Sufi masters', which were considered as sacrosanct and therefore had to be revered by the novice.

ʿibāda: devotion, worship, the observance of ritual practices.

iḥsān: the doing of good. *Iḥsān*, or 'the doing of good' for the good in itself, and not out of hope for reward or fear of punishment, is mentioned in the *Jawāmiʿ*, and in Sufi literature in general, as a characteristic quality of the sincere mystic. In the Qur'ān the term is mentioned more than once, as in Sura 55:60, where it is said: 'Is there any reward for good (*iḥsān*) other than good?' The term has also a more specific connotation in Sufi terminology, where it indicates the 'perfect virtue', or 'excellence', that consists, as the famous Hadith says, in adoring God 'as though thou sawest Him, for if thou dost not see Him, yet He sees thee' [Hujwīrī, *op. cit.*, p. 329]. In this sense, the quality of *iḥsān* represents the final stage of the process of interiorisation of religion: in fact, it is the last one of the three religious stations of Islam, after *al-islām* (*q.v.*; submission to God with its five pillars) and *al-īmān* (*q.v.*; faith). Those who have this spiritual virtue are called *al-muḥsinūn* ('the doers of good'): they turn their faces toward God alone, because their hearts are emptied of all alterities and their ego-self is extinguished in the Divinity.

ijtihād: effort. The term refers to the Sufi's striving on the path to God and his constant efforts to achieve spiritual realisation. See also *mujāhada*.

ikhlāṣ: absolute sincerity. The attitude of *ikhlāṣ* consists of turning wholly to God, acting solely for Him, and practising sincerity in every thought and action. *Al-ikhlāṣ* is purity of intention, that is, the purifying of one's acts from all concerns other than God and from any regard for praise and blame of the world. A model of *mukhliṣ* love in the history of Sufism is found in the ninth-century mystic Rābiʿa al-ʿAdawiyya, who was seen carrying a torch in one hand and a ewer in the other, and to those who asked her the reason for that, she answered: 'I am going to light fire in Paradise and to pour water on to Hell so that both veils may completely disappear from the pilgrims and their purpose may be sure, and the servants of God may see Him, without any object of hope or motive of fear' [Smith, Margaret, *Rābiʿa the Mystic and Her Fellow-Saints*, *op. cit.*, pp. 98–9]. An overemphasis on *ikhlāṣ* led to the attitude of the *ahl al-malāma*, or 'People of Blame', who would perform acts which might appear outwardly immoral in order to escape the risk of ostentation, but preserved absolute sincerity in their inward being. In this regard, some Sufis later on made a subtle distinction between the *mukhliṣ* mystic, such as the *Malāmatī*, and the *mukhlaṣ* one, the true Sufi who is 'made sincere' by God and not by an act that can be attributed to himself [cf. A. Schimmel, *op. cit.*, p. 87].

ikhtiyār: self-willing, or egocentric willing. In Sufi terminology the word can be also used in a positive sense, as meaning the choosing of God's willing instead of one's own, as Hujwīrī explains: 'By *ikhtiyār* they (i.e. the Sufis) signify their preference of God's choice to their own, i.e. they are content with the good and evil which God has chosen for them' [Hujwīrī, *op. cit.*, p. 388]. In the *Jawāmiʿ* the word is used with the first meaning (i.e., self-willing), as the author exhorts the Sufi to abandon *ikhtiyār*: yet, like for *tadbīr* (*q.v.*), it is not so much that one should give up making choices altogether as that he should choose according to God's injunctions and prohibitions.

ʿilm (pl. *ʿulūm*): science; intellectual, rational knowledge. The term is usually used to refer to traditional knowledge, or the knowledge acquired through the faculty of the intellect (*ʿaql*), and it is distinguished from the mystical knowledge (*maʿrifa, q.v.*). Its path entails observance of the law of the *sharīʿa* (*q.v.*). In the

Jawāmiʿ, *ʿilm* is also used in the plural in such expressions as *ʿulūm al-ḥaqīqa* and *ʿulūm al-bāṭin* to mean 'the sciences of the inward realities', 'the mystical sciences'. On the *adab* pertaining to *ʿilm*, see *Jawāmiʿ*, section 164.

īmān: faith; see *islām*.

imtiḥān: the probation of the heart of the mystic by various afflictions and tribulations sent by God, such as fear and grief. See also *balā'*.

irāda: discipleship, novitiate; will, determination. See also *murīd*.

islām: submission, reconciliation (to the will of God); the religion of Islam. The Sufis usually distinguished three religious stations (*anfās*) within Islam: *al-islām*, the devotional submission and complete surrender to God with the total acceptance of His commands and the observance of the five pillars of religion; *al-īmān*, faith, which represents the interior aspect of *al-islām* and consists of believing in God with a total inward conviction; and *al-iḥsān* (*q.v.*), excellence or perfect virtue.

istiqāma: integrity, rectitude; spiritual steadfastness. It is said in the Qur'ān (41 : 6): 'It is revealed to me by inspiration that your God is One God: so stand true to Him (*fa-'staqimū ilayhi*), and ask for His forgiveness.' Hujwīrī explains: 'The outward and inward rectitude (*istiqāmat*) of the seeker is founded on two things, one of which is theoretical and the other practical. The former consists in regarding all good and evil as predestined by God [...]; the latter consists in performing the command of God, in rightness of action towards Him, and in keeping the obligations which He has imposed' [Hujwīrī, *op. cit.*, p. 104]. The Sufi must *stand true* to God, and follow the path prescribed by His Word and by the Sunna: the mystic's rectitude, therefore, consists of being sincere in one's states, renouncing claims and pretensions, and exercising vigilance over one's inward beliefs and attitudes.

īthār: altruism. The term is usually interpreted as 'preference', from Qur'ān 59:9: 'and give them *preference* (*yu'thirūna*) over themselves even though they were in need of that'. Preference is one of the virtues of the Sufi and it consists basically in preferring other people to oneself, and, at the highest stage in the path, in preferring God's satisfaction to the satisfaction of those other than Him.

juhd, jahd: effort; spiritual struggle along the path. See also *mujāhada*.

karāma (pl. *karāmāt*): sing., nobility, as a sign of God's favour; pl., charisma, charismatic favour, gift of grace, miracle. The term designates the miracle of the *walī* (*q.v.*), from the same root of the verb *karuma*, as Abū Saʿīd ibn Abī'l-Khayr explains: 'whosoever belongs entirely to the Giver—*karīm*—, all his acts are *karāmāt*, 'gifts of grace'' [Schimmel, *op. cit.*, p. 243]. It must not be confused with the miracle of the prophets, which is called *muʿjiza* (pl. *muʿjizāt*), i.e., 'what makes others unable to do the same'. The difference between the two is that, as Hujwīrī puts it, '*muʿjizāt* involve publicity and *karāmāt* secrecy, because the result of the former is to affect others, while the latter are peculiar to the person by whom they are performed' [Hujwīrī, *op. cit.*, p. 220]. Islamic hagiography abounds in legends about Sufis' miracles that often resemble the legends of Christian saints and the tales of the Buddhist tradition. Fertility miracles, miraculous rescues from danger and recoveries from illness, tales of Sufis injuring themselves without feeling any pain or converting people to Islam by using their extraordinary powers: stories of this kind, that so delighted the crowds, contributed to nourishing popular saint worship, especially in the rural areas. Although it is probable that many of the miracles worked by mystic saints were authentic and real, it is also true that the desire for fame and approval frequently led alleged saints to indulge in using their charismatic talents for impure and worldly purposes. This explains, as Schimmel puts it, the 'aversion of the spiritually advanced mystics for the kind of miracle-mongering that constituted part of the activities of the "shopkeeper sheikhs" and pseudo-mystics' [Schimmel, *op. cit.*, p. 212]. Hence, Sulamī's advice to the Sufi, who has achieved a certain stage on the path, to conceal the charismata that he would acquire by virtue of his spiritual purity [*Jawāmiʿ*, 147]: working miracles, and thus gaining popularity among the masses, would be in fact much easier than pursuing spiritual realisation, and it would most probably keep the mystic from further progress on his way towards God.

khalq: creature; people, mankind; the Creation, as opposite of *al-Ḥaqq* (*q.v.*).

khalwa: isolation, spiritual retreat, seclusion. The term designates the period of spiritual isolation during which the mystic must devote himself totally to ascetic exercises. For Sulamī, through isolation one can preserve his integrity and concentrate with his whole being in the remembrance of the Divinity and the contemplation of it.

khāṣṣa (pl. *khawāṣṣ*): people of distinction, élite; in the *Jawāmiʿ*, probably referring to the spiritual elite.

khaṭara: *khaṭara ʿalā qalbī*, 'it occurred to my mind'. This expression signifies the occurrence in the mind of a passing thought (*khāṭir*), i.e., a thought, notion, or inclination that strikes a person and that is quickly removed by another thought. All minds are subject to *khāṭir*, but it is the quality of the mystic always to follow the first 'passing thought' in 'matters which come directly from God to Man' [Hujwīrī, *op. cit.*, p. 387]. In Sufi terminology the expression is used along with another, *waqaʿa fī qalbī*, 'it sank into my mind', which signifies instead the appearance of a thought in the mind of a fully realised mystic and its remaining therein.

khirqa: the Sufi patched frock, with which the adept was invested after he had performed the initial years (usually three) of service, and by which the disciple would acquire some of the blessing and mystical power (*baraka*, *q.v.*) of the master. It was considered the badge of aspirants to Sufism and its intention was to show that the Sufi had detached himself from the world and what relates to it. The *khirqa* was 'usually dark blue. It was practical for travel, since dirt was not easily visible on it, and at the same time it was the color of mourning and distress' [Schimmel, *op. cit.*, p. 102; see also Hujwīrī's description of the

Sufi *muraqqaʿa* (*q.v.*), which seems to be referring rather than the *khirqa*]. Warnings against attributing too much importance to the Sufi frocks were frequent, as some mystics would consider these externals so essential that they even invented rules for the sewing and stitching of them. For this reason, a mystical interpretation of the *khirqa* was given by some, who regarded the wool dress as a merely exterior sign of one's purity, whereas true poverty is hidden and proves true only in the secret relation between the mystic and God. In Sufi terminology *khirqa* is sometimes used interchangeably with *muraqqaʿa* (*q.v.*), although, as in the *Jawāmiʿ*, the former is more often identified with the symbolic garment of the sincere Sufi, while the latter has a more general, and also more negative, connotation.

khulq, *khuluq* (pl. *akhlāq*): character, natural disposition; morals. The Sufis' *adab* is based directly on the behaviour of the Prophet himself, whose character (*khuluq*) represents the highest degree of conformity to God's precepts as laid down in the Qur'ān and is therefore the model which it is incumbent upon the Sufis to follow. The notion of character is a basic one in Sufi literature: the mystic must know the qualities and potentialities of human beings, which are accorded by divine decree and are innate components of their character. Sulamī talks about character traits (*akhlāq*) as the innate temperament of a person, though that temperament can change through the cultivation of certain habitual practices: by following the rules of conduct laid down in the Holy Book, the Sufi can improve his character in his relationship both with people and with God. Working on one's temperament is therefore a duty for the mystic, who must 'elaborate' (*istaʿmala*) his own *khuluq* constantly in order to perfect it and purify it.

madhāq: taste. See *dhawq*.

maqām (pl. *maqāmāt*): station; one's 'standing' on the path of God. On his way to the Truth, the Sufi must walk through different stations until he attains total spiritual realisation. The Sufis distinguished between *maqām*, station, and *ḥāl* (*q.v.*), state: a state is something which descends upon a person independent of his will, whereas a station, quoting Qushayrī, is 'the particular place along the path of refinement (*adab*) realised by the godservant through a kind of behaviour and through a form of quest and self-discipline' [Sells, *op. cit.*, p. 102]. Therefore, the *maqām* is a lasting stage that one reaches, to a certain extent, through a self-directed effort. While the states are considered gifts of grace, the stations are the result of one's acts. The wayfarer must fulfil the obligations pertaining to each station and keep it 'until he comprehends its perfection' [Hujwīrī, *op. cit.*, p. 181], that is to say, he cannot move to the next station before having attained perfection in the station in which he dwells. The mystics differ in their classification of the stations and in their description of certain spiritual experiences, which are seen sometimes as stations, sometimes as states. However, the sequence of the *maqāmāt*, as it is described for instance in Sulamī's works, always includes: repentance (*tawba*), watchfulness (*waraᶜ*), renunciation (*zuhd*), poverty (*faqr*), patience (*ṣabr*), trust (*tawakkul*), and acceptance (*riḍā*). In the *Jawāmiᶜ*, the term is used both with the verb *salaka* (*q.v.*), in the expression *salaka al-maqāmāt*, 'to travel along the (spiritual) stations', and with the technical verb *nāzala* (*q.v.*), 'to pass through, to experience the (spiritual) stations'.

maᶜrifa: 'knowing', gnosis. With the English 'knowing' I have rendered the Arabic term *maᶜrifa*, which is used in Sufism to refer to 'mystical knowing' or gnosis, as distinguished from *ᶜilm* (*q.v.*), the traditional knowledge acquired through learning. Many Sufis have seen the archetype of mystical knowledge in the special wisdom of Adam, who was taught 'all the names' by God, before being placed as a regent (*khalīfa*) on the earth (Qur'ān, 2:30–34). The path of *maᶜrifa* and that of *sharīᶜa* (*q.v.*) are correlative and interdependent, as the one is the ground and basis of the other: along with observance of the divine laws, the path of knowing entails constant devotion and concentration on God, through which the Sufi achieves the mystical intuition of the Real. The faculty of knowing is the heart, wherein the voyager on the path experiences intimate union with the Divinity; the person who has experienced *ma*ʿ*rifa* is called ʿ*ārif* (*q.v.*) or 'realised knower', 'gnostic'. In the *Jawāmi*ʿ, however, Sulamī seems to use the two terms ʿ*ilm* and *ma*ʿ*rifa* almost interchangeably, even though the second acquires sometimes a more spiritual connotation.

*mu*ʿ*āmala* (pl. *mu*ʿ*āmalāt*): one's dealing with or treatment of people and God (and vice-versa).

mujāhada: effort, spiritual struggle; self-mortification. The term *al-mujāhada* is used to indicate the effort made by the mystic in his spiritual voyage toward God. The Sufi use of the word is founded upon a Qur'ānic verse which is frequently mentioned in the *Jawāmi*ʿ, 'Those who strive to the utmost (*jāhadū*) for Our sake, We will guide them into Our ways' (Qur'ān, 29:69), and upon a famous Hadith as well: '[The Prophet] said: We have returned from the lesser war (*al-jihād al-aṣghar*) to the greater war (*al-jihād al-akbar*). On being asked, "What is the greater war?" he replied, "It is the struggle against one's self (*mujāhadatu 'l-nafs*)."' Thus the Sufis strictly relate the two terms *al-mujāhada* and *al-jihād*, the latter being also the verbal noun of the third form verb *jāhada*, which is used to refer to the holy war against the *nafs*. On this basis, in his translation of the *Kashf al-maḥjūb*, R. A. Nicholson renders *al-mujāhada* as 'self-mortification', 'purgation' [Hujwīrī, *op. cit.*, pp. 200–7]. Similarly, in her translation of Sulamī's *Risālat al-Malāmatiyya*, Giuditta Sassi interprets the word as 'la grande guerra santa dei conflitti spirituali' ('the great holy war of the spiritual conflicts') [see Sassi, *I custodi del segreto, op. cit.*, p. 20]. This effort must be constant (*al-mudāwamatu* ʿ*alā 'l-mujāhada*) and is differently directed according to the mystic's stage on the path: from the effort of the initiate, who struggles against the attachment to worldly possessions, through that of the seeker, who fights the inclinations of the self, to the effort of the realised Sufi, who concentrates on God alone and on the continual recollection of Him. Hujwīrī explains *mujāhada* as being 'an indirect means (*asbāb*) of attaining contemplation (*mushāhada*)' [Hujwīrī, *op. cit.*, p. 201]. In the *Jawāmi*ʿ, the terms *al-juhd* (*q.v.*) and *al-ijtihād* (*q.v.*) are used at times with the same meaning as *al-mujāhada*.

munāzala: 'encounter'; more often in the plural form *munāzalāt*, 'encounters'. It is the Arabic verbal noun in the form of *mufāʿala* of the third form verb *nāzala*, 'to encounter'. However, the exact meaning of these expressions remains quite obscure. In the *Jawāmiʿ*, Sulamī often uses the word in expressions such as: *nāzala al-aḥwāl*, *munāzalatu 'l-ḥāl*, *nāzala al-maqāmāt*, 'to experience the (mystical) states', 'to encounter a spiritual condition', 'to pass through the (mystical) stations'.

murāqaba: concentrated attention on the Divinity, attentive control of oneself. The world being multiple by its very nature, there is a natural inclination in human beings to being attracted by its many and various manifestations; however, when the heart is occupied only with created things, it gets trapped in multiplicity, and wherever it turns, its goal remains the same as its departure. On the contrary, the mystic, while living in this world, should be 'vigilantly attentive' to the Divine Presence in the heart, for that is the only Reality, everything else being imperfect and ephemeral.

muraqqaʿa (pl. *muraqqaʿāt*): the patched frock, which some ascetics used to wear as a mark of their poverty. In his *Kashf al-maḥjūb*, Hujwīrī describes at length how this frock should be made, saying it was mostly blue, because this colour was practical for travel, and because 'a blue dress is the badge of the bereaved and afflicted, and the apparel of mourners, and this world is the abode of trouble ... and the cradle of tribulation' [Hujwīrī, *op. cit.*, pp. 45, 48 and 53]. In the *Jawāmiʿ*, Sulamī shows some criticism toward the habit of wearing *muraqqaʿāt*, as he believes it to be a merely exterior token and often a means of gaining worldly reputation and respect. See also *khirqa*.

murīd (pl. *murīdūn*): the 'seeker' of the Truth, the novice who has set out on a spiritual journey; lit. 'the one who wants or desires (God)'.

murūwa: 'the ideal of manhood, comprising all knightly virtues, esp. manliness, valour, chivalry, generosity, sense of honour' [Wehr, *op. cit.*, p. 902]; pre-Islamic equivalent to Latin 'virtus'. The ideal of *mūruwa* closely resembles that of *futuwwa* (*q.v.*): it requires the discipline of both outward and inward behaviour, and includes all those virtues and morals that the Sufi needs in order to attain the highest degree of conformity to the *adab* prescribed by God.

mushāhada: contemplation, witnessing. This word, which derives from the same root as *shahāda* (the Islamic witness or testimony 'There is no god but God and Muḥammad is His Prophet'), occupies an important place in Sulamī's terminology and in Sufi language in general. In the first section of *Sūrat al-Najm* (Qur'ān, 53:1–18) Muḥammad's prophetic vision is depicted: 'Then (the Prophet Muḥammad) drew near and descended/ at a distance of two bows' lengths or nearer/ He revealed in His servant what He revealed/ the heart did not lie in what it saw/ will you then dispute with him on his vision?', and in a second passage, where the divine voice describes another vision of the Prophet, we read: 'He saw it descending another time/... / his gaze did not turn aside nor did it overreach/ he had seen the signs of his Lord, great signs.' On this key passage the Sufis centred their debate on the possibility of beholding the deity in this world, and in particular the verse on the 'gaze' of the Prophet, which neither swerved aside nor exceeded, became the paradigm for Sufi understanding of the mystical gaze and the nature of Sufi vision of the divine. In *al-Risāla al-Qushayriyya*, Qushayrī speaks of 'witnessing' as the highest state, in which one witnesses nothing other than God. Indeed, that of contemplation is one of the most intense experiences for the Sufi, when duality is overcome and the ego-self is totally annihilated in mystical union 'for the appearance of the real, Most Praised, is the disappearance of the creature' [Sells, *op. cit.*, p. 132]. The locus of this spiritual vision is the heart, wherein mystical knowledge and love abide.

nadāma, nadam: contrition. In the *Jawāmiʿ* it is usually mentioned along with repentance (*tawba, q.v.*), of which it is considered as a fundamental part. It is the feeling of contrition, which is gained through past repentance and which makes the Sufi resolved not to commit a sin again, 'even though he should have the power and means of doing so at some future time'. It is mainly due to three causes, which are: 'fear of Divine chastisement and sorrow for evil actions, desire of Divine favour and certainty that it cannot be gained by evil conduct and disobedience, and shame before God' [Hujwīrī, *op. cit.*, pp. 295–6].

nafas (pl. *anfās*): breath. The *nafas* is explained by Qushayrī as 'the inspiriting of the hearts with the subtle essences of the unknown' [Sells, *op. cit.*, p. 142]. It is often used in Sufi language in association with *waqt* to indicate a unit of time which is much shorter and subtler than the moment itself. For the realised mystic each breath is an act of worship of God and a renewal of his affirmation of unity (*tawḥīd*, *q.v.*): the Sufi is aware that he will be called to account for every breath he takes, because not a breath does he expire but a divine decree has made it go forth.

nafs (pl. *nufūs*, *anfus*): self; the soul, the subtle reality of the individual; the lower soul, the ego. The term *nafs* is used in Arabic to mark reflexive grammatical constructions, such as 'he saw himself' (*ra'ā nafsahu*); it is also used to refer to a man's soul or to his personality as a whole. In Sufi literature, and in works on ethics in general, the word comes to mean the ego-self, the lower soul, as the locus of blameworthy traits and of self-centred life. Sulamī dedicated a whole treatise to the subject, with the title *ᶜUyūb al-nafs wa-mudāwātuhā* ('The Defects of the Soul and their Remedy'): in it Sulamī lists many of human sins and base qualities and suggests a cure for them. In the *Jawāmiᶜ* the word *nafs* appears sometimes in the usual sense, that of *nafs* as 'the whole personality'; however, it appears more often in the restricted Sufi sense. In many passages of the *Jawāmiᶜ*, the Sufi is called to fighting his *nafs*, the seat of his baser inclinations, and humbling his self, so as to pass away from the attributes of his own individuality and see God as the only reality.

nāzala: see *munāzala*.

niyya: intention. The Muslim utters the *niyya* at the beginning of religious acts, when he expresses the intention to perform his prayer. In the same way, the mystic, when undertaking an action, should formulate intention to act only for God and turn away from everything created. The Sufi must deepen his path with God in view, as it is said in the Qur'ān (53:42): 'And that the final end is unto thy Lord.' The Sufis frequently cite the following Hadith to point out the importance of intention in the path: 'Therefore, he whose flight is for God and His Messenger, then his flight is for God and his Messenger; and he whose flight is for worldly gain or marriage with a woman, then his flight is for that which he flees to' [Ibn ʿAṭā'illāh al-Iskandarī, *Sūfī Aphorisms* (*Kitāb al-Ḥikam*), translated by V. Danner, *op. cit.*, p. 31]. The purity of one's intentions is, therefore, essential in one's actions, because intentions depend entirely on man, and the Sufi will be held to account for his intentions on the Day of Judgement.

qadar: destiny, or the 'predestined Decree' as settled by divine will.

qalb (pl. *qulūb*): the heart. In Sufi literature it corresponds to the physical heart in its centrality: it can become the locus of sentimentality and passion or the receptacle of virtue and knowledge, depending on the case. It can also be the faculty of contemplative intuition (*maʿrifa*, *q.v.*). In Sulamī's work, the heart as a potential source of virtuous aspirations appears usually as the antithesis of the *nafs*: when the self is humbled, the heart is purified, and when the ego boasts of itself, the heart is sealed and turns away from God.

qanāʿa: satisfaction; contentment; also, temperance and moderation, especially when tempted to yield to one's appetites and desires (*shahawāt*, *q.v.*). From the same root, and with the same meaning, we find also the word *qunūʿ*.

quʿūd ʿalā 'l-futūḥ: to practise trust in God the Maintainer, by relying on Him totally for one's sustenance. As explained in the *Jawāmiʿ*, this practice consisted properly in sitting (*al-quʿūd*) and waiting for God to bestow one's sustenance (*al-futūḥ*). While practising the *quʿūd ʿalā 'l-futūḥ*, the mystic should refrain from begging and he should trust that God will find a way to provide him with nourishment.

riʿāya: vigilance, surveillance. The term is used in Sufi terminology to refer to both God's surveillance over His servants, and the mystic's surveillance of his heart, i.e., his taking care that his interior be totally devoted to God.

riḍā: acceptance; the quality of 'taking pleasure in', 'being content with something or someone'. In the *Jawāmiʿ*, as in Sufi literature in general, the word is often used to refer both to God's satisfaction and good favour in regard to His servants, and to man's acceptance and satisfaction in whatever the divinity has forewilled for him. In short, 'Divine satisfaction really consists in God's willing that Man should be recompensed (for his good works) and in His bestowing grace (*karamāt*) upon him. Human satisfaction really consists in Man's performing the command of God and submitting to His decree' [Hujwīrī, *op. cit.*, p. 177]. The virtue of *riḍā* is mentioned in the Qur'ān, where it is said (5:119) 'God was accepting of them and they of Him', and (9:72) 'Acceptance from God is greater'. It is important to note that the mystic's acceptance 'is not a passive virtue; for the Sufis, a person's active accepting and good-pleasure in his life will lead to an empowerment to act effectively in fulfilling the divine will, which in Qur'anic spirituality centres on justice and resisting the unjust' [Sells, *op. cit.*, pp. 209–10]. Therefore, *riḍā* is not merely a patient bearing of all the adversities of life, but joy in poverty and affliction: quoting Dhū'l-Nūn al-Miṣrī, it is 'the delight of the heart with the passing of the Decree' [*ibid.*, p. 210]. This inward happiness and this perfect agreement with divine decrees result from love: *riḍā* is the attitude of a loving heart, inasmuch as the lover is pleased with what pleases his beloved [cf. Hujwīrī, *op. cit.*, p. 179].

riyā': hypocrisy, ostentation, conceited self-display. Al-Ḥārith al-Muḥāsibī, the master of psychological analysis in early Sufism, treated extensively *riyā'* in his *Kitāb al-waṣāyā* or the 'Book of Counsels' [see, Sells, *op. cit.*, pp.174–5], as well as in his *Kitāb al-riʿāya li-ḥuqūq Allāh* [*ibid.*, pp. 188–193]. In his discussion of egoism, Muḥāsibī explains that *riyā'* results from 'love of human praise for the good act', and manifests itself in that one 'is zealous in front of others, that he is lazy when no one is watching, and that he desires to be praised in all his acts' [*ibid.*, p. 175]. *Riyā'* can engender a host of other faults, such as pride (*kibr*), powerlust (*ri'āsa*), vaunting (*tafākhur*), and rivalry (*ḥubb al-ghalaba*).

riyāḍa (pl. *riyāḍāt*): training; discipline. The term indicates the training of one's character for asceticism through spiritual practices and exercises.

rubūbiyya: Lordship or Lordliness of God; the quality of God as the Lord; the opposite of *al-ʿubūdiyya* (*q.v.*).

rūḥ: spirit. In Sufi terminology, the term usually indicates the vital spirit, intermediary between body and soul, and it is considered higher than the *nafs* (*q.v.*). Sufis held that the spirit is a substance, which is corporeal and not eternal, as it is said in Qur'ān (17:87): 'Answer, "The Spirit belongs to that which (i.e. the creation of which) my Lord commanded"' [cf. Hujwīrī, *op. cit.*, p. 261]. It is also used to refer to the divine spirit, the uncreated *rūḥ al-ilāhī*, and in this sense it represents the innermost being or secret (*al-sirr*, *q.v.*) in man.

rūḥāniyya, al-: spirituality, that is, what relates to the higher senses of the word *al-rūḥ* (*q.v.*). It refers to all that concerns the life of the spirit, distinguished in that from *al-nafsāniyya*, which is the psychological life or life of the *nafs* (*q.v.*), and from *al-jismāniyya*, which is the physical life or life of the body.

ru'ya: the vision of things with the eyes of the *nafs*. As long as the Sufi looks at things from the point of view of his self, he cannot free himself from bondage to his *nafs*. Therefore, he must strive to look with the eyes of the truth: thus, he will view his actions as coming not from himself alone, but from God, because all true acts come from the one actor, the Real. The term is also used in the *Jawāmiʿ* to mean 'vision' (of God) and 'seeing' in a more general sense.

sabab (pl. *asbāb*): living, means of subsistence (like money, food, or any kind of possessions); profession, trade; cause, motive.

ṣabr: patience. Being patient in God and for God, the sincere Sufi endures difficulties, without being overcome by anxiety or yielding to complaint. The virtue of patience, which is complementary to that of gratitude (*shukr*, *q.v.*), is seen as an essential stage in the progress of the mystical path, and an essential quality to be acquired by the Sufi in general. It is founded upon the Qur'ānic verses (16:127): 'And endure you patiently (*wa-'ṣbir*), your patience (*ṣabruka*) is not but from God', and (39:10): 'The patient (*al-ṣābirūna*) will be paid their due without measure.' Patience is considered by Sufis as being an essential part of faith [cf. Qushayrī's and Ghazālī's views on *ṣabr* in Smith, *op. cit.*, pp. 58–9], and is usually divided into three stages: 'first, to leave off complaining, and this is the stage of the repentant; second, to be satisfied with what is decreed, and this is the rank of the ascetics; third, to love whatever his Lord does with him, and this is the stage of the true friends of God' [*ibid.*, p. 58].

safar (pl. *asfār*): journey. The travelling of the Sufi was seen as a symbol of the mystic's search of the truth and as a means for detaching oneself from worldly concerns, while practising ascetic exercises and concentrating totally on the remembrance of God. In the *Jawāmiᶜ*, Sulamī deals at length with the practice of travelling and the rules (*ādāb*) of it. See also *siyāḥa*.

salaka: 'to travel' (along the spiritual path). See: *maqām*, *sālik* and *sulūk*.

sālik: one who follows the spiritual path. The term is commonly used in Sufi terminology to refer to the voyager on the mystical path, the training Sufi who follows the path methodically, in that being guided by the shaykh, the master who has achieved spiritual realisation. In the last section of the *Jawāmiᶜ*, however, Sulamī gives the term *al-sālik* a connotation which is very close to that of *al-shaykh*, as he uses it to designate the novice's guide or master (elsewhere referred to also as *imām*, or *ᶜālim nāṣiḥ*).

samāᶜ: lit. hearing; mystical audition, mystical concert and dance. The *samāᶜ* is one of the most widely known expressions of Sufi life: it has been practised in Islam from early times, although it became famous through the mystical dance of the 'whirling dervishes' of the Mevleviyya, a Sufi order tracing back to the Persian mystic Jalāl ad-Dīn Rumi (d. 1273). On the issue of *samāᶜ* the opinions of the Sufi theologians were divided (on the controversy about *samāᶜ* in Islamic contexts see Nelson, Kristina, *The Art of Reciting the Qur'an*, Cairo: The American University in Cairo Press, 2001, chapter 3 'The samāᶜ Polemic', pp. 32–51). In particular, some of the sober orders would ban dancing and listening to music as illegitimate attempts to gain by self-willed effort a state that can be bestowed only by God. Therefore, they would denounce the dangers inherent in *samāᶜ* and would warn novices against attending musical concerts lest they might be depraved by them. Yet, notwithstanding the orthodox aversion to it, *samāᶜ* became a common practice in most fraternities, as it offered an outlet for the religious feelings of people, especially for the masses who needed an emotional kind of worship. As early as the second half of the ninth century, there were founded in Baghdad the *samāᶜ khāna*, houses in which the Sufis could attend freely sessions of music and dancing. The symbolic meaning of *samāᶜ* was also used in mystical literature, especially by the poets who applied the symbolism of music and dance to their verses and praised *samāᶜ* as the medium for uplifting the soul. As for Sulamī's position in this matter, in the *Jawāmiᶜ*, the author seems to advocate a moderate approach to *samāᶜ*. In fact, it is said [*Jawāmiᶜ*, 165] that mystical audition, as well as *khalwa* (*q.v.*), are appropriate only for the 'divinely learned man' (*ᶜālim rabbānī*, *q.v.*); it is also said [*Jawāmiᶜ*, 125] that the novice should remain calm and silent when participating in a mystical concert, because 'he who attempts to reach an ecstatic state by external means and whose ecstasy-inducing measures are not conducive to spiritual enhancement (*ziyāda*, *q.v.*), must feel ashamed and repent.' In the *Risālat al-Malāmatiyya*, Sulamī explains the *Malāmatīs*' position in the matter of *samāᶜ*, saying that they do not disapprove of the ritual auditions, although they abstain from them for fear that they may lead them to manifest their inward states, and that, therefore, only those who know perfectly how to conceal their spiritual experience may participate in the *samāᶜ* sessions [see *Uṣūl al-Malāmatiyya,* n. 8, in the translation of the *R. al-Malāmatiyya* by G. Sassi, *op. cit.*, pp. 38–9].

shahwa (pl. *shahawāt*): carnal desire, passion; any of the instincts and inclinations coming from the lower soul (*nafs*, *q.v.*). The Sufi must not yield to his desires and he must strive to abandon his passions, lest he become a slave to them and be led into the darkness of his ego-self.

sharᶜ: see *sharīᶜa*.

sharah: avidity. See *ḥirṣ*.

sharīᶜa: the revealed law of Islam (see *ḥaqīqa*); more often referred to as *al-sharᶜ*.

shukr: gratitude. 'But few of My servants are grateful' (Qur'ān, 34:13), and again: 'And God will give reward to those who are grateful' (Qur'ān, 3:144). In the Qur'ān we find many passages on gratitude, which is seen as the quality of the true believer, often as opposite of *kufr*, a word meaning both ingratitude and unbelief. In Sufism gratitude, which is the complementary quality to patience (*ṣabr*, *q.v.*), means to acknowledge the favours which God bestows on man and to see everything that happens to him, be it a cause for joy or sorrow, as emanating from God. Sufis considered gratitude a station on the mystical path, and divided it 'into different ranks: gratitude for the gift, gratitude for not giving, and gratitude for the capacity to be grateful. For though the common man deserves to be applauded when he expresses his gratitude at receiving a gift, the Sufi should give thanks even if his wish is not fulfilled or a hope is withheld' [Schimmel, *op. cit.*, p. 125]. As it is said in the *Jawāmiᶜ*, gratitude must extend to misfortunes as well as blessings. The genuine mystic, therefore, is thankful even in adversity, because he can have an insight into the wisdom of God's working and thus 'see with the heart's eye the blessings veiled in affliction' [*ibid.*, p. 126]. Related to *shukr* is the mystical station of *riḍā* (*q.v.*).

ṣidq: truthfulness, sincerity. Usually it is used in Sufi terminology with the same meaning as the word *ikhlāṣ* (*q.v.*), i.e., 'acting with regard for God alone, without regard for human praise or blame'.

sirr (pl. *asrār*): the term is used at times to refer to the 'secret' or 'mystery', and at times to the faculty or locus of the heart associated with that secret. In this sense, the *sirr*, or 'secret heart', is the inmost and most private area of consciousness which has contact with the Infinite and where the intimate (and secret) relation between the human and the Real takes place. In Sufi language it is also the locus of witnessing (*mushāhada, q.v.*), and it represents what must be protected and concealed between the servant and God. As it 'witnesses' the encounter with the Reality, the secret heart must remain inviolable; hence, the Sufi must be constantly 'vigilant and attentive in keeping his secret (*rāqaba sirrahu*)', because to disclose it would be an act of betrayal. In the *Jawāmiʿ* Sulamī advises the Sufi to disguise his innermost states, by assuming an outward behaviour which would not attract people's attention and reverence: this attitude helps the mystic escape the subtle traps of vanity and, at the same time, preserve the secret of his spiritual condition. The term *sirr* is also used by Sulamī in the *Jawāmiʿ* in the expression *adab al-sirr* to refer to the inward *adab* (along with *adab al-bāṭin*, see *bāṭin*).

siyāḥa (pl. *siyāḥāt*): the travelling that was the practice of some mystics, and especially of the early ascetics, who would wander for devotional reasons, living a life of poverty and spiritual seclusion.

siyāsatu 'l-nufūs: self-management. The expression is used in the *Jawāmiʿ* to mean both the tendency of the *nafs* (*q.v.*) to managing and directing man's life and the capacity to govern one's *nafs* and exercise control and domination over it. In the first case the word *nufūs* is a subjective genitive and the expression has a negative connotation, whereas in the second case it is an objective genitive and gives the expression a positive connotation.

su'āl: asking; begging. In the *Jawāmiʿ*, begging (also referred to as *al-kudya*) is frowned upon. The Sufi should not abstain from working and gaining his living [*Jawāmiʿ* 47], at least until he has perfected the stage of *tawakkul* (*q.v.*). Only when he has realised the true *tawakkul* [*Jawāmiʿ*, 53], can he give up working and totally rely on God for his sustenance. In both cases, however, the mystic must refrain from asking others for anything, and never resort to begging as a means to get his living [*Jawāmiᶜ*, 51, 144]. Yet, Sulamī seems to allow the practice of begging when it is done with the object of training the lower soul (by enduring the humiliation of asking, *Jawāmiᶜ*, 154), that is to say, in Junayd's words, when it is done 'for the sake of discipline, not for the sake of profit' [Hujwīrī, *op. cit.*, p. 359].

ṣūfī: the mystic, the Sufi. The name comes, according to many, from the wool (*ṣūf*) clothes that the first ascetics of Islam used to wear. Massignon also indicates other possible—although less probable—etymologies of the word: *ṣafā'* (purity), *ahl al-ṣuffa*, 'the people of the bench' (of the mosque in Medina, at the time of the Prophet Muḥammad), *sophos* or *sophía* (wisdom), and *al-ṣaff al-awwal*, 'the first rank' (before God) [See, Massignon, Louis, *Essai sur les origines du lexique technique de la mystique musulmane, op. cit.*, pp. 155–156]. *Al-ṣūfiyya*: the collective noun from *al-ṣūfī*.

sulūk (used in the expression *sulūk al-ṭarīq*): the Sufi's proceeding in his way to God. It designates the mystic's progression in the path towards the divine reality, and also the behaviour and conduct to be observed on the path. See also *sālik*.

tadbīr: forethought; self-planning. The term is used in Sufi literature to refer both to self-direction and to 'God's direction'; therefore, it can be both positive and negative, depending on whether it conforms to God's will or not. Talking about *tadbīr*, Victor Danner says: '*Tadbīr* implies egocentric concern for one's direction in life, and more particularly in one's daily existence, to the point where it blots out the obligations due to God. In that case, which is self-direction, the *tadbīr* is negative and should be eliminated. But if the planning or direction is in conjunction with God's directives, then it is positive [...]. It is not so much that all future planning should be set to one side as it is that one should repose in the knowledge that one's future has already been taken care of by providential arrangements' [al-Iskandarī, Ibn ᶜAṭā'illāh, *op. cit.*, pp. 23–4]. According to Sulamī, one should refrain from planning independently for his future (*tark al-tadbīr*), that is to say that he should not let his ego-self direct his plans, but he should trust in God and in the providential arrangement of his existence.

taḥaqquq: spiritual realisation. The term is also used as a participle in the expression *murīd mutaḥaqqiq*, which in the technical sense designates the novice who is following a method (*ṭarīqa*, *q.v.*) to achieve spiritual realisation. However, we can also interpret the term as having a more general meaning, i.e., that of 'a novice who has set out on his path with sincerity and conviction.'

tajrīd: isolation; the denuding one's self of worldly things. It is used in Sufi terminology to refer to isolation for the purpose of contemplation, as opposed to being in the world to gain one's living (*sabab*, *q.v.*). He who is engaged in *tajrīd* is called *mutajarrid*: he totally deprives himself of everything, and lives a life of absolute poverty, usually withdrawn from society. He is opposed to the *mutasabbib*, the mystic who lives in the world to gain his living. Both attitudes are praiseworthy, as long as the *mutasabbib* gains only what suffices him, without indulging greed and yielding to the desires of his *nafs*, and as long as the *mutajarrid* does not choose to practise begging as a profession. Usually both orientations are innate in human beings, as we read in *Kitāb al-ḥikam*: 'Your desire for isolation, even though God has put you in the world to gain a living, is a hidden passion. And your desire to gain a living in the world, even though God has put you in isolation, is a comedown from supreme aspiration' [Ibn ʿAṭā'illāh al-Iskandarī, *op. cit.*, p. 23]. The orientation of the mystic results from his vocation, predetermined by the natural inclinations of the individual, and eventually it can be controlled by the mystic's shaykh or master. However, as Sulamī states in the *Jawāmiʿ*, one's behaviour must be in keeping with one's way of life, and therefore the Sufi who is engaged in *tajrīd* or stays with those who practise it, should abide by the rules of it altogether, and, for instance, he should 'not sit with people who practise absolute poverty and isolation while he has means of livelihood with himself' [*Jawāmiʿ*, 39].

taqrīb al-ajal: awareness of the prospect of sudden death; *taqṣīr al-amal*: restraint of expectation. These concepts are two leitmotifs in Sufi literature. Man does not rely on God totally and he often carries out his religious duties in a spirit of indifference, arising from the false belief that a long life still lies ahead and that the day when he will be called to account for his actions will be indefinitely postponed. The Sufi instead is constantly aware of the transitory nature of this world, and of the significance of the present moment, which must be wholly taken up by acts of sincere devotion to God. In Sulamī's *Jawāmiʿ*, the concepts of *taqrīb al-ajal* and *taqṣīr al-amal* are complementary to that of *al-waqt* (*q.v.*).

taqṣīr al-amal: see *taqrīb al-ajal*.

taqwā: self-vigilance; piety. The quality of *taqwā* is mentioned frequently in the *Jawāmiʿ* as an essential virtue of the genuine mystic, who is godfearing and always on guard and vigilant against the wiles of his own ego-self.

ṭarīq (pl. *ṭuruq*): religious path; method of spiritual training; path.

ṭarīqa: This term, which means 'path' or 'way', is used in Sufi language to refer to 'the way of proceeding' of the mystic along the spiritual path. This way is interdependent with the *sharīʿa*, or the revealed law of Islam, as Schimmel explains: 'The *ṭarīqa*, the 'path' on which the mystics walk, has been defined as the *path* which comes out of the *sharīʿa*, for the main road is called *sharʿ*, the path, *ṭarīq*. This derivation shows that the Sufis considered the path of mystical education a branch of that highway that consists of the God-given law, on which every Muslim is supposed to walk' [Schimmel, *op. cit.*, p. 98]. The mystic way is acquired by the novice through his master's teachings, and varies according to the method and the approach of the master himself. Later on, the term *ṭarīqa* (pl. *ṭuruq*) came to designate the various Sufi 'orders', wherein groups of mystics associated and organised themselves following the specific methods of instruction, initiation and asceticism suggested by their master. In the *Jawāmiʿ*, the term is used at times with the general meaning of 'way of behaviour', 'way of acting', and at other times in the sense of 'mystical way', 'spiritual path'.

tark (or: *mujānabat*) *al-ḥuẓūẓ* (pl. of *ḥaẓẓ*, fortune, fate): the giving up of thoughts about one's fate and fortunes. As he trusts in God totally and unreservedly, the Sufi does not occupy himself with thoughts and conjectures about his fortune: he does not think of the future but concentrates only on the present moment.

taṣawwuf: the Sufi way of life, Sufism. The term is a verbal noun of the fifth form (*tafaʿʿala*), which can imply 'taking trouble', 'making effort' in doing something. In the *Jawāmiʿ*, the participle, *mutaṣawwif*, is used along with the more common term *ṣūfī*, with the implicit meaning of 'the one who makes efforts in the spiritual path'. We can well apply Hujwīrī's explanation of the term: 'The *Sūfī* is he that is dead to self and living by the Truth; he has escaped from the grip of human faculties and has really attained (to God). The *mutaṣawwif* is he that seeks to reach this rank by means of self-mortification (*mujāhadat*) and in his search rectifies his conduct in accordance with their (the Ṣūfīs') example' [Hujwīrī, *op. cit.*, p. 35].

taṣḥīḥ al-aḥwāl: to rectify one's 'states'. In the *Jawāmiʿ*, Sulamī often exhorts the Sufi to rectify and perfect his spiritual condition, which means that he should maintain an attitude of honesty and purity of heart, while experiencing the various states and stations of his spiritual realisation, and abstain from false claims and pretensions (see *daʿwā*).

tawajjuh: the turning of one's face toward God, which for the mystic means to trust God unreservedly and make Him alone the goal of his whole existence. In Sufi esoteric language *tawajjuh* means the orientation of the contemplative in his inner voyage to the Real.

tawājud: ecstasy-inducing measures; 'making-ecstatic' [Sells, *op. cit.*, pp. 111–112]. In the *Jawāmiʿ*, Sulamī distinguishes between *wajd* and *tawājud*, yet another term based on the Arabic *w/j/d* radical. The term *tawājud* is the verbal noun of the sixth form verb *tawājada*; this form can take on several senses, like attempting to do something, affecting something, or doing something in a studious or deliberate manner. As all of these meanings apply in the case of *tawājud*, I have adopted Sells' phrase 'making-ecstatic' in the intransitive sense: one who makes ecstatic attempts to reach an ecstatic state by a self-conscious effort (*takalluf*) and by external means, like, for example, listening to music or dancing. As it was this attempting to reach ecstasy by indulging in the *samā*ᶜ that was criticised both by the orthodox and the moderate Sufis, the term *tawājud* acquired often the negative connotation of forced ecstasy. Hujwīrī explains the word as 'taking pains to produce *wajd*, by representing to one's mind, for example, the bounties and evidences of God, and thinking of union (*ittiṣāl*) and wishing for the practices of holy men.' He goes on to speak of an unlawful *tawājud*, which is that of those who 'do this *tawājud* in a formal manner, and imitate them (i.e. the holy men) by outward motions and methodical dancing and grace of gesture.' Yet, there is another form of *tawājud*, which is considered permissible by Hujwīrī, and which consists in doing it 'in a spiritual manner, with the desire of attaining to their (i.e. the holy men) condition and degree' [Hujwīrī, *op. cit.*, p. 415]. In the *Jawāmi*ᶜ, Sulamī uses *tawājud* both with the neutral sense of 'entering into a state of ecstasy' (150) and with the negative sense of 'affecting a state of ecstasy' (125): in both cases, however, the term refers to a state which is usually induced by outward means and does not reflect the true *wajd*.

tawakkul: trust in God, the relying on Him unreservedly. The concept of *tawakkul* is a basic one in Sufi literature; in the Qur'ān there are many verses underlying the notion of *tawakkul*: God directed the believers to nothing outside Himself and enjoined them to put their trust in Him unconditionally, 'for whoever trusts in God, God is his sufficiency' (Qur'ān, 65:3). According to Sarrāj, *tawakkul* is 'a noble station' and can be divided into three categories: the *tawakkul* of the novice, that is 'the living for a single day and the silencing of care for tomorrow', the *tawakkul* of the select, that is 'the death of the self upon the disappearance of its share in the motives of the world and of the afterlife', and finally the *tawakkul* of the realised mystic, which is 'the bending toward God alone' [Sells, *op. cit.*, pp. 208–9]. ʿAbd Allāh al-Anṣārī al-Harawī talks about *tawakkul* as one of the patterns of behaviour (*muʿāmalāt*) of the Sufi voyager on the path, along with vigilance, respect, sincerity, confidence in God and total submission to Him: the heart of the mystic relies upon God in all its conditions, because He is the Only Agent (*al-Wakīl*) and the Lord of everything [al-Anṣārī, ʿAbd Allāh al-Harawī, *op. cit.*, p. 74]. For Sulamī, *tawakkul* is seen as an essential condition for the mystic who aims at achieving unity with the Divinity, and the acquisition and the practice of *tawakkul* are frequently mentioned in the *Jawāmiʿ* as the necessary 'provisions' for the Sufi's spiritual journey.

tawba: repentance. We read in the Qur'ān (66:8): 'O ye who believe! Turn to God with sincere repentance (*tūbū ilā 'llāh tawbatan naṣūḥan*).' Etymologically the word means 'return' and it involves the turning back from one's sins and from God's prohibitions in general. It usually comprises three stages, namely, 'remorse for disobedience, immediate abandonment of sin and determination not to sin again' [Hujwīrī, *op. cit.*, p. 296]: the Sufi's repentance must be sincere and must be accompanied by the firm intention of never relapsing into the same error that one has repented of. In the *Jawāmiʿ*, as in Sufi literature in general, it is considered as the very first station on the spiritual path, because it implies the novice's abjuring of every worldly concern. A fundamental part of repentance is contrition (*nadāma*, *q.v.*).

tawḥīd: the profession of the Oneness of God, the affirming of the absolute divine unity at all levels of knowledge. The Qur'ān mentions constantly the Oneness of God, Who is (Qur'ān, 112:1–4) 'the One/ God the Self-Sufficient Master./ He begets not, nor was He begotten/ and there is none co-equal or comparable unto Him.' *Tawḥīd* is one of the two bases of Islamic belief, as codified in the Muslim's testimony (*shahāda*) 'There is no God but God (and Muḥammad is the Messenger of God)'. The common meaning of this affirmation is that there is only one divinity: therefore, to affirm any other divinities besides God is to be guilty of 'associationism' (*shirk*). However, for the Sufis, this is only the first stage of *tawḥīd*, that of the common people and of the initiate on the path. The Sufi interpretation of *tawḥīd* is indeed much more complex, and vast and varied is the Sufi literature dealing with this subject. According to Junayd, whose meditation on *tawḥīd* is one of incomparable theological intensity, there are four grades of affirmation of unity. The first consists in the Muslim's credal affirmation, which we have already seen. The second consists of the total harmonisation of the person to the one God in the exterior, through the performance of the ritual obligations, whereas the third occurs on the plane of both exterior and interior actions, as the person harmonises his inward life around the single centre. In the last stage, the mystic realises *tawḥīd* through the annihilation of the self in union with the divine. With the disappearance of 'he', the Sufi returns to his being 'as he was before he was', that is to say, in the original state associated with the pre-eternal covenant (Qur'ān, 7:171) of 'Am I not your lord? Yes, indeed!' [Sells, *op. cit.*, pp. 253–6].

ta'wīl (pl. *ta'wīlāt*): symbolic or metaphorical interpretation of the Qur'ānic text. As concerns the application of the principles of interpretation, the Qur'ānic exegetes distinguished between two main domains: the *tafsīr* and the *ta'wīl*. In the preface to his translation of the *Ta'wīlāt al-Qur'ān* by ʿAbd al-Razzāq al-Qashānī, Pierre Lory explains the *tafsīr* as the kind of exegesis which aims at 'la compréhension la plus complète possible du texte littéral du Coran', by resorting to the sources of Arabic grammar and lexicography, by collecting all the possible information on the circumstances of the revelation and by referring to the prophetic Hadiths on the same subjects. As for *ta'wīl*, Lory distinguishes between the *ta'wīl ʿaqlī*, which 'consiste en l'introduction de l'opinion personnelle du commentateur (*ra'y*), de sa réflexion individuelle après un emploi exhaustif des ressources de la langue et de la Tradition,' and the *ta'wīl kashfī*, or esoteric exegesis, which he defines as 'la voie du dévoilement intérieur—par une saisie directe et intuitive' of the meaning of the Qur'ānic passages. The *ta'wīl kashfī* found its development in Sufi exegesis, in particular with the commentary attributed to Jaᶜfar al-Ṣādiq (d. 765) and the *Ta'wīlāt al-Qur'ān* by ᶜAbd al-Razzāq al-Qashānī (d. 1329). The Sufis based their spiritual exegesis on the polarity of *ẓāhir–bāṭin*: in this sense, the *ta'wīl kashfī* consisted properly of 'the unveiling' of the original and interior meaning of a passage, and would thus apply to all Qur'ānic verses. However, this type of exegesis was openly criticised by some Sufis, who considered it as resulting merely from a personal interpretation of the Qur'ānic text and therefore regarded it as misleading. [For the quotations above, see Lory, Pierre, *Les Commentaires ésotériques du Coran d'après ᶜAbd ar-Razzāq al-Qashānī*, Paris: Les Deux Océans, 1980, p. 10]. In the *Jawāmiᶜ* the term is used once in the plural *ta'wīlāt* to mean a kind of loose interpretation, to which some would resort in order to make the application of the Qur'ānic prescriptions easier and avoid tough duties and restrictions.

taᶜẓīm: reverence. The term means the acknowledgment of God's omnipotence and the humbling of oneself before it. The reverent mystic glorifies his Lord and reveres the divine precepts and decrees; at the highest degree, he reveres God Himself, that is to say he sees in Him the Only Agent and Cause of everything. The term also designates the novice's respect and reverence towards his spiritual master.

ᶜubūdiyya: servanthood. The term refers to the state of obedience of the godservant, which consists in fulfilling the rights due to the Lordship (*rubūbiyya*, *q.v.*) of God. In the technical Sufi use of the term, the word *ᶜubūdiyya* means the intermediate state of the seeker between *ᶜibāda* (*q.v.*), the mere observance of ritual obligations (term which appears in the *Jawāmiᶜ* along with *ᶜubūdiyya*) and *ᶜubūda*, the total devotion to God.

ᶜujb: narcissistic vanity; conceit; pride. It is one of the various forms of egoism, deriving from man's attachment to his *nafs* (*q.v.*) and his yielding to the inclinations of his nature (*ṭabᶜ*). The person who falls into vanity becomes blind to his sins, loses fear of doing wrong and strays into error while thinking he is doing right.

Through vanity, 'one perishes in error by waxing self-important, becoming arrogant, and turning pretentious' [Sells, *op. cit.*, p. 173]. An interesting discussion on vanity is found in Muḥāsibī's *Kitāb al-riʿāya li-ḥuqūq Allāh*, or 'The Book on the Observance of the Rights of God', where the author examines attentively the stations and moments of egoism, the various forms it can take, and the methods of overcoming it [*ibid.*, pp. 171–3].

ʿulūm al-ḥaqīqa: see *ʿilm*.

uns: intimacy (with God). See *hayba*. In the *Jawāmiʿ* the term *uns* is not present but we find, from the same root, the fourth form verb *ānasa*, 'to become intimate (especially, with God)'.

ʿuzla: retreat, seclusion; synonymous with *khalwa* (*q.v.*).

waḥsha: retreat, solitude; estrangement. The word is synonymous with *khalwa* (*q.v.*).

wajd: the emotion of mystical ecstasy. The word is a verbal noun and means, literally, 'the experiencing of a strong emotion': it is used in Sufism to denote a state which manifests itself in audition (*samāʿ*, *q.v.*), i.e., the state of emotional upset during the mystical rapture. It is often rendered as 'ecstasy', although, as Sells observes [Sells, *op. cit.*, p. 111], one may note the difference in metaphor between the Latinate term ecstasy (*ex stasis*) as 'standing outside of oneself' and the Arabic term *wajd*, which combines the meaning of 'intense feeling' with the notion of 'finding' (*wujūd*). In Sufi terminology, the lexical field of *wajd* also includes the frequently recurrent term *wujūd*, 'existence' or 'ecstatic existentiality'. Qushayrī explains the Sufi concept of *wajd* as 'the result of encounters', which 'happens upon your heart and comes upon it without any intention or self-conscious effort', and quotes the known saying by Abū ʿAlī al-Daqqāq on ecstasy: '*Tawḥīd* entails the encompassing of the servant. Ecstasy (*wajd*) entails the immersion of the servant. *Wujūd* entails the extinction of the servant. It is like one who witnesses the sea, then sails upon the sea, then drowns in the sea' [Sells, *op. cit.*, pp. 110–116]. Hujwīrī explains *al-wajd* as 'a painful affection of the heart, arising either from jest or earnest, either from sadness or gladness [...].

He who feels *wajd* is either agitated by ardent longing in the state of occultation (*ḥijāb*), or calmed by contemplation in the state of revelation (*kashf*)' [Hujwīrī, *op. cit.*, pp. 413–4].

walī (*pl. awliyā'*): godfriend. The term, which is usually translated as 'saint', derives from *waliya*, 'to be near' and also 'to guide, govern, protect someone', and in this sense it means both 'friend, someone who is under special protection' and 'protector, patron'. The word is both active and passive: a *walī* is one whose affairs are led (*tuwulliya*) by God and who performs (*tawallā*) worship and obedience [see, Schimmel, *op. cit.*, p. 199]. In the Qur'ān (2:257) the word is applied to God, who is both the Friend and the Protector of the faithful; however, it is also used for the friends of God (*awliyā' Allāh*), as in Sura 10:62: 'Behold! Verily on the Friends of Allah there is no fear, nor shall they grieve.' The concept of *walī* developed during the early centuries of Sufism and it was adopted in Sufi vocabulary to refer to any believer who has reached a stage of proximity (*qurb*) to God. This person, who has become near to God both for individual merits and divine grace, progressively came to assume the characteristics of the saint in Christianity, and he was believed to perform miracles and bestow special blessings on people. Since the late ninth century, various theories on 'saintship' (*wilāya*, *q.v.*) developed and several essays were written on this subject [on *wilāya* and the lexical field of the word, see Chodkiewitz, Michel, *Le Sceau des saints: prophetie et saintité dans la doctrine d'Ibn ʿArabi*, Paris: Gallimard, 1986; on sainthood in Islam see also Bel, A., *L'Islam Mystique*, Paris: Adrien Maisonneuve, 1988, 'Les Saints', pp. 44–90]. In the *Jawāmiʿ*, and in his works in general, Sulamī uses the term *walī* with the sense of 'friend of God', or 'a person who has achieved a very high stage in the path toward the Divinity'. Therefore, rather than 'saint', I have translated the term *walī* as 'godfriend' or 'friend of God' [cf. Sells, *op. cit.*, p. 8], an interpretation which I believe is also more faithful to the original meaning of the word's etymology. Yet, Sulamī's notion of *walī* somehow resembles that of 'saint', in that, for example, the *awliyā' Allāh* are said to have the capacity to intercede with God for those who love them [*Kitāb al-futuwwa*, G. Sassi., *op. cit.*, p. 27].

waqt (pl. *awqāt*): the moment, the instant. The term is used by Sufis to refer to 'the time in which a person happens to be', the 'now' between the past and the future, the non-recurring moment in which the Sufi should invest all his efforts and energies. For this reason, the mystic is often called by Sufis 'a son of his moment' (*ibn waqtihi*), meaning that he is wholly occupied with the present moment and that he has concern neither for the moment past nor for the moment to come. A more technical interpretation of the term, which is often alluded to in many of Sulamī's expressions, explains the *waqt* as the period of the *ḥāl*, a 'time-out-of-time within time' [Sells, *op. cit.*, p. 100] that comes upon the Sufi without any choice or willed effort on his part and to which the self is given over completely.

waraᶜ: scrupulousness, watchfulness; piety. The term recurs frequently in the *Jawāmiᶜ* and represents one of the main qualities of the Sufi. In his *Kitāb al-lumaᶜ*, Sarrāj talks about the station of *waraᶜ* and distinguishes the *waraᶜ* of the common people, 'who are scrupulous in avoiding [...] whatever lies between the prohibited (*ḥarām*) and the permitted (*ḥalāl*)', from the *waraᶜ* of the gnostics, which consists in abstaining from everything that distracts one's heart from God [Sells, *op. cit.*, pp. 200–2]. In the *Jawāmiᶜ* the term is also used to designate 'piousness', which is reflected in one's behaviour, keeps one from having an improper conduct and makes one venerated in the eyes of people [*Jawāmiᶜ*, 138].

wārid: the 'oncoming'; in Sufi terminology means inspiration in the sense of a spiritual insight, a good inclination that comes upon the heart independent of any intention on the part of the mystic. It is from the same root as the verb *warada*, *yaridu*, which indicates the 'coming upon' the heart of a state or mode of consciousness, such as happiness and sorrow, or of any praiseworthy inclinations by way of inspiration. In the *Jawāmiᶜ* the term '*wārid*' is used usually to designate a particular moment (*waqt*, *q.v.*), state (*ḥāl*, *q.v.*), or circumstance which God sends down to the mystic, and the verb '*warada*' to indicate the 'coming upon' the mystic of that moment or state.

wilāya: special friendship with God, saintship (see *walī*).

wird (pl. *awrād*): 'specified time of day or night devoted to private worship (in addition to the five prescribed prayers); a section of the Qur'ān recited on this occasion' [Wehr, *op. cit.*, *warada*, I. p. 1060]. In Sufism, the *awrād* designated also certain formulae or litanies, which the spiritual master would teach to his disciples and which were recited after the ritual prayer or for any special occasion.

wuṣla: union. It refers to the mystical union with the Divinity, which comes as an act of grace from God and through which man experiences true knowing (*maʿrifa*, *q.v.*) and witnesses the Real. In the *Jawāmiʿ*, it is used, along with *wuṣūl* (*q.v.*), as synonymous with the more common *al-ittiṣāl*.

wuṣūl: arriving at God, attaining the truth through union with the Divinity.

yaqīn: certitude; certain faith. It is 'the unquestioning faith that eventually becomes deeply rooted in the soul and turns into unshakable certitude' [Schimmel, *op. cit.*, p. 253]. The 'reality of certitude' (*ḥaqq al-yaqīn*) is the highest station of the mystic and is attained when the Sufi annihilates his individuality in union with the Divinity [Ḥallāj has symbolised the stations of *yaqīn* as the way of the moth, which experiences the 'knowledge of certitude' when it sees the light of the candle, the 'vision of certitude' when it draws near and feels its heat, and the 'reality of certitude' when it is, finally, burned and consumed by the flame; cf. al-Ḥāllaj, Ḥusayn ibn Manṣūr, *Kitāb aṭ-ṭawāsīn, texte arabe avec la version persane d'al-Baqlī*, edited and translated by L. Massignon, Paris: Geuthner, 1913].

zāhid (pl. *zuhhād*): ascetic, 'the one who renounces the world', 'the one occupied with *zuhd* (*q.v.*)'.

ẓāhir: see *bāṭin*.

ziyāda (pl. *ziyādāt*): enhancement (*fī 'l-aḥwāl*, in one's states), spiritual growth. The Sufi must seek always to raise his mystical states to the highest levels of spiritual perfection. Thus, for instance, the experience of a state should always be accompanied by the enhancement in one's spiritual condition (*ziyāda*), as a mystical ecstasy that does not upraise the Sufi's inwardness is not sincere but is merely a manifestation of the self.

zuhd: renunciation of the world, detachment from worldly concerns; asceticism. In the Qur'ān (11:86) we read: 'The remainder which God left for you is better for you, if you are believers.' On this Qur'ānic principle was grounded the *zuhd* or 'ascesis' practised by the early mystics, which consisted of the renunciation of worldly possessions and the giving up of any desire for anything but what God has left for our bare necessities. The attitude of *zuhd*, which recalls that of the Christian anchorites, was especially typical of the mystics of the first centuries of Islam: they would live alone in retreat with a very simple lifestyle, away from people and society, renouncing any form of attachment to earthly things and indulging in the performance of supererogatory acts of devotion. *Zuhd*, which was considered by the ascetics a privileged means for drawing near to God, came to be regarded by later Sufis as a (somehow imperfect) stage of the spiritual path, between the stage of the *ʿābid* (*q.v.*), the devotee who is occupied with the external acts of devotion, and that of the *ʿārif* (*q.v.*), the gnostic who has achieved spiritual realisation. Many Sufis talked about *zuhd* as a 'station' (*maqām*, *q.v.*): from the *zuhd* of the novices, which is in Junayd's words 'that the hands are free of possession and the hearts are free of craving', to the *zuhd* of 'those who have realized renunciation', which is, according to Ruwaym, 'the giving up of all goods or benefits for the self from whatever exists in the world'. Those who have realised renunciation renounce also 'the goods for the self', that is 'the tranquillity, honor, praise, and status among the people' that come with renunciation of the world [see, Sells, *op. cit.*, pp. 202–3]. At the highest spiritual level, however, the Sufi's meditation goes beyond the idea itself of 'renunciation'. In fact, for the realised mystic, who is totally concentrated on God and on the contemplation of Him, the world is not any more something separated from his Creator but is a manifestation of Him, and within the world, and not outside it, he finds his true realisation as a mystic [cf. *Risālat al-Malāmatiyya*: G. Sassi, *op. cit.*, p. 27]. References to *zuhd* as 'renunciation of earthly things' are frequent in the *Jawāmiᶜ* and many are the passages where Sulamī stresses the importance of renouncing pleasure in worldly possessions and concerns. Yet, throughout the book, one can detect a certain (often implicit) criticism against *zuhd* practices, especially when conceived as merely exterior acts performed in the hope of gaining merits and reward in the afterlife.

Appendix

Biographical Notes on Some Major Sufi Figures*

ʿABD ALLĀH B. AL-MUBĀRAK: he was born in 118/736 and died in 180/796. He was the exponent of an ascetic trend in mysticism, which was rigorously traditionalist, and which from ʿAbd Allāh's spiritual master Sulaymān Taymī, through his disciples Sufyān al-Thawrī, Sufyān b. Uyayna and Wakīʿ, finally arrived at Ibn Ḥanbal and through him became the distinctive feature of the Ḥanbalite school (Massignon, *Essai*, p. 236).

ABŪ'L-ʿABBĀS AḤMAD B. MUḤAMMAD B. SAHL B. ʿAṬĀ' AL-ĀDAMĪ AL-WALĪ: born in Baghdad, he died in 309/921

* For the biographical notes I have referred to: Sulamī's *Ṭabaqāt al-ṣūfiyya*, edited by J. Pedersen, *Kitāb Ṭabaqāt al-Ṣūfiyya: Texte arabe avec une introduction et un index,* Leiden: E. J. Brill, 1960; Farīd al-Dīn al-ʿAṭṭār's *Tadhkiratu 'l-awliyā'*, in the translation by L. Pirinoli, *Tadhkirat al-awliyā: Parole di Ṣūfī,* Grandi Pensatori d'Oriente e d'Occidente, Le Tradizioni: 2, Milan: Luni Editrice, 1994; Hujwīrī's *Kashf al-maḥjūb* in Nicholson's translation, *The Kashf al-maḥjúb, the oldest Persian treatise on Sufiism by ʿAlí b. ʿUthmán al-Jullábí al-Hujwírí*, translated from the text of the Lahore Edition, compared with Mss. in the India Office and British Museum, by R. A. Nicholson, London: Luzac and Company Ltd., 1967; Abū'l-Qāsim ʿAbd al-Karīm al-Qushayrī, *al-Risāla al-Qushayriyya*, Cairo: Dār al-Kutub al-Ḥadītha, 1966; Abū Naṣr al-Sarrāj, *Kitāb al-lumaʿ fī 'l-taṣawwuf*, edited and translated by R. A. Nicholson, Leiden and London: E. J. Brill, 1914; *The Encyclopaedia of Islam*, new edition, Leiden: E. J. Brill, 1986–7; L. Massignon, *Essai sur les origines du lexique technique de la mystique musulmane*, Paris: J. Vrin, 1954; M. Molé, *I Mistici Musulmani*, Milan: Adelphi, 1992; A. Schimmel, *Mystical dimensions of Islam*, Chapel Hill: The University of North Carolina Press, 1975.

or 311/923. 'He was one of the masters (*mashā'ikh*) of the men of wisdom and of the most intelligent (*ẓirāf*) Sufis. [...] He was the disciple of Ibrāhīm al-Māristānī, al-Junayd b. Muḥammad, and the masters above them (*fawqahumā*). He was held in high esteem by Abū Saʿīd al-Kharrāz' (Sulamī, *Ṭabaqāt*, p. 260).

ABŪ ʿABD ALLĀH B. AL-JALLĀ', MUḤAMMAD (OR AḤMAD) B. YAḤYĀ: born in Baghdad, he spent most of his life in Ramla and Damascus. He was one of the greatest shaykhs of Syria. He was the disciple first of his father Yaḥyā al-Jallā', and then of Abū Turāb al-Nakhshabī, Dhū'l-Nūn al-Miṣrī and Abū ʿUbayd al-Busrī. He died in 306/918.

ABŪ ʿABD ALLĀH AL-MAGHRIBĪ, MUḤAMMAD B. ISMĀʿĪL: he was the disciple of ʿAlī b. Razīn. He died in 279 or 299/911.

ABŪ ʿALĪ AL-RŪDHBĀRĪ: 'he was a great Ṣúfí and of royal descent. Many signs and virtues were vouchsafed to him. He discoursed lucidly on the arcana of Ṣūfiism' (Hujwīrī, *The Kashf al-maḥjūb*, p. 157). He died in 322/934.

ABŪ ʿAMR AL-ZUJĀJĪ, MUḤAMMAD B. IBRĀHĪM B. YŪSUF AL-NAYSĀBŪRĪ: a native of Nīshāpūr, he was a disciple of Abū ʿUthmān al-Ḥīrī and then of the great masters of Baghdad, Junayd, Ruwaym and Ibrāhīm al-Khawwāṣ. He settled in Mecca where he himself became a Sufi master. He died there in 348/957.

ABŪ BAKR AL-KATTĀNĪ, MUḤAMMAD B. ʿALĪ B. JAʿFAR: he was born in Baghdad and lived in Mecca, where he died in 322/933. He was a disciple of Junayd, Abū Saʿīd al-Kharrāz and Abū'l-Ḥusayn al-Nūrī.

ABŪ BAKR AL-WARRĀQ, MUḤAMMAD B. ʿUMAR AL-ḤAKĪM: he was born at Tirmidh, a city standing on the right bank of the Oxus, and died in 370/980. He spent most of his life in Balkh and was the disciple of Tirmidhī and Ibn Khiḍrawayh.

ABŪ ḤAFṢ AL-ḤADDĀD 'THE BLACKSMITH', ʿAMR B. SĀLIM AL-NAYSĀBŪRĪ: he was born at Kūradābādh, near Nīshāpūr. He was a disciple of ʿAbd Allāh b. Mahdī al-Abīwardī

(d. c. 267) and of ʿAlī al-Naṣrābādhī, and one of the companions (*rāfaqa*) of Aḥmad b. Khiḍrawayh. With him are connected Shāh b. Shujāʿ al-Kirmānī and Abū ʿUthmān Saʿīd al-Ḥīrī. With Ḥamdūn al-Qaṣṣār, he was an exponent of the *Malāmatiyya*. He probably died in 265/879.

ABŪ'L-ḤUSAYN AL-NŪRĪ, AḤMAD (OR MUḤAMMAD) B. MUḤAMMAD: he was born in Baghdad and died in 295/907 or in 286/899. 'None in his time followed a better path (*ṭarīqa*) or spoke in such a subtle way' (Sulamī, *Ṭabaqāt*, p. 151 and ff.). He was a disciple of al-Sarī al-Saqaṭī and Muḥammad b. ʿAlī al-Qaṣṣāb, and consorted with Aḥmad b. Abī'l-Ḥawārī (d. 230/844). He is one of the greatest representatives of the concept of pure and unconditioned love: his enthusiastic utterances and his speaking of himself as God's 'lover' (*ʿāshiq*) were often misinterpreted and condemned, and earned him the accusation of heresy.

ABŪ ISḤĀQ IBRĀHĪM B. SHAYBĀN AL-QIRMĪSĪNĪ: he was a disciple of Abū ʿAbd Allāh al-Maghribī and Khawwāṣ; he died in 348/959.

ABŪ'L-KHAYR AL-AQṬAʿ: he was born in al-Tīnāt, in Morocco, and died in c. 343/954. He was one of the disciples of Abū ʿAbd Allāh b. al-Jallā'.

ABŪ MUḤAMMAD AL-JURAYRĪ, AḤMAD (OR AL-ḤASAN) B. MUḤAMMAD B. AL-ḤUSAYN (OR AL-ḤASAN): he was 'one of the disciples of al-Junayd and of Sahl b. ʿAbd Allāh al-Tustarī [...] He succeeded al-Junayd in his assembly (*majlis*) because of the height of his spiritual state (*ḥāl*) and the truth (*ṣiḥḥa*) of his knowledge. He died in 311 (923)' (Sulamī, *Ṭabaqāt*, p. 253 and ff.).

ABŪ SAʿĪD AL-KHARRĀZ 'THE COBBLER', AḤMAD B. ʿĪSĀ: he was a disciple of Dhū'l-Nūn al-Miṣrī, Saqaṭī, and Bishr al-Ḥāfī. According to Sulamī, 'he was the first who spoke about the science of "annihilation" (*fanā'*) and "subsistence" (*baqā'*)' (*Ṭabaqāt*, p. 223 and ff.). He died in Cairo in 277/890 or 286/899.

ABŪ SULAYMĀN AL-ʿANSĪ AL-DĀRĀNĪ, ʿABD AL-RAḤMĀN B. ʿAṬIYYA (OR ʿABD AL-RAḤMĀN B. AḤMAD

B. ʿAṬIYYA): born at Dārāyā, a quarter of Damascus, he died in 215/830. He was a disciple of ʿAbd al-Wāḥid b. Zayd (ascetic and disciple of Mālik b. Dīnār in Basra, who died in 177/793) and the spiritual master of Aḥmad b. Abī'l-Ḥawārī. He was 'the best of his times; he had no equals in the practice of austerity and in the moderation of desires, a virtue which none practiced better than him. He possessed the mysteries of the knowledge of God' (ʿAṭṭār, *Tadhkira*, p. 247).

ABŪ TURĀB AL-NAKHSHABĪ, ʿASKAR B. ḤUṢAYN (OR ʿASKAR B. MUḤAMMAD B. ḤUṢAYN): he was born in Nakhshab in the Transoxiana, between Bukhāra and Balkh. He was the disciple of Abū Ḥātim al-ʿAṭṭār al-Baṣrī and of Ḥātim al-Aṣamm al-Balkhī, and he was the master of Abū ʿUbayd al-Busrī and of Ibn al-Jallā'. He was an authority in the field of Hadith. The surname 'Abū Turāb', or 'father of the dust', was the same as the one given to ʿAlī b. Abī Ṭālib. He died in 245/860.

ABŪ ʿUTHMĀN AL-ḤĪRĪ, SAʿĪD B. ISMĀʿĪL (OF HIRA, A QUARTER OF NĪSHĀPŪR): a native of Rayy, he was a disciple of Yaḥyā b. Muʿādh al-Rāzī and Shāh b. Shujāʿ al-Kirmānī, and then moved to Nīshāpūr, where he associated with Abū Ḥafṣ al-Ḥaddād, whose daughter he married. According to Sulamī (*Ṭabaqāt*, p. 159 and f.), Ḥīrī was the first who divulged the way of *taṣawwuf* in Nīshāpūr. He has been considered the third great master of the *Malāmatiyya*, after Abū Ḥafṣ al-Ḥaddād and Ḥamdūn al-Qaṣṣār. He was known as the *zāhid*, or 'the ascetic', and the *wāʿiẓ*, or 'the preacher'. According to Hujwīrī (*Kashf*, p. 134), 'he is the author of sublime treatises on various branches of this science (i.e. Sufism)' and consorted with famous Sufi masters of Baghdad, among whom Junayd and Ruwaym. He died in Nīshāpūr in 298/910.

ABŪ ʿUTHMĀN AL-MAGHRIBĪ, SAʿĪD B. SALLĀM: 'he was an eminent spiritualist of the class who have attained "fixity" (*ahl tamkīn*), and was profoundly versed in various departments of knowledge. He practised austerities and is the author of many notable sayings and excellent proofs concerning the observation of spiritual blemishes (*ru'yat āfāt*)' (Hujwīrī, *Kashf*, pp. 158–9). He died in 373/984.

AḤMAD B. KHIḌRAWAYH, ABŪ ḤĀMID AL-BALKHĪ: he was 'one of the greatest masters (*mashā'ikh*) of Khurāsān. He was a disciple of Abū Turāb al-Nakhshabī and of Ḥātim al-Aṣamm; he travelled to see Abū Yazīd al-Bisṭāmī ... and went to Nīshāpūr to visit Abū Ḥafṣ al-Naysābūrī' (Sulamī, *Ṭabaqāt*, p. 93). Like other masters of the school of Khurāsān, Aḥmad b. Khiḍrawayh professed the doctrine of absolute *tawakkul* and the principle of *inkār al-kasb* (see Shaqīq b. Ibrāhīm al-Balkhī). He died in 240/852.

ʿALĪ B. BUNDĀR B. AL-ḤUSAYN AL-ṢAYRĀFĪ ABŪ'L-ḤASAN: a disciple of Abū ʿUthmān al-Ḥīrī, he became an eminent shaykh of Nīshāpūr. He travelled frequently and had among his spiritual masters many famous Sufis of Baghdad, among whom Junayd, Ruwaym and Sumnūn al-Muḥibb (d. after 287/900). He was also a collector of traditions. He died in 359/970.

BAYAZĪD (ABŪ YAZĪD) AL-BISṬĀMĪ, ṬAYFŪR B. ʿĪSĀ B. SURŪSHĀN: born at Bisṭām, in northwestern Iran, he was one of the greatest personalities of early Persian Sufism. He was the second of three brothers and 'all were ascetics (*zuhhād*) and pious servants of God (*ʿubbād*), and they were possessed of mystical states (*arbāb aḥwāl*)' (Sulamī, *Ṭabaqāt*, p. 60). First of the 'intoxicated' Sufis, he developed the doctrine of 'annihilation' in God (*fanā*). He conceived it as a total extinction of the traces of the self and mostly expressed himself in paradoxical sentences (Molé, *I Mistici Musulmani*, p. 66). He was also the first to describe the mystical experience by using the image of the *miʿrāj*, the heavenly journey of the Prophet. He died in 261/874.

BISHR AL-ḤĀFĪ 'THE BARE-FOOTED ONE', ABŪ NAṢR BISHR B. AL-ḤĀRITH B. ʿABD AL-RAḤMĀN B. ʿAṬĀ AL-ḤĀFĪ: he was born in 150/767 and died in 227/841. A native of Merv, he spent most of his life in Baghdad, where he died, and consorted (*ṣaḥiba*) with Fuḍayl b. ʿIyāḍ (Sulamī, *Ṭabaqāt*, p. 33). He emphasised the Sufi concept of *ikhlāṣ*, or 'absolute sincerity'.

DHŪ'L-NŪN AL-MIṢRĪ, ABŪ'L-FAYḌ THAWBĀN B. IBRĀHĪM: born in Ikhmīm in Upper Egypt, he died in Gīza in 245/860. He was accused of being a philosopher and a magician and works of alchemy and 'science of the letters' (*ʿilm al-ḥurūf*) have been attributed to him. He was the first to formulate the Sufi notion of *maʿrifa*, or 'gnosis', as opposed to *ʿilm*, or discursive knowledge. He also dealt for the first time with the classification of the mystical states.

AL-DUQQĪ, MUḤAMMAD B. DĀWŪD ABŪ BAKR: born in Dīnawār, he lived in Damascus. He was a disciple of Jallā' and Abū Bakr al-Miṣrī. He died in c. 359/970.

AL-FUḌAYL B. ʿIYĀḌ, ABŪ ʿALĪ B. MASʿŪD AL-TAMĪMĪ AL-YARBŪʿĪ: he was born near Merv and died in Mecca in 187/804. He was a disciple of Abān b. Abī ʿAyyāsh and Sufyān al-Thawrī and devoted himself to the study of the Prophetic traditions in Kufa. He is a typical representative of early orthodox asceticism (*zuhd*), in that he disdained the company of people and, although he was married, he considered family life a great obstacle on the path to God.

AL-ḤAKĪM AL-TIRMIDHĪ, ABŪ ʿABD ALLĀH MUḤAMMAD B. ʿALĪ: according to Sulamī (*Ṭabaqāt*, p. 212), he associated with Nakhshabī and he was a disciple of Yaḥyā al-Jallā' and Aḥmad b. Khiḍrawayh. He was the spiritual master of Abū Bakr al-Warrāq. Tirmidhī, who followed the Shāfiʿite doctrine, was a famous Sufi. Yet he was expelled from Tirmidh and charged with infidelity because of the theories he expounded in two of his works: the *ʿIlal al-sharīʿa*, where he explained the motives and the meaning of Islamic rites, and the *Khātam al-awliyā'*, where he asserted that the saints hold a 'seal' (*khātam*) like the prophets. The doctrines of Tirmidhī greatly influenced later metaphysicians and in particular the famous Ibn ʿArabī (d. 638/1240). He died in 285/898.

AL-ḤALLĀJ, ABŪ MUGHĪTH AL-ḤUSAYN B. MANṢŪR 'THE COTTON CARDER': born at Bayḍā, in the province of Fārs, he grew up in Wāsiṭ and Tustar. He was the disciple of Junayd, Abū'l-Ḥusayn al-Nūrī, and ʿAmr al-Makkī (d. c. 297/909). The figure of this mystic is a peculiar one in the history of Sufism. The fact that he dared to proclaim the secret of mystic love openly, by uttering sentences such as the famous *anā 'l-Ḥaqq*, 'I am the Truth', made more sober mystics, among whom was also his master Junayd, accuse him of propagating false religious claims. Ḥallāj's behaviour, along with the strong impact of his teachings on the political and social sphere, led to his imprisonment; finally he was put to death in 309/922.

ḤAMDŪN AL-QAṢṢĀR, ABŪ ṢĀLIḤ B. AḤMAD B. ʿUMĀRA AL-NAYSĀBŪRĪ: shaykh of the *ahl al-malāma* or 'people of blame' in Nīshāpūr, he became the leading figure of the *Malāmatiyya* movement. He was the disciple of Sālim b. al-Ḥasan al-Bārūsī, Abū Turāb al-Nakhshabī and ʿAlī al-Naṣrābādhī. He died in 271/884. 'The way (*ṭarīqa*) that he followed was peculiar to him (*yakhtaṣṣu huwa bihā*) and among his disciples none followed him as faithfully as ʿAbd Allāh b. Muḥammad b. Munāzil did. [...] Al-Qaṣṣār died in Nīshāpūr in 271 and was buried in the cemetery of Ḥīra' (Sulamī, *Ṭabaqāt*, p. 114).

AL-ḤĀRITH AL-MUḤĀSIBĪ, ABŪ ʿABD ALLĀH B. ASAD AL-ʿANAZĪ: he was born in Basra in c. 165/781 and died in Baghdad in 243/857. Sulamī considers him 'the master of the most part of the Baghdadian Sufis' (*Ṭabaqāt*, p. 49). He belonged to the Shāfiʿī school of law, as did Junayd, but he also adopted the vocabulary of the 'rationalist' theological school of the Muʿtazila, which attracted criticism from the Hanbalites. His surname is derived from the word *muḥāsaba*, which means 'examination of conscience' or 'the analysis of the secret motions of man's inward being'. In his writings, where he contributed to giving Sufism a developed technical language, he provided the reader with a subtle psychological analysis of every thought and a scrupulous guide for spiritual training. In particular, his examination of the concept of 'hypocrisy' (*riyā'*) and his methodological approach were essential to the development of Sufi thought.

IBRĀHĪM B. ADHAM (ABŪ ISḤĀQ IBRĀHĪM B. ADHAM B. MANṢŪR AL-ʿIJLĪ): he was born in Balkh and died in Syria in 161/777 or 162/778. According to the legend, he renounced the princely life and became a paragon of poverty and abstinence. In Mecca he associated with Sufyān al-Thawrī and Fuḍayl b. ʿIyāḍ.

IBRĀHĪM AL-KHAWWĀṢ (ABŪ ISḤĀQ IBRĀHĪM B. AḤMAD B. ISMĀʿĪL): he was 'one of those who followed the way of *tawakkul* [...]. He was a contemporary of al-Junayd and al-Nūrī [...] and he died in the great mosque of Rayy in 291(904)' (Sulamī, *Ṭabaqāt*, p. 283).

AL-JUNAYD, ABŪ'L-QĀSIM B. MUḤAMMAD B. AL-JUNAYD AL-KHAZZĀZ: born in Nihawand (Iran), he settled in Baghdad, where he died in 297/910. He studied law according to the Shāfiʿite school. In Sufism he was educated by his uncle al-Sarī al-Saqaṭī, and then continued with Muḥāsibī and Maʿrūf al-Karkhī. The greatest master of the Sufis of Baghdad, he was one of the first theorisers of mysticism. Like others, he spoke about the various stations and stages on the path, among which he particularly praised poverty (*faqr*). He emphasised the state of sobriety (*ṣaḥw*) as opposed to that of intoxication (*sukr*), an attitude which appears also in his treatises, where he spoke mainly by *ishārāt*, or subtle allusions. The central theme of Junayd's speculation is the notion of *tawḥīd*, or 'to declare that God is One'. According to him, only when he witnesses the unity and oneness of the Divinity, can man reach the state 'in which he was before he was', i.e., the state of the primordial covenant (*al-mīthāq*, Qur'ān, 7:171), when man 'was but an idea in God and did not have a separate existence' (Molé, *I Mistici Musulmani*, p. 78). However, the most perfected state for a mystic is that of the 'second sobriety', when, after the intoxication of ecstasy, man 'comes back to the world' and, fully aware of his individuality, he lives in total intimacy with God (*ibid.*, p. 79).

MAʿRŪF AL-KARKHĪ (ABŪ MAḤFŪẒ MAʿRŪF B. FAYRŪZ): he was a disciple of Dāwūd al-Ṭā'ī (d. 165/781) and of Abū Bakr b. Khunays al-Kūfī. He was the spiritual master of al-Sarī al-Saqaṭī. According to Farīd al-Dīn al-ʿAṭṭār, he was called Maʿrūf because 'he was "well-known" for his being an *ʿārif*, who possessed the science of the knowledge of God (*maʿrifa*)' (*Tadhkira*, p. 269). He died in Baghdad in 200/815.

MUḤAMMAD B. AL-FAḌL, ABŪ ʿABD ALLĀH B. AL-ʿABBĀS B. ḤAFṢ AL-BALKHĪ: he was born in Balkh, from where he was exiled, and lived in Samarkand, where he died in 319/931. 'He was a disciple of Aḥmad b. Khiḍrawayh and one of the wisest men of Khurāsān' (ʿAṭṭār, *Tadhkira*, p. 333) and 'Abū ʿUthmān (al-Ḥīrī) had a predilection for him (*kāna yamīlu ilayhi*) more than for any other sheykh' (Sulamī, *Ṭabaqāt*, p. 206).

MUḤAMMAD B. KHAFĪF AL-ḌABBĪ AL-SHĪRĀZĪ, ABŪ ʿABD ALLĀH: he lived in Shīrāz and died in 371/981. According to Sulamī, 'this sheykh of princely lineage (*min awlād al-umarā'*) was the master of the masters of his time. He was the disciple of Ruwaym, al-Jurayrī and Abū'l-ʿAbbās b. ʿAṭā' al-Dimashqī; he knew al-Ḥusayn b. Manṣūr (al-Ḥallāj)' (*Ṭabaqāt*, p. 485). Ibn Khafīf was Ashʿarite in *kalām* (theology) and Shāfiʿite in *fiqh* (jurisprudence).

AL-MURTAʿISH, ABŪ MUḤAMMAD ʿABD ALLĀH B. MUḤAMMAD AL-NAYSĀBŪRĪ: 'he was the disciple, in Nīshāpūr, of Abū Ḥafṣ and Abū ʿUthmān (al-Ḥīrī). He knew al-Junayd and became his disciple, and he lived in Baghdad till he became one of the masters and spiritual leaders (*a'imma*) of Iraq. [...] The masters of Iraq would say: "Three are the wonders of Baghdad: the metaphors (*ishārāt*) of al-Shiblī, the anecdotes (*nukat*) of al-Murtaʿish, and the stories (*ḥikāyāt*) of Jaʿfar al-Khuldī"' (Sulamī, *Ṭabaqāt*, p. 356). He died in Baghdad in 328/939.

AL-NAṢRĀBĀDHĪ, ABŪ'L-QĀSIM IBRĀHĪM B. MUḤAMMAD: he was a Shāfiʿī scholar of Hadith who became a Sufi at the hands of Abū Bakr al-Shiblī at Baghdad. According to Hujwīrī, 'he was like a king in Nīshāpūr, save that the glory of kings is in this world, while his was in the next world. Original sayings and exalted signs were vouchsafed to him. Himself a pupil of Shiblī, he was the master of the later Shaykhs of Khurāsān. He was the most learned and devout man of his age' (*Kashf*, p. 159). He educated Sulamī in Sufism and from him Sulamī received the *khirqa*, or the Sufi frock of investiture. He died in 367/977–8.

RUWAYM (ABŪ MUḤAMMAD RUWAYM B. AḤMAD, OR B. MUḤAMMAD, B. YAZĪD B. RUWAYM): he was born in Baghdad and died in 303/915. A friend of Junayd, he was known as a spiritual master, as a jurist (*faqīh*) of the Ẓāhirite school, and as a *muqri'*, or Qur'ānic reader. Unlike many of his contemporaries, he did not overstress the practice of asceticism and austerity: for him, *tawakkul* did not mean to shun this world totally, but simply to trust God's promise to look after His creatures (Sarrāj, *Kitāb al-luma*ᶜ, p. 52).

SAHL AL-TUSTARĪ, ABŪ MUḤAMMAD SAHL B. ᶜABD ALLĀH B. YŪNUS B. ᶜĪSĀ AL-TUSTARĪ: he was born in Tustar in Khūzistān in 203/818 and died in Baṣra in 273 or 283/896. According to Qushayrī and Sulamī, Tustarī met Dhū'l-Nūn al-Miṣrī in Mecca, during a pilgrimage. Tustarī's most frequently mentioned theory is that concerning repentance (*tawba*), which should be a permanent state in the believer. An austere ascetic, he wrote an extensive commentary on the Qur'ān and became famous for his theories of saintliness and his idea of a 'pillar of light' constituted from the souls of those who are predestined to become saints and achieve the 'secret mystery of Lordliness' (*sirr al-rubūbiyya*). The teachings of Tustarī were continued by his disciple Ibn Sālim (d. 296/909) and, therefore, their school was known as the Sālimiyya.

AL-SARĪ AL-SAQAṬĪ (ABŪ'L-ḤASAN SARĪ B. AL-MUGHALLIS AL-SAQAṬĪ): a disciple of Maᶜrūf al-Karkhī, he was the uncle and the master of Junayd, and also the master of Abū'l-Ḥusayn al-Nūrī, al-Kharrāz and Khayr al-Nassāj. Sulamī says that 'he was the Imām of the sheykhs of Baghdad at his time, and the most part (of the sheykhs) of the second *ṭabaqa* (i.e. of the generation of al-Junayd) are connected with him' (*Ṭabaqāt*, p. 41). According to tradition, he was the first to discuss the various mystical states and to define the relation between man and God as one of 'real mutual love'. He also dealt with the issue of *tawḥīd*, which was later elaborated by his nephew Junayd. He died in c. 257/870.

SHĀH B. SHUJĀ῾ AL-KIRMĀNĪ, ABŪ'L-FAWĀRIS: 'he came from a royal family (*min awlād al-mulūk*). He was a disciple of Abū Turāb al-Nakhshabī and of Abū ῾Ubayd al-Busrī' (Sulamī, *Ṭabaqāt*, p. 183). He was also the master of Abū ῾Uthmān al-Ḥīrī. He died between 270/883 and 300/912.

SHAQĪQ B. IBRĀHĪM AL-BALKHĪ, ABŪ ῾ALĪ: according to Sulamī (*Ṭabaqāt*, pp. 54–59), he was among the most famous Sufi masters in Khurāsān. A disciple of Ibrāhīm b. Adham and spiritual master of Ḥātim al-Aṣamm, Shaqīq was the first Sufi to classify the concept of *tawakkul* as a spiritual state: he also developed the doctrine of the *inkār al-kasb*, then endorsed by the Khurāsānian school, according to which man is denied any right to possess or desire anything. He died in 194/809.

AL-SHIBLĪ, ABŪ BAKR DULAF B. JAḤDAR (OR ABŪ BAKR JA῾FAR B. YŪNUS): a native of Khurāsān, he was born in Sāmarrā, and lived in Baghdad. 'He was a disciple of al-Junayd and of the masters of his time [...]. He was a sage and a jurist according to the school of Mālik, and wrote many Hadiths. [...] He died in 334 (945)' (Sulamī, *Ṭabaqāt*, p. 340).

SUFYĀN B. SA῾ĪD AL-THAWRĪ: he was born in Kūfa and died in Baṣra in 161/777. A disciple of Wuhayb b. Ward and Yūnus b. ῾Ubayd, he became the spiritual master of Ibn ῾Uyayna al-Ḥilālī, Ibn ῾Iyāḍ and Dārānī. He also founded a juridical school (*madhhab*).

YAḤYĀ AL-JALLĀ': the father and spiritual master of the more famous Abū ῾Abd Allāh Aḥmad b. Yaḥyā al-Jallā' (*q.v.*).

YAḤYĀ B. MU῾ĀDH AL-RĀZĪ (ABŪ ZAKARIYYA YAḤYĀ B. MU῾ĀDH B. JA῾FAR): born in Rayy (near present Tehran), he spent part of his life in Balkh and died in Nīshāpūr in 258/871. According to Sulamī (*Ṭabaqāt*, p. 98), he attached much importance to the concept of hope in God (*rajā'*) and he and his two brothers, Ismā῾īl and Ibrāhīm, were considered ascetics (*zuhhād*). Probably a disciple of Ibn Karrām, he was the master of Abū ῾Uthmān al-Ḥīrī, Yūsuf b. al-Ḥusayn al-Rāzī and Ibrāhīm al-Khawwāṣ. Known as *al-Wā῾iẓ*, the Preacher, he is one of the most mentioned masters in spiritual literature, whose sayings 'are delicately moulded and pleasant to the ear and subtle in substance and profitable in devotion' (Hujwīrī, *Kashf*, p. 123).

YŪSUF B. AL-ḤUSAYN AL-RĀZĪ, ABŪ YAʿQŪB: 'sheykh of Rayy and of the region of Media (*al-jibāl*), he was unparalleled in the path; he disregarded honours (*al-jāh*), gave up affectation and artificial behaviour (*taṣannuʿ*), and practised sincerity (*ikhlāṣ*). He was the disciple of Dhū'l-Nūn al-Miṣrī and Abū Turāb al-Nakhshabī; he accompanied Abū Saʿīd al-Kharrāz during some of his travels. He was wise and devout (*dayyin*)' (Sulamī, *Ṭabaqāt*, p. 175). He died in 304/935.

BIBLIOGRAPHY

ʿAbd al-Bāqī, Muḥammad Fu'ād, *al-Muʿjam al-mufahras li-alfāẓ al-Qur'ān al-Karīm*, Cairo: Dār al-Ḥadīth, 1996.

al-ʿAfīfī, Abū'l-ʿAlā', *al-Malāmatiyya wa-'l-ṣūfiyya wa-ahl al-futuwwa*, Cairo: Dār Iḥyā' al-Kutub al-ʿArabiyya, 1364/1945.

Anawati, G. C., and Gardet, L., *Mistica islamica: aspetti e tendenze, esperienze e tecniche*, Turin: SEI, 1960.

al-Anṣārī, ʿAbd Allāh al-Harawī, *Manazil al-Sa'irin: Les Étapes des Itinérants vers Dieu. Édition critique avec introduction, traduction et lexique par S. De Laugier De Beaurecueil O. P.*, Cairo: Imprimerie De L'Institut Français d'Archéologie Orientale, 1962.

Arberry, Arthur J., *The Koran Interpreted*, New York: Macmillan Publishing, 1974.

——, *Sufism: An Account of the Mystics of Islam*, London: Allen & Unwin, 1979.

al-ʿAṭṭār, Farīd al-Dīn, *Tadhkirat al-awliyā: Parole di Ṣūfī,* tr. by Laura Pirinoli, Grandi Pensatori d'Oriente e d'Occidente, Le Tradizioni: 2, Milan: Luni Editrice, 1994.

al-Baghdādī, ʿAbd al-Qāhir Ibn Ṭāhir, *al-Farq bayna al-firaq*, Cairo: Maktabat Ibn Sīnā, 1989.

Bausani, Alessandro, *L'Islam*, Milan: Garzanti, 1987.

——, *Il Corano*, traduzione e commento, Milan: Biblioteca Universale Rizzoli, 1990.

Bel, A., *L'Islam Mystique*, Paris: Adrien Maisonneuve, 1988.

Biberstein-Kazimirski, Albert de, *Dictionnaire Arabe-Français*, Cairo: Imprimerie V. R. Égyptienne, 1875.

Bonebakker, S. A., '*Adab* and the concept of *Belles-lettres*', in *The Cambridge History of Arabic Literature: ʿAbbasid belles-lettres*, ed. by Julia Ashtiany et al., Cambridge: Cambridge University Press, 1990, chapter 1, pp. 16–30.

Böwering, Gerhard, 'Al-Sulamī', in *The Encyclopaedia of Islam*, new edition, vol. IX, ed. by H. A. R. Gibb et al., Leiden: E. J. Brill, 1998, pp. 811–12.

——, 'The Qur'ān Commentary of Al-Sulamī', in *Islamic Studies Presented to Charles J. Adams*, ed. by W. B. Hallaq and D. P. Little, Leiden: E. J. Brill, 1991, pp. 41–56.

——, *The Minor Qur'ān Commentary of Abū ʿAbd ar-Raḥmān Muḥammad b. al-Ḥusayn as-Sulamī (d.* 412/1021*), edited with introduction by-*. Recherches (Collection publiée sous la direction de la Faculté des Lettres et des Sciences Humaines de l'Université Saint-Joseph, Beyrouth), vol. XVII-Nouvelle Série: Language Arabe et Pensée Islamique, Beirut: Dār el-Mashriq, 1995.

Brinner, William M., 'Prophet and Saint: The Two Exemplars of Islam', in *Saints and Virtues*, ed. by J. S. Hawley, California: University of California Press, 1987.

Brockelmann, Carl, *Geschichte der Arabischen Litteratur*, vol. I, Weimar: Verlag Von Emil Felber, 1898.

——, Supplement Bände, vol. I, Leiden: E. J. Brill, 1937.

al-Bukhārī, Muḥammad b. Ismāʿīl, *Ṣaḥīḥ al-Bukhārī*, Riyad: Bayt al-Afkār al-Dawliyya li'l-Nashr, 1998.

Calverley, E. E., 'Nafs', in *The Encyclopaedia of Islam*, new edition, Leiden: E. J. Brill, 1993, vol. VII.

The Cambridge History of Arabic Literature, vol. 2: *ʿAbbasid belles-lettres*, ed. by J. Ashtiany, T. M. Johnstone, J. D. Latham, R. B. Serjeant and G. Rex Smith, Cambridge: Cambridge University Press, 1990.

The Cambridge History of Islam, vol. 2: *The Further Islamic Lands, Islamic Society and Civilization*, ed. by P. M. Holt, A. K. S. Lambton, B. Lewis, Cambridge: Cambridge University Press, 1970.

Chodkiewitz, Michel, *Le Sceau des saints: prophetie et saintité dans la doctrine d'Ibn ʿArabi*, Paris: Gallimard, 1986.

Collins: Concise Dictionary of the English language, third edition, London: HarperCollins Pub., 1995.

Denny, Frederick M., 'God's Friends: The Sanctity of Persons in Islam', in *Sainthood: Its Manifestations in World Religions*, ed. by R. Kieckhefer and G. D. Bond, California: University of California Press, 1988; ch. III, pp. 69–97.

The Encyclopaedia of Islam, new edition, ed. by H. A. R. Gibb et al., Leiden: E. J. Brill, 1960–.

al-Fāwī, ʿAbd al-Fattāḥ Aḥmad, *al-Taṣawwuf: al-wajh wa'l-wajh al-ākhar, maʿahu taḥqīq kitāb uṣūl al-malāmatiyya wa-ghalaṭāt al-ṣūfiyya, li'l-imām Abī ʿAbd al-Raḥmān al-Sulamī* (412 *H*), Cairo: Maktabat al-Zahrā', 1995.

Fowler, Henry W., *The Concise Oxford Dictionary of Current English*, Oxford: Clarendon Press, 1964.

Gabrieli, Francesco, *La letteratura araba*, Florence: Sansoni/Accademia, 1967.

——, 'Adab', in *The Encyclopaedia of Islam*, new edition, vol. I, Leiden: E. J. Brill, 1986–7.

Gibb, H. A. R., *Studies on the civilization of Islam*, Boston: Beacon Press, 1962.

——, *Arabic literature: an introduction*, second (revised) edition, Oxford: Clarendon Press, 1963.

—, 'ʿArabiyya: Arabic literature', in *The Encyclopaedia of Islam*, new edition, vol. I, Leiden: E. J. Brill, 1986.

Goldziher, Ignaz, *A short history of classical Arabic literature*, Hildesheim: Georg Olms Verlagsbuchhandlung, 1966.

Guénon, René, *Il Simbolismo della Croce*, Milan: Luni Editrice, 1998.

al-Ḥallāj, Ḥusayn ibn Manṣūr, *Kitāb aṭ-ṭawāsīn, texte arabe avec la version persane d'al-Baqlī*, ed. and tr. by L. Massignon, Paris: Geuthner, 1913.

Ḥasan, Aḥmad, *Principles of Islamic Jurisprudence*, Islamabad: Islamic Research Institute, 1993.

Hava, J. G., *Al-Farā'id: Arabic-English Dictionary*, Beirut: Dār al-Mashriq, 1970.

Hitti, Philip K., *History of the Arabs: from the earliest times to the present*, New York: Macmillan St Martin's Press, 1970.

Honerkamp, K. L., Heer, N., *Three Early Sufi Texts*, Louisville: Fons Vitae, 2003.

al-Hujwīrī, ʿAlī b. ʿUthmān al-Jullābī, *The Kashf al-maḥjúb, the oldest Persian treatise on Sufiism*, tr. by Reynold A. Nicholson, London: Luzac and Company Ltd., 1967.

Ibn ʿArabī, Muḥyī 'l-Dīn, *Voyage vers le Maître de la Puissance*, tr. by Rabia Terri Harris and Corine Derblum, Monaco: Le Rocher, 1987.

——, *What the seeker needs: with Ibn ʿArabi's glossary of* 199 *Sufi technical terms*, tr. by Shaikh Tosun Bayrak al-Jerrahi and Rabia Terri Harris al-Jerrahi, New York: Threshold Books, 1992.

Ibn Manẓūr, Muḥammad b. Mukarram, *Lisān al-ʿArab*, Beirut: Dār Iḥyā' al-Turāth al-ʿArabī, 1988.

Ibn al-Nadīm, *Kitāb al-fihrist*, second edition, Tehran: Marvi Offset Printing, n.d.

al-Iṣfahānī, Abū'l-Faraj, *Kitāb al-aghānī*, ed. by Ibrāhīm al-Ibyārī, Cairo: Dār al-Shaʿb, 1969.

al-Iṣfahānī, Abū Nuʿaym, *Ḥilyat al-awliyā' wa-ṭabaqāt al-aṣfiyā'*, Beirut: Dār al-Maʿrifa, 1967.

al-Iskandarī, Ibn ʿAṭā'illāh, *Ṣūfī aphorisms* (*Kitāb al-Ḥikam*), tr. with an introduction and notes by Victor Danner, Leiden: E. J. Brill, 1984.

——, *al-Ḥikam*, ed. by Aḥmad ʿIzz al-Dīn ʿAbd Allāh, Cairo: Al-Maktaba al-Azhariyya li'l-Turāth, 1996.

—, *The Key to Salvation & the Lamp of Souls* (*Miftāḥ al-Falāḥ wa Miṣbāḥ al-Arwāḥ*), tr. by Mary Ann Koury Danner, Cambridge: The Islamic Texts Society, 1996.

al-Jurjānī, ʿAlī b. Muḥammad al-Sayyid al-Sharīf, *Kitāb al-taʿrīfāt* (*A Book of Definitions*), Beirut: Librairie du Liban, 1985.

al-Khafājī, Muḥammad ʿAbd al-Munʿim, *al-Adab fī'l-turāth al-ṣūfī*, Cairo: Maktabat Gharīb, 1980.

——, *al-Adab al-ʿarabī wa-taʾrīkhuhu: fī ʾl-ʿaṣrayn al-umawī waʾl-ʿabbāsī*, Beirut: Dār al-Jīl, 1990.

Kinberg, Leah, 'What is Meant by *Zuhd*', in *Studia Islamica* 61 (1985), pp. 27–44.

——, *Ibn Abī al-Dunyā: Morality in the guise of dreams: A critical edition of Kitāb al-Manām*, Leiden: E. J. Brill, 1994.

Lane, E. W., *An Arabic-English Lexicon*, Cambridge: Islamic Texts Society, 1984.

Lings, Martin, *What is Sufism?*, Cambridge: Islamic Texts Society, 1993.

Lory, Pierre, *Les Commentaires ésotériques du Coran d'après ʿAbd ar-Razzāq al-Qāshānī*, Paris: Les Deux Océans, 1980.

Makkī, Abū Ṭālib Muḥammad b. ʿAlī, *Qūt al-qulūb*, Cairo: Dār al-Rashād, 1991.

Massignon, Louis, *Essai sur les origines du lexique technique de la mystique musulmane*, Paris: J. Vrin, 1954.

——, *Essai sur les origines du lexique technique de la mystique musulmane*, Paris: Les Editions du Cerf, 1999, pp. 273–286.

——, *al-Islām waʾl-taṣawwuf*, Cairo: Dār al-Shaʿb, 1979.

——, *Le Dīwān d'al-Ḥallāj*, Paris: Cahiers du Sud, 1955.

Meier, Fritz, 'Ein Knigge für Sufi's', in *Rivista degli Studi Orientali* 32 (1957), pp. 485–501.

——, 'Ein wichtiger Handschriftenfund zur sufi: Abū ʿAbdarraḥmān Muḥammad b. al-Ḥusayn as-Sulamī (gest. 412/1021)', in *Oriens* 20 (1967), pp. 91–106.

Molé, Marijan, *I Mistici Musulmani*, Milan: Adelphi, 1992 (Italian translation of: *Les mystiques musulmans*, Paris: Les Deux Océans, 1982).

al-Muḥāsibī, Abū ʿAbd Allāh al-Ḥārith, *al-Riʿāya li-ḥuqūq Allāh*, ed. by ʿAbd al-Ḥalīm Maḥmūd and Ṭaha ʿAbd al-Bāqī Surūr, Cairo: Dār al-Kutub al-Ḥadītha, n.d.

al-Muʿjam al-wasīṭ, third edition, 2 vols., Cairo, 1980.

al-Munjid fī ʾl-lugha waʾl-aʿlām, Beirut: Dār al-Mashriq, 1994.

Nallino, Carlo Alfonso, *La letteratura araba: Dagli inizi all'epoca della dinastia Umayyade. Lezioni tenute in arabo all'Università del Cairo.*

Traduzione italiana di Maria Nallino (Estratto da C. A. Nallino, *Raccolta di scritti editi ed inediti*, vol. VI), Rome, 1948.

Nelson, Kristina, *The Art of Reciting the Qur'an*, Cairo: The American University in Cairo Press, 2001.

Nicholson, R. A., *A Literary History of the Arabs*, Cambridge: Cambridge University Press, 1930.

——, *The Mystics of Islam*, London: Routledge and Kegan Paul, 1963.

Nwyia, Paul, *Exégèse Coranique et langage mystique: Nouvel essai sur le lexique technique des mystiques musulmans*, Beirut: Dar el-Machreq SARL Éditeurs, 1991.

al-Qāshānī, ʿAbd al-Razzāq, *Iṣṭilāḥāt al-ṣūfiyya*, ed. by ʿAbd al-Khāliq Maḥmūd, Cairo: Dār al-Maʿārif, 1984.

——, *A Glossary of Sufi Technical Terms*, tr. by Nabil Safwat, revised and ed. by D. Pendlebury, London: The Octagon Press, 1991.

al-Qushayrī, Abū'l-Qāsim ʿAbd al-Karīm, *al-Risāla al-Qushayriyya*, Cairo: Dār al-Kutub al-Ḥadītha, 1966.

——, *Principles of Sufism: Selections from al-Risāla al-Qushayriyya*, tr. by B. R. Von Schlegell, Berkeley: Mizan Press, 1990.

Ragazzini, Giuseppe, *Dizionario Inglese-Italiano, Italiano-Inglese*, third edition, Milan: Zanichelli, 1995.

al-Sarrāj, Abū Naṣr, *Kitāb al-lumaʿ fī'l-taṣawwuf*, ed. and tr. by R. A. Nicholson, Leiden and London: E. J. Brill, 1914.

Sassi, Giuditta, *I custodi del segreto: Risālat-ul-Malāmatiyya, ovvero, Epistola della Gente della riprovazione*, Milan: Luni Editrice, 1997.

——, *La Cavalleria spirituale: Kitāb-ul-Futuwwa*, Milan: Luni Editrice, 1998.

Scattolin, Giuseppe, *L'esperienza mistica di Ibn al-Fārid attraverso il suo poema Al-Ta'iyyat al-Kubrā: un'analisi semantica del suo linguaggio,* Tesi di dottorato, Rome, 1986.

Schimmel, Annemarie, *Mystical dimensions of Islam*, Chapel Hill: The University of North Carolina Press, 1975.

——, *As through a Veil: Mystical Poetry in Islam*, New York: Columbia University Press, 1982.

Sells, Michael A., *Early Islamic Mysticism: Sufi, Qur'an, Miʿraj, Poetic and Theological Writings*, New York: Paulist Press, 1996.

Sezgin, Fuat, *Geschichte des Arabischen Schrifttums*, Leiden: E. J. Brill, 1967.

Shorter Encyclopaedia of Islam, ed. by H. A. R. Gibb and J. H. Kramers, Leiden and London: E. J. Brill, 1953.

Smith, Margaret, *Studies in early mysticism in the Near and Middle East*, Amsterdam: Philo Press, 1973.

——, *Rābiʿa The Mystic and Her Fellow-Saints*, Cambridge: Cambridge University Press, 1984.

al-Sulamī, Abū ʿAbd al-Rahman, *Early Sufi Women: Dhikr an-niswa al-mutaʿabbidāt aṣ-Ṣūfiyyāt by Abū ʿAbd al-Raḥmān al-Sulamī*, tr. with notes by Rkia E. Cornell, Louisville: Fons Vitae, 1999.

——, *Jawāmiʿ Ādāb al-Ṣūfiyya and ʿUyūb al-Nafs wa-Mudāwātuhā by Abū ʿAbd al-Raḥmān al-Sulamī*, ed. with an introduction by Etan Kohlberg, The Max Schloessinger Memorial Series, Texts 1, Jerusalem: Jerusalem Academic Press, 1976.

——, *Kitab Ādāb aṣ-Ṣuḥba by Abū ʿAbd ar-Raḥmān as-Sulamī*, ed. by M. J. Kister, Jerusalem: The Israel Oriental Society, 1954.

——, *Kitāb Ṭabaqāt al-Ṣūfiyya: Texte arabe avec une introduction et un index*, ed. by Johannes Pedersen, Leiden: E. J. Brill, 1960.

al-Tirmidhī, al-Ḥakīm, *The Concept of Sainthood in Early Islamic Mysticism: Two works by al-Ḥakīm al-Tirmidhī (Bad' and Sīrat al-awliyā')*. An annotated translation with introduction by Bernd Radtke and John O' Kane, Richmond: Curzon Press, 1996.

Trimingham, J. Spencer, *The Sufi orders in Islam*, London: Oxford University Press, 1971.

Vadet, Jean-Claude, *L'Esprit courtois en Orient dans les cinq premiers siècles de L'Hégire*, Paris: éd. Maisonneuve & Larose, 1968.

Vaglieri Veccia, Laura, *Grammatica Teorico-Pratica della Lingua Araba: Volume Secondo*, Rome: Istituto per l'Oriente, 1989.

Vocabolario Arabo-Italiano, 2 vols., Rome: Istituto per l'Oriente, 1989.

Wahba, Magdi, *A Dictionary of Literary Terms: with French and Arabic Indexes*, Beirut: Librairie du Liban, 1974.

Wehr, Hans, *A Dictionary of Modern Written Arabic*, ed. by J. Milton Cowan, Beirut: Librairie du Liban, 1980.

Wright, W., *Arabic grammar*, third edition, 2 vols., Cambridge: Cambridge University Press, 1964.

Yūsuf ʿAlī, ʿAbd Allāh, *The Holy Qur'ān*; *text, translation and commentary*, Cairo: Al-Zahrā' li'l-Iʿlām al-ʿArabī, 1990.

INDEX

ʿabd (servant) 1, 4, 29, 31, 43, 49, 63, 66, 68, 83;
- *adab* xxxvi, 4, 11, 39–40;
- *dhikr* 76;
- duty 30;
- faith xxxiv, 4;
- *ghafla* 70;
- *ḥarām* 78;
- humility 72;
- *ʿibāda* 63;
- Master 8–9, 54, 88;
- *nafs* 27;
- obedience 11, 54, 85;
- poverty 49;
- *ṣuḥba* xx;
- *tawakkul* 17;
- see also *ʿābid*; *ʿibāda*; *ʿubūdiyya*

ʿAbd Allāh b. al-Mubārak xxxi, 7, 12, 21, 28, 34, 63, 75

abdāl (the 'substitutes') 26

ʿābid (devotee) 4, 89;
- see also *ʿabd*; *ʿibāda*

Abū Bakr al-Ṣiddīq 74

Abū Saʿīd b. Abī'l-Khayr xli–xlii

Abū Turāb al-Nakhshabī 14, 18, 22, 41, 64

acceptance, see *riḍā*

adab 1, 2, 71–2;
- *adab al-sirr* 12, 71;
- *ādāb al-ẓawāhir wa'l-bawāṭin* xxxvi, 1, 61;
- *adīb* xxv, xxvii;
- disregard 4, 11, 12, 63, 70, 72;
- excellence 4;
- gnostic, *adab* of 5, 21;
- importance 3, 11, 62–3;
- *Jawāmiʿ ādāb al-ṣūfiyya* xxxv–xxxvi, xxxviii–xxxix;
- knowledge, *adab* of 55;
- *mandūb* 71;
- meanings xxiv–xxix, xxxv, xxxviii, xlviii, 4;
- perfection 10;
- piety, *adab* of 55;
- poverty, *adab* of xxxvii, 7, 25, 29, 48–9;
- Prophet Muḥammad, *ādāb* of 2, 3, 62;
- Qur'ān xl, 58;
- religion 3;
- servant, *adab* of xxxvi, 4, 11, 39–40;
- spiritual master xxxv, 10, 21, 37;
- spiritual realisation xxiv, xxxv, xxxviii, 40;
- Sunna xl, 12, 37, 58, 72;
- *taṣawwuf*, *adab* of 35;
- travelling, *adab* of 7, 22;
- with God xxxvi, 2, 3, 8–9, 39, 61, 68;
- with godservants xxxvi, 4, 11, 39–40;
- see also *adab* literature

adab literature xvii, xxiv–xxxiii;

reverence, see *taʿẓīm*
riʿāya (vigilance) 22, 55, 79;
see also *taqwā*
riḍā (acceptance, contentment) xxxi, 24, 76, 77;
riḍā ʿan al-nafs xxiv
rifq (kindness) 67, 68
riyāʾ (hypocrisy) xxiv, 36, 72, 82
riyāḍa (discipline, spiritual exercise) 23, 36, 78;
riyāḍāt al-nafs 15
rubūbiyya (Divine Lordship) 38, 83
al-Rūdhbārī, Abū ʿAlī 47, 48;
Adab al-faqīr xxxii
rūḥ (spirit) 78, 88
al-rūḥāniyya (spirituality) 25
Ruwaym b. Aḥmad, Abū Muḥammad 7, 34, 35, 47

sabab (means of subsistence) 6, 20, 67;
mutasabbib xxxvi, 66;
see also *tajrīd*; working
ṣabr (patience) xxxi, 3, 16, 22;
al-Ḥasan al-Baṣrī 70
al-Tustarī, Sahl xliii, 4, 12, 13, 14, 15, 24, 36, 45, 54, 72
saints, see *awliyāʾ*
saintship, see *wilāya*
salaka ('travelling' along the spiritual path) xxxvii, 42, 58;
sulūk al-ṭarīq 40
see also *maqām*; *sālik*
sālik (follower of the spiritual path) 58, 90;
samāʿ (mystical audition and dance) xxxv, xxxvii, 41, 49, 83–4;
see also ecstasy
al-Sarī al-Saqaṭī, xlviii, 5, 7, 9, 13, 17, 31–4, 36, 45, 56
al-Sarrāj, Abū Naṣr:
Kitāb al-lumaʿ fī'l-taṣawwuf xlvii, 63, 78
scrupulousness, see *waraʿ*
secret, see *sirr*
self-management, see *siyāsatu'l-nufūs*
self-mortification, see *dhilla*; *mujāhada*
self-planning, see *tadbīr*
self-vigilance, see *taqwā*
self-willing, see *ikhtiyār*
servant, godservant, see *ʿabd*
servanthood, see *ʿubūdiyya*
Shāh b. Shujāʿ al-Kirmānī, 14
shahwa (passion) 5, 15, 32;
see also passion
Shaqīq al-Balkhī, 3, 14
sharʿ, see *sharīʿa*
sharah (avidity) 36–7, 82;
see also *ḥirṣ*
sharīʿa (religious law) 19, 25, 63;
taʿẓīm al-sharʿ 57
shaykh (spiritual master) 40–1, 58, 70, 75, 86;
adab xxxv, 10, 21, 37;
ʿālim nāṣiḥ 58, 90;
blessings 40, 47, 58;
obedience to 11, 20, 23–4, 28, 29, 32, 40, 57, 75;
respect to xx, 41;
sālik 58, 90;
see also *al-akābir*; *ʿālim*; *murīd*
al-Shiblī, Abū Bakr xv, xliii, 23, 39, 51, 87
shukr (gratitude) xxxi, 4, 55, 77, 89
sickness 26, 42, 45, 85
ṣidq (sincerity) 15, 36;
see also *ikhlāṣ*